A WALK IN ANCIENT ROME

A VIVID JOURNEY BACK IN TIME

JOHN T. CULLEN

ibooks
new york

DISTRIBUTED BY SIMON & SCHUSTER, INC.

A publication of ibooks, inc.

Distributed by Simon & Schuster, Inc.
1230 Avenue of the Americas, New York, NY 10020

ibooks, inc.
24 West 25th Street
New York, NY 10010

The ibooks World Wide Web Site address is:
www.ibooks.net

Cover art: A Capriccio of Classical Ruins by Giovanni Paolo Panini
Cover © Christie's Images/CORBIS

ISBN: 1-4165-0417-6
First ibooks printing 2005
10 9 8 7 6 5 4 3 2 1

Printed in the U.S.A.

CONTENTS

PART ONE | SALT ROAD

PART TWO | AVENTINE DISTRICT

PART THREE | GREAT RACEWAY DISTRICT

PART FOUR | ROMAN FORUM DISTRICT

PART FIVE | PALATINE HILL DISTRICT

PART SIX | PUBLIC POOL DISTRICT

DEDICATION

For Prof. and Mrs. James F. Mormile, Ph.D.
Also for Jim and Mary, lifelong friends.
"Quando il nieve, bene si beve."

For Andrew and Carolyn, with love.

My great thanks to Byron Preiss for his vision and patience,
as well as Dwight Jan Zimmerman for his invaluable input,
and, for their excellent work,
April Isaacs, Maria Reyes, Marianne Paul.

PART ONE

SALT ROAD

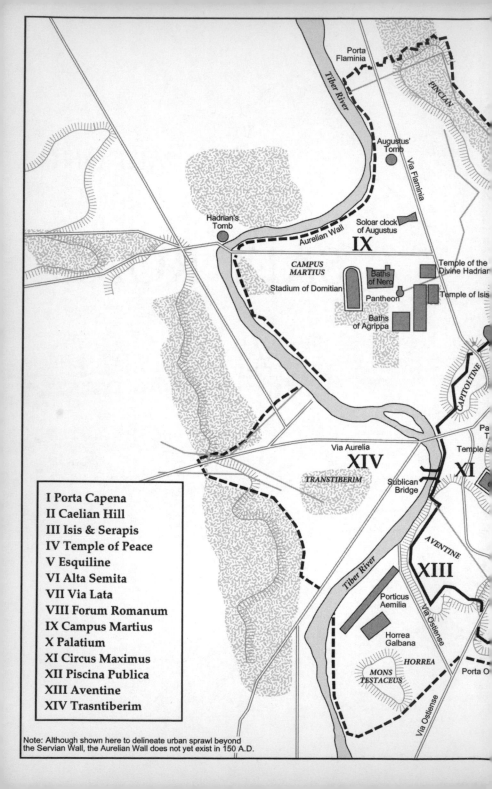

Porta
Flaminia

Tiber River

PINCIAN

Augustus'
Tomb

Via Flaminia

Hadrian's
Tomb

Soloar clock
of Augustus

Aurelian Wall

IX

CAMPUS
MARTIUS

Temple of the
Divine Hadrian

Stadium of Domitian

Baths
of Nero

Pantheon

Temple of Isis

Baths
of Agrippa

CAPITOLINE

Pa
T

Via Aurelia

XIV

TRANSTIBERIM

Temple c

XI

Sublican
Bridge

Tiber River

AVENTINE

XIII

Porticus
Aemilia

Via Ostiense

I Porta Capena
II Caelian Hill
III Isis & Serapis
IV Temple of Peace
V Esquiline
VI Alta Semita
VII Via Lata
VIII Forum Romanum
IX Campus Martius
X Palatium
XI Circus Maximus
XII Piscina Publica
XIII Aventine
XIV Trasntiberim

Horrea
Galbana

MONS
TESTACEUS

HORREA

Porta O

Via Ostiense

Note: Although shown here to delineate urban sprawl beyond
the Servian Wall, the Aurelian Wall does not yet exist in 150 A.D.

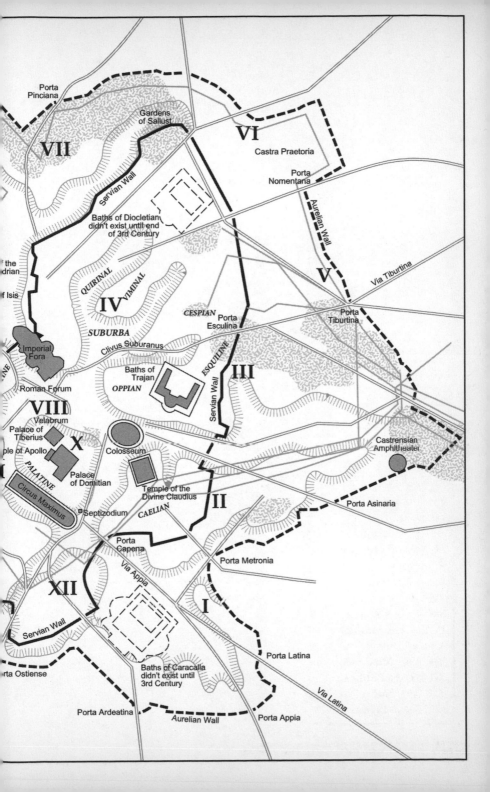

Porta
Pinciana

Gardens
of Sallust

VII

VI

Castra Praetoria

Servian Wall

Porta
Nomentana

Baths of Diocletian
didn't exist until end
of 3rd Century

Aurelian Wall

QUIRINAL

the
drian

V

Via Tiburtina

of Isis

IV VIMINAL

CESPIAN Porta
Esculina

Porta
Tiburtina

SUBURBA

Imperial
Fora

Clivus Suburanus

ESQUILINE

III

Roman Forum

Baths of
Trajan

Servian Wall

OPPIAN

VIII

Velabrum

Palace of
Tiberius

X

Colosseum

Castrensian
Amphitheater

ple of Apollo

PALATINE

Palace
of Domitian

Circus Maximus

Temple of the
Divine Claudius

II

Septizodium

CAELIAN

Porta Asinaria

Porta
Capena

Porta Metronia

Via Appia

XII

I

Servian Wall

Porta Latina

rta Ostiense

Baths of Caracalla
didn't exist until
3rd Century

Via Latina

Porta Ardeatina

Aurelian Wall

Porta Appia

CHAPTER 1

ALONG
THE TIBER

Under the early morning sun of a fresh, windy day, we leave the ancient port city of Ostia and begin our walk to Rome on the *Via Ostiensis* (Ostia Road).

Behind us, Ostia's wharves bristle with the masts of ships bringing goods from around the world. Ostia's dwellings rise up to six stories above the wealth of her many warehouses. Her unique mosaic-decorated streets boldly declare the rich commerce of her merchants. Ostia, for all her glory, is but prelude to the great city of Rome herself.

It is the Year 150 A.D., and the well-liked Antoninus Pius is Emperor. This is that moment in time when the Roman Empire is at its zenith of power, prosperity, peace, and self-confidence.

At this time of year the days are bright and balmy, but the evenings become brisk and autumnal. A touch of frost may even breathe thin sheets of ice across puddles and water jars, but the morning sun quickly warms everything. In places, our road is shaded by huge willow trees, while the level-cut stones of the Ostia Road start to gather the heat and dust of a long summer-like day.

The immutable stone blocks in the two-lane road rumble steadily with wooden cartwheels and clattering hooves. A great deal of cargo heads to Rome each day, in preparation for entering the city by night. Rome is so crowded that it is forbidden to bring wagons of produce and other goods into the city during daylight hours. By torchlight after dark, the city is an insomniac's pitch-flickering hell. One hears a constant rumbling of wheels, laughter, and the crack of whips. Draft animals continuously whinny or low. Owners sharply bark orders at their slaves.

This morning, 25 kilometers (16 miles) from Rome, the air is filled with laughter, conversation, and an occasional shout. The crowd is a human stew that thickens as we approach the city. From Ostia, as we gaze expectantly over the lush tree crowns hoping to catch a glimpse of the city, but all we see is a smudge of ashen smog. This cloud extends from horizon to horizon, caused by the cooking fires, smelters, lanterns, and temple votive lamps of an estimated 1.2 million urban dwellers. Romans call it either *gravioris caeli* (oppression from the sky) or *aer infamis* (outrageous air).

On our left, the surface of the Tiber River is a hypnotic sheet of shifting colors. Among the natural blessings of Rome, without which she could not have become what we are about to marvel at, the Tiber is the most prominent river in the mid-Italian Peninsula. It is a turbulent river, fed by runoff starting at Mount Fumaiolo in the Apennine Mountain Range. It runs 406 km (252 mi), and near its mouth it drains into a basin estimated to be 18,000 square km (6,845 square miles). So much silt washes out in the powerful currents, that the shoreline grows outward by four meters per year.[1] The Tiber meanders into the Tyrrhenian Sea through a low-lying swampy plain hemmed in on three sides by mountains. Its plentiful, fast-flowing supply of fresh water from the mountains is a key factor in the survival and growth of Rome.

Rome, as we shall see, is a city of aqueducts with almost limitless capacity. They power the public baths, as well as the public latrines. Aqueducts provide power to a sophisticated underground sewer system that helps keep the city clean. They also sustain the city's large population.

A steady procession of shallow-draft, broad-beamed wooden barges ply their way on Rome's watery trade artery. Some are powered by single banks of oars, or lean forward into a broad, billowing bowsprit sail. Others have a mast set especially close to the bow, for towing from shore if the wind direction is wrong. Most river boats have two large steering oars in front and two more in the rear. They ride low in the water when full of cargo, approaching the city's river port. Often, if the current is swollen with flood waters, the captains order towing ropes thrown around the frontal mast, and then slaves and pack animals alike must pull from towing paths at the water's edge (much like on the 1840s Erie Canal).

The boats ride high in the water when they depart to sea, empty, to import another load. High also ride the hopes of their sponsors, that the boats won't join the thousands already on the bottom of the *Mare Nostrum* (Our Sea, as the imperial Romans style the Med). Trips are funded by vast pools of imperial and private corporate money, to bring the next shipment of oil or grain to sustain the city's million or more inhabitants.

High or low, the boats are huge, and move with dreamlike slowness like so much in this ancient world, where time seems to flow more casually everywhere except in the arena downtown. There the knife blade that is faster comes away glittering red with the other's spilled lifeblood.

Along the edge of the river, it's possible to see sand shimmering in the shallows amid tall river reeds. Insects buzz about, and birds snap down to eat the insects. The water gets murkier and dirtier toward the center. In the Tiber's center (on average about 42 meters, or 140 feet from the bank) flows a greenish-black miasma of sewage from city outflows. The black effluent shoots along surprisingly fast, judging by the thick layer of trash on top. Bits of broken wood, scraps of cloth, puddles of oil, and the occasional dead dog or cat float swiftly along. Whenever the wind shifts, we get a whiff of sewer gas and corruption.

The swift and turbulent flow of the Tiber itself (or 'himself,' since the Romans have deified the river, like virtually all else in their lives) gives us a palpable sense of power. At the worst of times, it has torn heavy stone bridges apart. Even in the 21st Century, torn piers of ancient Roman bridges will remain visible deep down as ghostly shapes.

Everything about Rome seems to revolve around power. Rome is muscular, assured, often bitterly cruel, but just as often unforgettably brilliant.

The Tiber soon meanders north, while we continue eastward (we and the Tiber will meet again as we approach the city). There is a sweet pastoral smell of mown grass, mainly from the hay bales for sale along the right side of the road. Oranges, plums, and arbutus add their blossom perfume in season. Myrtle, heather, sarsaparilla bloom. Owls and hawks abound in the marshes that fill the Tiber estuary and vast surrounding marshes. Walking east toward

One could well argue that the Western Roman empire died during the siege by Gothic general Vitiges in 537 A.D. (61 years after the last emperor, a boy named Romulus Augustulus, was deposed). Gothic besiegers broke down the aqueducts in the hills outside the city. Defending Byzantine general Belisarius blocked the water channels on the city side, to prevent entry by the enemy. The resulting devastation marked not so much the start of a drought, but rather the end of the city's baths. (There had been about two dozen huge thermae and nearly 1,000 small, privately run neighborhood establishments called balnea or balinea.) The great baths offered not only recreation, but relief and hygiene for crowded, stressed Roman citizens. They also housed libraries, sponsored learned lectures, offered gymnastics, and much more.

The architecture of St. Peter's Basilica in the Vatican, and Grand Central Station in New York City, are examples of design influenced by these large public baths.

Rome on the Ostia Road, we sense the businesslike urgency of the people around us. We are part of a great flow of people, animals, and conveyances going east, in an irresistible tide of marching shoes and sandals. We hear an almost musically ringing horseshoes, and the duller and more plodding but more powerful tread of teams of bullocks. A momentary touch of gaiety comes from a donkey under a bright red blanket. Tied to each side are blocks of salt in a net of hempen rope. The donkey is in good spirits. He tosses his head, making a choir of bells around his neck chime rhythmically, while his sharp little hooves click on the stones. His handler, a sullen boy with a willow cane draped over one shoulder, seems relieved not to have to expend energy beating the animal.

A remarkable discovery one makes about the Romans is that one moment they seem to be much like us, and the next instant, it seems as if we are looking at an inexplicably alien culture. Like the Tiber, these people are a rapidly and unpredictably shifting river containing different cultural streams. One moment it's modern Europe, the next it's the Far East. One moment it's Classical Mediterranean, the next moment it is the archaic Bronze Age or the early Iron Age. In this cosmopolitan culture, we rub elbows with remarkably dissimilar persons: an Etruscan augur, a Roman senator, a Syrian eunuch-priest, an Egyptian Horus-priest, and a Christian bishop from Morocco. We also come across a Spanish export millionaire, a Jewish schoolboy on his way to synagogue, British Celt, a Nubian chamberlain, and a Greek librarian. We meet a German gladiator who escaped becoming a human sacrifice to Freya and fell into the hands of Belgian slave traders. They sold him to the Swiss who sold him to the Ludus Magnus by the Colosseum.

A cultural explosion has transformed Rome's ancient and simple culture. They've gone from Republic to Empire. Small business changed into global corporations. Family farms gave way to huge plantations worked by slave labor.

We are visiting at a moment when it all seems to work. As one tries to look closely at Roman culture, one has a delightful sense of peering into the clockwork of a different civilization. One can get the sense of setting sandals on a foreign street; at the same time one has a disquieting sense of being more 'there' than 'here' as the lens keeps changing focus. Sometimes everything seems alien and scary, as we will see at unexpected moments throughout our walk. At other times, things appear to be downright homey.

Except for their clothing, the people around us on the Ostia Road could well blend into a crowd of bustling pedestrians on Fifth Avenue in Manhattan during a typical work day. We see the pleased look of a matron who has just gotten her only son accepted into a prestigious college of priests. We observe the calculating eyes and licked lips of a businessman newly arrived from Ostia to conclude a complex deal for international grain shipping. We glimpse the mysterious smile on the face of a poor but beautiful young seamstress in long dress. Her head is modestly veiled, but her eyes sparkle with secrets as she thinks about someone very special in her life. She carries a bolt of fine blue cloth on both arms before her, probably to show a wealthy lady in Ostia. By contrast, we cannot make out the expression of a wealthy woman being carried in a litter by four slaves. All we see, through the expensive Chinese silk curtains of her litter, is her shadow with a high, ornately piled hairdo, which is currently in vogue at the Imperial court. Her delicate fingers apply a salve to her pouting lips. Some of the passers-by ignore us, while others stare back with amused curiosity. Others, slaves, flit by like gray shadows, looking ahead with hunger or back in fear.

Most of the people we see are shorter than the average modern. They are of slighter build, probably due to both diet and heredity. We do see some tall Northern Europeans, including blond Anglish or Saxon slaves. A brown-haired North Italian cavalry officer, in gilded parade armor, is out for a morning ride on his horse. Since the Emperor Antoninus Pius sports a full head of curly hair and a full beard, many of the men we see today are bearded. However, the norm in Roman history is short hair and a clean-shaven face. A few men wear bulky, unwieldy togas that signal the owner is a teacher, priest, or manager.

This mode of dress, like those unwieldy long fingernails of the Chinese Mandarin class, signals a magisterial life; someone else must do the lifting. Romans usually wear the traditional toga on special occasions. They require the assistance of at least two other persons to get the complicated wrapping pattern just right. It's a heavy, expensive wool wrapping, roughly semicircular, about 5.5 meters (18 feet) long and 2.1 meters (7 feet) wide. It's not, in other words, a practical garment.

A toga gives a Roman added body language in public—most notably, when he pulls its edge over his head. We see this, for example, in reliefs of emperors making sacrifices. When the Roman pulls the edge of his toga over his head, he enters a spirit world of which we will hear much more. This is a key to the Roman soul and to understanding all that we are about to see.

Most of the free-born Roman men and women, on this warm day, wear some variation on a much more practical garment, the *tunica* (tunic). The tunica is sleeveless like a large T-shirt, belted at the waist. Some *tunicae* are plain white, while others are quite colorful. Some have elaborate borders at the sleeves and hem. A two-wheeled carriage passes us, pulled by a pair of ponies guided by a slave boy. In the carriage, with the curtains open, is a matron wearing a *stola*. This is a long dress covering all but the head and forearms, and gathered in a belt high above the waist.

In the air, and in the attitudes of people we meet, is a sense of assuredness. Even the average slave knows things could be a lot worse. Our fellow passers-by feel just fine about their world, since it's all they know. They are filled with a sense of security and rightness. They believe with utter certainty that things in the world are the best they have ever been. There seems to be no reason why it can't go on like this forever. This is a phenomenon that comes rarely in history, and lasts all too short a time.

Like all Roman roads, this one is designed according to the old Republican Laws of the Twelve Tables. It must be 4.8 m (15' 9") wide so two wagons or chariots can pass can pass side by side. This is comparable to a modern U.S. neighborhood street. Considerably wider roads might be built in cities, harbors, and the like.

Unlike traffic on a 21st Century two-lane street, opposing traffic directions don't stay to the left or right. Thus, pedestrians, horsemen, slave-borne litters, and horse-drawn wagons weave chaotically around each other. Mind you, not everything with wheels is a chariot. We see a variety of two-wheeled and four-wheeled vehicles. These range from a lithe hunting chariot with two arrogant-looking, wealthy teenage boys inside, to a lumbering hay wagon pulled by two bullocks. In many places, there is a wide apron of beaten earth on either side of the road. Some of the heavier wagons travel there

This is Rome's sublime moment. It's the *Pax Romana* (Roman Peace), the era of the Good Emperors (all four of them) as modern historians will one day call it. Most historians consider the Pax Romana as lasting from the accession of Augustus in 27 B.C. to the accession of the worthless Commodus in 180 A.D.

Commodus you may know from the movies: (1) Ridley Scott's *Gladiator*, released 2002, which is almost historically true except, for example, that Commodus didn't die in the arena. In real life, Maximus was murdered early on, and the physically robust Commodus died a death reminiscent of Rasputin's: stabbed, strangled, and drowned. But that's about 40 years ahead of this wonderful sunny day where we are just now walking. (2) *The Fall of the Roman Empire*, 1964, dir. Anthony Mann, with an all-star cast including Rex Harrison, Sophia Loren, and many others. Most memorable scene: Praetorian Guards auctioning off the Roman Empire to the highest bidder against a background of flames and smoke (it really happened).

rather than on the stone roadbed. That's because the softer earth is easier for the wooden wheels to bear, and in any case the later Byzantine emperors imposed taxes and restrictions on the weight allowed, to spare excess wear on the roads.

We begin to see small shrines, graves, and memorials along the southern side of the street. Rome burns its dead and forbids the ashes to be buried within city limits. Hence, cemeteries have sprung up outside the city. Land being increasingly valuable the closer the city, the rich bury their dead in ostentatious tombs along the great roads near the city.

As we begin our approach to the city itself, we start seeing lovingly tended family shrines, some for the dead of nearby villages. However, as we get closer to the city, more and more of the shrines are those of middle class Roman families. We pass small temples, as well as roadside inns, stables, smithies for shoeing horses. Here and there one sees a tavern or a brothel. Often, the walls are marked with charcoal graffiti, advertising a lost dog, or a cheer for the Greens or Blues (great chariot racing teams). One might also see a plug for the local aedile in the next election. Lacking neon lighting and sixty second TV sound bites, the Romans use public thoroughfares to advertise their status in life. One fellow, a freed slave who went on to become a fabulously wealthy commercial bakery owner, built his tomb in the shape of a huge bread oven which is still visible in the city in modern times. One might say he got his money's worth on his funeral.

When in Rome, we do as the Romans do, so we walk constantly. There is no public transportation to speak of. We could rent a chariot or a horse, but most people can't afford to do so, or if they could afford it, they'd just buy one. Now and then, we rest in the shade of a huge willow tree. We buy drinks of water from dirty looking little children who could be either slaves or else the offspring of very poor parents. These children are barely clothed, in scraps and castoffs. One would think they would have sad eyes or gloomy countenances, but for the most part they stare with razor-sharp, hungry attention at the small copper coins we drop in their cupped, muddy hands. Off they go to the next customer, scratching bloodied louse bites as they scramble to be first. The eldest of that particular pack,

Get Your Kicks on Route LXVI. Eventually the Roman Empire is serviced by some 83,000 kilometers (about 50,000 miles) of major post roads in addition to myriad unpaved segments. For an interesting point of comparison, consider the imperial domain as very roughly rectangular and superimpose it on the modern U.S. Our rectangle is roughly 1600 km (1000 miles) north/south (from the Baltic Sea to the Sahara) and 4000 km (2400 miles) east/west distance from Wales to the Mesopotamian. Compare this with the continental United States of the 21st Century, which is very roughly 2500 km (1550 miles) north/south and 5000 km (3000 miles) east/west. The Roman Empire superimposed on this map would roughly extend east/west from Atlantic City, New Jersey to Salt Lake City, Utah; and north/south from New Orleans on the Gulf of Mexico to Chicago, Illinois at the southern end of Lake Michigan.

a boy of ten, lugs a leather sack. His much younger siblings, two tousle-haired girls and a boy, wave clay cups and yell that the water is pure, from a spring guarded by nymphs. The sloshing sack has a rough drawing of Mercury and Daphne scratched on its brown sides. This is supposed to make us believe that the water comes not from the Tiber but from a spring on the other side of the road. As we sip the water, sparingly at first, then greedily, we find that it does indeed seem fresh. The enterprising young water-kids have probably used a good village well nearby. No time to peer into the depths of our cups, for grimy hands appear out of nowhere and tear the empty containers away for the next customer's indulgence.

Gratias! the children cry in slurred street accents as they flee to the next deal. *Multae gratiae. Benedicta domne Miherculi Dafnisque Neptuni at Diuspitri!* "Many thanks. Blessings on you from Hercules (a demigod hero), Daphne (a water nymph), Neptune (the god of seas and water), and Jupiter (the Father God)!" It takes a few moments to sort out their grammar. Everyone is *dominus, domina* (lordship, ladyship) because the children have no time to sort out who is what. So *domne* (your lordship) might be a white-haired schoolteacher striding along with his leather satchel of books (yes, they have them, not just scrolls) and writing implements. It could also be some rich kid's scrambling child slave. It doesn't matter, as long as they buy water and drop an *as* in a grimy hand.

Small villas pop up left and right on high spots in the marshes. We see long, low storefronts where one can buy fruits or dried fish or little bits of fried meat (usually dormouse, the Roman McBurger, made from a small hamster-like rodent). The bread here is excellent. We can smell it from afar, being fresh-baked in ovens that never cool. *Far* (wheat) is a staple of the Roman diet; it's also an essential ingredient in Roman religion.

Get used to this; everything in daily life has a sacred and traditional aspect. Thus, in a humble grain of wheat, we see one of the essential unities of Roman history. Sacred and traditional go hand in hand, because the Romans are a very conservative and traditional people. Even as their society is for centuries torn apart by rapid expansion and population explosion, they hold their own. The high point of our walk will be the Pantheon, dedicated around 125 A.D. to welcome and unite all gods (Gr *Pan* all + *theoi* gods).

The Ostia and Port Roads replace paths trod by ancient salt-traders of Latium. Salt is a *sine qua non* (without which, not) of life. People living in the Apennine Range and its foothills needed salt. Salt could easily to be collected at the Tiber estuary. A regular trade sprang up for the precious commodity.

Fish Sauce a Delicacy. The first of many Asian-seeming touches is the ever-present fish sauce in which the Romans drown their food. Think of modern Vietnamese *nuoc nam* or Thai *nam pla*. In ancient Rome, fish sauce is called *garum*. It's a lot like modern-day Asian varieties, and the Romans put it on everything. Garum, on the low end, might be a common sauce to throw over a fish that's been dead awhile, while on the high end it's a delicacy costing large sums of money per small jar.

Interestingly, garum also has its sacred component in that its primary ingredient, after fish, is salt. Salt is, like the Tiber, a key to understanding the archaic Roman soul.

On our walk, we see more touches that suggest Asia as much as Europe. The point of mentioning this is not to suggest that there was contact with Asia, but that Classical Mediterranean civilization wasn't really either European or Asian—it was a third thing. At times the Romans seem quite modern, yet in a blink of an eye they are once again unreachably distant.

In one place we see a booth by the side of the road, with a woman soothsayer sitting on a little platform. She is wearing a round-brimmed hat, flat at the edges and sloping up gently all around, coming to a high, pointy peak in the center. She is swathed in a cloud of gauzy silk robes. She delivers news of his future to a middle-aged working man in a frayed tunic and simple woolen cloak. He bows gratefully and kisses her hand as he passes coins to her.

> The Romans sometimes pay their legionaries in salt, because in some areas it is easier to trade with the locals in salt than gold, and it is easier for the military postal service to ship salt than gold. If you receive a regular paycheck from an employer, it's called your salary (from *sal*, salt). It is a foregone conclusion that you are 'worth your salt,' and you are 'salt of the earth.'

We see two giggling young Roman ladies wearing colorful silk robes with many folds. They are in the company of a rather surly younger sister who, by her willful and selfish pout, radiates a sense of always getting what she wants. The women's robes may well be Chinese in origin. They have been brought across the great Asian deserts and the Himalayan Mountains via the Silk Road. Each young lady carries an *umbrella* ('small shade,' from *umbra*, 'shade') as they walk on high, stylish clog sandals. The two women have stepped from a gilded four-wheeled carriage with an ornate, rounded vault-roof of inlaid wood. The younger sister stays behind, glowering after them. Perhaps she really wants be near some boy to whom she's taken a fancy. We'll never know who won this argument.

A horde of slaves and private guards stand about while the two companions mince to a nearby picnic spot for refreshment. Perhaps they are secretly going to a (frowned upon) theater in Ostia this evening, where they will see a comedy of Plautus. They will enjoy some slapstick provided by chubby, pot-bellied comedians in short tunics with long, comically dangling genitals that are ever visible and swinging about. This vulgar touch provides no end of mirth to the common Roman audience—the bumbling, white-haired, and white-bearded characters have the brains of addled old men, but the prowess of donkeys.

The first permanent stone theater, built by Pompey, was built in the 1st Century B.C. under the guise of a temple, outside the sacred *Pomerium*. At the same time, the Romans inherited from the Etruscans a cult of phallus-reverence typical of fertility cults around the world (the Etruscans equally venerated the vulva). Prominent on the entrances of many public buildings in Rome, like the Circus Maximus, are stylized posts (herms) with a Hermes head on top and an erect phallus and testicles in front. The generative organ figures prominently in Dionysiac rites pictured in Pompeian wall murals.

Similar rituals, mixing the ribald with religion, are still found in modern Japan, at the Tagata Shrine near Nagoya, during the annual *Hounen Matsuri* festival when a giant phallus is paraded around town by merry festival-goers, and it's considered good luck for young women to touch the phallus for having healthy babies. It's not surprising that early Roman nature worship (buried under layers of imported Greek and then Asian and finally Christian religiosity) was very similar to Japanese Shinto still practiced today.

CHAPTER 2

SALT SLAVE

Let's look back through the haze of millennia and meet a youth named Rumo. About 17, Rumo is a slave brought here as a child by Sabine warriors from the mountains in return for salt. Rumo (whose real name was lost with the deaths of his entire village during a booty raid) has spent most of his life working around the mouth of this river. There are a few huts here, and traders simply call the area 'river mouth.

What is it that Rumo and his fellow slaves do on that beach that is so economically and strategically important that it helps give rise to the mighty Roman Empire? Against a nearly timeless setting of sunshine and windy marshes, the natives set out clay pots on the beach. These fill with sea water as the tide rises. The tide falls, and the water in the clay pots evaporates, leaving a residue of sea salt. This process repeats itself over and over again, until the clay pot is full of dry salt. Putting Rumo on the job speeds things up and ensures nobody comes down from the hills at night to steal a pot of salt. Rumo and other slaves work a kiln near the beach, where they make these simple vessels. Once a pot is full of salt, Rumo smashes the pot, leaving a pot-shaped block of salt. The salt is sold to traders coming down from the hills. Tying the blocks in pairs

Os is the Latin for 'mouth'—hence later the Roman city of Ostia (archaic variant is *us*, Ustia).

Rumo also happens to be an archaic name of the River Tiber. This offers an alternative to the story of how Rome got her name from a fellow named Romulus (unless Romulus got his name from the river).

with rope, the hill people can sling them over a donkey. Then they carry them into the mountains and to trade for other commodities.

Life is short, violent, and scary. In the dim memory of his childhood lies the destruction of his village. He vaguely recalls the trip to the river mouth here, while tied to a horse. He can also remember the callousness of his owners. When conditions became intolerable, the slaves rioted, killed their owners (an Etruscan gang), and escaped into the hills upriver. There, they were enslaved by a gang of renegade Alban Latins who dominated the river crossing. They extorted money to let people pass. Rumo and several friends escaped again, back to the mouth of the river. There they potted salt for the traders who came down from the mountains.

During this time, Rumo marries a pretty young woman named Almo. They plan to make a family, but their joy is short-lived. Rumo is away gathering wood when a Greek trader from *Neapolis* (Gr. 'new city,' later Naples) comes to the mouth of the river with a half dozen brutal mercenaries with their own potting slaves. Almo and the other women run away into the marshes. The men make a stand, but the Greeks kill them. When Rumo returns, they capture him. He finds his woman gone, his friends dead, and himself in shackles.

The Greek potting slaves don't speak Rumo's Latin tongue, and they bully him as they themselves are bullied. They may be slaves, but they are from the great cities of the Greeks. One of the slaves has been among the Etruscans. They have only contempt for a wild mountain child like Rumo with his rustic, stupid name.

One time, the Greek merchant takes several men including Rumo on a trading trip to Neapolis. It is is several days' journey by shore roads south of the river. Now Rumo sees marvels he had never imagined. This is far greater than the small Etruscan and Alban settlements around Latium.

Rumo bides his time, ignoring the shackles on his ankles and the longing for Almo. He ignores the taunting and bullying of the brutes who are his fellow slaves. He ponders the wonders he has seen in Neapolis. Rumo believes, somehow, that he is destined for something more than this miserable life.

One day, when Rumo is 19, and sleeping alone on the beach, a boy creeps down from the rushes in the darkness and speaks with him. "Almo sent me," the boy tells him. "She has spoken to the freedmen and we wish to seize the salt works. She says you have seen the wonders of Megale Hellas" (Gr., L. *'Magna Graecia* or 'Great Greece;' the southern third of Italy, plus Sicily, colonized by Greek city-states since 750 B.C.) "and know about the world. Will you show us what to do?"

Realizing how innocent the boy's people are, Rumo tells him: "Keep your people hidden so they will be safe. I have a plan, but I must choose the right moment." Rumo has an instinct for people. He knows there is not much time, or the people will move on to some other idea. They will tire of Almo, unless he quickly delivers something of value. Rumo works hard, thinks hard, remains silent as he forms his plan. It's more than just a plan for escape. It's a plan for the future.[2]

Rumo must wait for his opportunity, and bides his time. One day after a big shipment of furs that will fetch a high price in Neapolis, the Greeks and their slaves are all dead drunk on the beach. Rumo seizes the moment. Gasping from exertion, and terrified lest they wake up, he pounds a rock on his shackles so they break. He knows his owners may come hunting for him, so he picks up a bronze sword and, one by one, slices the mercenaries' throats.

He makes an important decision at that moment, that will govern the future of the settlement he is about to found. All men will be welcome, slave or free, without questions asked. He doesn't kill the three slaves who have behaved so badly toward him, but leaves them tied up. When they awaken, they can decide whether to run away or join his people—if bandits don't kill them first.

Rumo washes the sword in the sea, then runs inland on the salt trade trails. We catch a last glimpse of him, running down a path of beaten earth beside the great river. As night falls, the fires burn down slowly and go out. When dawn comes, the beach is deathly still except for packs of vultures and sea birds. These scavengers are busy pecking at the dozen bodies sprawled on the sand. The corpses of the merchant and his mercenaries lie rotting in the sun.

Rumo and Almo found a new settlement atop a hill near the great bend in the Tiber. There is a defensible position on a hill in the marshes. The hill will one day be called the Palatine. Across the swampy field of rocks and brambles that will come to be called the

Forum Romanum lies another hill that will one day be called the Capitoline. Here is where the outlying huts of the Sabine people stand, along with their small shrines of stone and wood.

Days later, Rumo and Almo return with a couple of mules to take over the salt works that supply the mountain kingdoms. They bring with them a motley but collegial crew of men and women much like themselves, who have escaped from servitude and now eke out a wild but free life in the gloomy and haunted landscape— of cemeteries and sucking swamp holes, where owls hoot in the dark, and veiled figures are said to walk on moonless nights—that will one day become the Forum Romanum.

Rumo knows that the river mouth is indefensible. There are too many enemies on all sides. Pirates[3] could strike from the sea or from the river. Etruscan, Alban, or Greek raiders could attack from the north and the south. Sabines and Samnites might come from the east. The small neighboring Latin towns are also a threat as are the bandits like the slaves he frees who live in the marshes.

Rumo wants to control the salt trade. In order to do that he must control both the production of the salt at its source, the crossing point at the Tiber, and the heights above. He isn't worried about the outlying towns, or the bandits who will either perish or join his nation. He knows the Etruscans and the Greeks will one day be a problem, but that will be for his successors to worry about. He is already thinking of how to play the surrounding rulers against each other.

Rumo knows that the mountain cities need salt. They will support him if he keeps the salt trade safe. That's the grand strategy, which Rumo develops in a simple but burningly clear analysis. It means the nation that guards the salt trade, and collects taxes at the river crossing, must be above suspicion. They must be a moral people who take only what is just, and offer protection to all. They must be strong at arms, and clever in strategy. It is imperative that they zealously appease the *numina* (including *penates* and *lares*), nameless deities who cohabit their world with humans.

Rumo and Almo vanish into the mists of history. It's not clear whether it is his plan, or that of someone like him, that will mesh with the opportunities offered by this spot, at this nexus of history. The historic empire that will explode from this pinprick settlement may simply have been inevitable with the only question being who would emerge as the winner. The historical verdict is in: a group of Latins who take their name from the river that created their history.

CHAPTER 3

HOTEL BALBI

Halfway to the city, the Tiber swings back south as it meanders. Its zigzagging banks stay within our sight as we continue our walk along the Ostia Road. As the sun begins to set, a gilded, almost silvery light fills the shady trees all around. It softens the harsh but lovely views. This could be the same glow as on our street at home, and yet there are such touches of strangeness here that we almost get goose bumps. In the many shrines and memorials around us, the honeyed light of evening seems to almost rise up from the groves beyond.

We almost feel that we belong here, yet we know we can never quite manage that. Just when we feel for an instant that we could just as well be in our modern hometown (minus cars, traffic lights, neon, and overhead jets) something always jars us out of our comfort zone. Perhaps it's the sight of a gang of blond-haired slave men with downcast eyes and hopelessly vacant expressions. They stagger in rags, each man carrying his part of the chain in a row. They march together, at a slow pace uncaring of time, to a nearby barracks. Those that have tried to run away will spend the night in leg irons after eating a bowl of gruel. All will be locked up under guard. They committed no crime, and weren't even captured on the battlefield. Many were children peacefully tending their parents' fields or flocks years ago on the far pale of Belgium, in Frisia, when they were captured by privateering raiders and sold in a slave market at Augusta Treverorum (modern Trier, Germany).

An agent of a state *latifundium* (plantation) near Ostia bought the lot and shipped them by sea to Rome as raw labor. Those that did not die along the way, nor perished in the Tiber marshes trying to escape, will eke their miserable lives out among others like them from a thousand places around the Empire. They aren't violent or criminal, or they would wind up either in the arena or, much worse, in the mines (salt, silver, gold, lead, or a dozen other commodities). There, men labor like half-blind moles by oil lamps, while salt and other chemicals corrode their vision and rot their skin.

Standing here, inhaling the brisk, fresh wind in the reeds, and the road dust with its tang of manure and straw, and a whiff of river effluent when the lazy, balmy wind shifts a bit, we too feel the overwhelming power of the Roman world. It's an almost cloying, overpowering sense that we could well become part of this world and its sometimes strange logic. We cannot resist the temptation to judge, but we must overcome our occasional revulsion or even fear if we are to make this journey.

The roadhouse of Balbus is an enormous structure on the south side of the Ostia Road. At first glance, it reminds one of a motel complex by any modern highway. It's a rectangular building four stories high, with shops along the front street floor. The dusty square in front resembles a parking lot, and indeed has several wagons parked at odd angles (no painted parking stalls here). Several creamy-colored tents stand around the edges of the square. We walk into a cacophony of noise, smoke, and food smells—a harbinger of what's to come when we reach Rome.

The crowd in front of Balbus' hotel is a miniature of Roman society. The tents—some with rollup windows and doors—are for the slaves and servants of the wealthiest travelers. Their master and his family will sleep in an apartment in the hotel.

Brightly colored blue, red, white, yellow, and green canvas overhangs shelter the shops forming an arcade around the front of the building. People crowd in tightly, laughing and gossiping, as they buy snacks

We are in Rome of 150 A.D. not to judge or compare, but to learn. In so doing, we may learn more about ourselves. We'll have to develop a strong stomach to get past certain things, like slavery, that the Romans take for granted. Are there things in our world that we don't think about much, that a visitor from our future might find horrifying? Perhaps we are more like the Romans than we realize.

and wine, or fruit drinks. Just off the sidewalk at the far corner, a trio of musicians play. They've had a few cups of wine, and the crowd laughs and claps around them. A little monkey on a slender chain, wearing his own tunica, scampers about collecting coins. Comically, he bites them as if to see that they are real. The crowd roars with laughter. The oldest musician, a mustached man with graying hair and sun-lined coppery features, leans forward in a little dance while tapping a large tambourine. He wears tunica whose blue border matches that of the monkey's tunica; on his head, slightly askew, sits a mock laurel wreath—a king of buffoons.

Accompanying him are his wife, strumming chords on a harp, and a boy on a double flute. On the curb, a toothless little bald man sits tapping out a fast, catchy rhythm on the bottom of a leather bucket; his face is upturned with a wide laugh that makes bystanders titter as his tongue wriggles over his pink gums. It's a happy moment, which passes just as quickly, as the crowd turns its attention to a fight in progress in the middle of the lot.

Two men raise a cloud of dust as they fight for some reason—an insult, a dirty look, or a petty theft. Luckily, they aren't *sicarii*—knifemen, gangsters—but just two freedmen laborers who've had too much to drink. Several armed guards step in. They have been guarding the expensive litters and wagons of a wealthy family. From another side come two of Balbus' hired guards. All wear quasi-military gear, including leather body armor from a bygone age. Instead of helmets they wear Phrygian caps (sort of a sock upturned on the head). No two uniforms are alike from one man to the next. One man is missing an eye and walks with a limp, but his body is powerful, his stride intimidating, and his one eye authoritative. He is probably one of the thousands of military veterans who eke out a living any way they can. In a huge, brawling society like Rome's, there is an unending need for guards, so they always find work. There are police and fire cohorts in the city, but they aren't numerous enough to guard every corner and stop every brawl.

Leaving their swords and knives sheathed, the guards step in quickly with wooden clubs, but there is no need to strike. A bucket of water splashes amid the two combatants, settling the dust and their anger. The two fighters disperse, and the guards return to watching their master's tents and transports. They also protect several of his slave women, who busily wash and cook in a corner of the lot.

Balbus' rent-a-cops step back onto the portico to eyeball the crowd. The musicians have moved to another corner, and resume their merry music to a round of cheers. Balbus' guards keep an eye on two near-naked and crippled beggar men who creep up on all fours in their rags, with a hand upheld and piteous chalky faces. The guards lean forward in alarm, looking for signs of leprosy, but the emaciated, jaundiced faces simply indicate the men are slowly dying of some internal disease. The guards relax, and one actually fumbles in his belt, around a massive belly, for a little coin to toss. In the harshest moments, there is a soft touch. Without that, the greatest of societies could not survive a year, much less a thousand years.

Dusk settles, and lanterns flicker into light. Around the shopping arcades, grease-driven fires flare inside the snack shops. Smoke continues to drift out from cooking fish and other delicacies. The smell of fresh bread is ever in the air. A cooling breeze becomes noticeable, ruffling the hair and bringing goose bumps as night presses in from the marshlands. Not far away, torchlight flickers as the endless cavalcade of ships in and out of the city harbor continues. One hears the occasional crack of leather—usually not a whip on a slave's back, as one might imagine, but the snap of reins, accompanied by a sharp yell or whistle, as draft animals are pushed on.

We notice now the thick press of carts and animals of all descriptions in the road. This is part of the mighty daily rhythm of Rome from sundown to sunup. Since late Republican times, all cargo in and out of the city must move by night. This includes every imaginable cargo from furniture to fish, vegetables to vanities, from marble slabs for wealthy homes to whitewash for hovels Some of it is hauled in large four-wheeled wagons pulled by oxen or horses. Some comes in smaller two-wheeled donkey or horse carts. Some carts may be driven by two or four slaves, guiding and moving the cart by means of poles slung on either side and protruding in parallel at front and rear. What one tends not to see here are bulk liquids (like olive oil) and grains, which generally move on the huge river barges.

The Romans seem to yell liberally at the lowly cargo slaves, but whipping them is a rare event. After all, these slaves are valuable property, and the cargo masters are accountable for damage not

Roman society has a perennial fear of slave revolts. The slave owner's dilemma is to purchase a healthy, productive slave with a mild temperament to avoid future trouble. If a slave must be flogged or even killed, it's a loss to the owner, and yet slaves must be kept in considerable fear of consequences to ensure their good behavior.

As time goes on, increasingly large numbers of citizens are either freed slaves, or descended from slaves. A slave is motivated to behave well and better himself, since the possibility of freedom lies within reach. Freed slaves never enjoy truly high status, even those few who become very wealthy. All hope to be granted manumission (literally, *manus*, hand + *mittere*, to send) a sacred ceremony for releasing household slaves from their bondage.

The Romans have a familial relationship with their household slaves. This may seem strange to modern eyes. However, one might be reminded that this same practice lasted until the 1860s in the U.S.

The Roman household slave enjoys a status somewhere between that of a child and a pet. The household slave goes by a single name (usually not Roman, but faux-Greek like Staphylos or Delphios). He or she might even have a nickname (*Felix*, happy) This is in sharp contrast to the Roman citizen who has a triple name (Gaius Julius Caesar). Male slaves of all ages may be called (affectionately, patronizingly) *puer*, boy.

Slaves enjoy increasing protection in law. Yet society must act quickly and with an iron fist to prevent another revolt like the one led by Spartacus in 73 B.C. He was the Thracian gladiator who fled his barracks near Pompeii and gathered, on Mount Vesuvius, a huge force of escaped slaves. Their number eventually grew to about 100,000. For two years, Spartacus led an armed insurrection across central Italy. He defeated several Roman armies in a series of brilliant maneuvers. He was eventually defeated by Crassus (future partner of Julius Caesar in the First Triumvirate) who fielded a huge army (eight to ten legions) at Bruttium. The Romans crucified thousands of the defeated slaves along the Appian Road. They stretched from Rome to Capua (an important crossroads city north of Neapolis, or Naples, where the Appian and Latin Roads or highways cross). That revolt was 200 years ago, and there has not been a similar one since. The cautionary tale of Spartacus will remain engraved as a horrible warning in the world's collective memory, for ages.

only to the goods, but to the handlers. For their part, the cargo slaves know their boundaries. If they argue back, it may mean a cut in rations or other punishment. If they strike back, the punishment is almost certainly execution on the spot.

The roadhouse, or hotel, of Balbus is a four-story brick building with a smaller rectangular inner courtyard. The roof is moderately pitched, or gabled, and covered with brick red clay tiles. Due to the damp marsh environment, the tiles are heavily covered with moss. Unlike the case of flimsy *insulae* (islands, tenements) in the city, that collapse suddenly and kill their occupants, Balbus had the money to build solidly. Imperial building codes are poorly enforced. Bribery, although illegal (and Rome is a litigious society, crawling with lawyers and law courts), is the common way for an unscrupulous contractor to scrimp on quality materials. Balbus, the eldest son of a freed slave, actually owns a chain of these hotels on roads all around the outskirts of Rome. He lives in luxury on the Caelian Hill in the city, and prefers to build for the long-term. This is considered an investment, to be passed along to his children. Thus, the walls of this hotel are a yard thick at the base and well secured on a spit of granite in the otherwise marshy soil.

It is cheaper for wealthy travelers to keep their households outside in tents, as we have seen. The family sleeps in expensive lodgings like those facing the quieter rear views of the marshes. These views offer a charming panorama of nature, whereas the inner courtyard tends to be noisy. The street in front is a bedlam of cargo movement.

Not all those staying here are wealthy families. Some are single business travelers forced into the safety of the hotel because they couldn't reach the city gates. They also may not want to risk the city streets at night. If we check with Filo, the Greek slave who manages the hotel accounts, we see that there are over 300 guests tonight. They include a wax merchant from Egypt and his male lover; and a wealthy Greek slave who is teacher and philosopher at a palace downtown. A Syrian eunuch priest, in white headgear and robes, keeps a small altar to Cybele in his room. A captain of infantry and his attendant slave are guests. An elderly lady dying of cancer is accompanied by her pretty granddaughter, heading to Ostia for a final sea voyage to the Sibylline cave in Cumae. The luxury suites

Roman brick used around here is not the standard modern or even Roman reddish brick, but the smaller, yellowier, almost glassy fired *bessales* that are light, porous, and energy-efficient. Such a square brick typically is 1.5 inches (38 mm) thick, and eight inches (197 mm) long on each side. The outer walls of the upper two stories are two bricks' width thick; in summer they keep the night's coolness on a hot day, and in winter they warm with the sun's rays by day, and retain that warmth into the evening and night hours. Along the road we see crews of men building high walls—one or two to enclose villa gardens, several in building small apartment buildings, atop roadside shops. The engineer and the property owner stand by, looking over plans, as the engineer points here and there explaining points of importance. A gang of freemen artisans, meanwhile, put up the wall with practiced speed and efficiency. They lay course after course of slightly irregular gray tufa (a sedimentary stone found in great abundance around Rome). They use mortar, which two slave assistants mix in a slight, hard depression in the ground. Every meter or so upward, the artisans stop while the engineer and a foreman use levels and sights to take readings. After this the artisans carefully lay a course of flat, thin Roman brick. They may lay two or three such leveling courses before going back to the stones. The brick not only levels the wall for strength, but adds a decorative touch. Roman walls all over the world often characteristically have these layers of yellowish or reddish brick inset among gray stone.

on the first floor rear are occupied by a Senator and two noticeably beautiful women of undetermined function. A host of businessmen of various nationalities and dress complete the roster. They are lacking all but cell phones and laptops, to distinguish them from modern conferees at a convention center in San Diego or London. Vast amounts of business deals have been sealed at places like the Balbi. These involve not only the cargo traffic around Rome, but the movement of camels on the Silk Road, or dhows on the Indian Ocean. Other deals involve slaves from Germany or Nubia, and tin and silver from Britain. To make his hotel useful to all sorts of travelers, including those cutting business deals or an inspirational philoso-

pher, Balbus has installed conference rooms around the second
floor mezzanine. These overlook pleasant fountains and gardens
crammed into the inner courtyard (though a barking dog, a yelling
kitchen slave, or a screaming night-lady cheated of her obol, mod-
ify the tranquility somewhat).

Each floor has a central hallway with whitewashed walls and
pleasantly tiled floors on which the daytime sunlight falls. It's a far
cry from the often wretched, stinking, dark tenements of the city. If
you want to play, you've got to pay, and it's no different at the Balbi.
It's expensive but, for a price, you can call (yodeling at the height
of your tonsils, since there is no telephone) or send a slave for numerous amenities. Snacks, drinks, massage, musical entertainment,
juggling dwarves, are available. One can also request strippers, language lessons, poetry reading, and philosophical chats. A come-
dian to tell jokes is at your beck and call.

People get about in the hotel by climbing wooden stairs in
stuccoed stairwells at each end of the building. The stairs are covered with black tile, here and there inset with white tiles. These
glow in the moonlight or by lamplight, to guide the night wan-
derer. Most people don't wander at night in a place like this. They
use chamber pots kept under the bed, emptied by slaves as needed.
Balbus has installed a square brick cistern, several meters high, behind the building. Its purpose is to hold rainwater for cleaning and
bathing. The hotel boasts a small bath house complete with hot,
lukewarm, and cold pools. However, it's small and always crowded,
and also expensive. Only the wealthiest guests can afford to use it.

The beds are, in a word, wretched. Guests sleep on a wooden
frame with cross slats, on which lies a straw mattress. For a copper
coin, one gets a male or female house slave (the Roman equivalent
of room service and housekeeping) to bring a few armfuls of fresh
straw to toss under the mattress. We bring our own blankets, and a
fly swatter for the occasional cockroach or marsh centipede. The
windows in the cheaper rooms have only wooden shutters with slats
to let air in and out. The more expensive rooms have glass windows
(more translucent than transparent, but great for keeping out winter cold or a morning breeze, while allowing a warm greenish or
golden light into the room). All windows on the first two floors
have iron bars to prevent thieves from getting in. In several places,

we see small balconies big enough for one or two persons to sit and enjoy the sun. They can pass the time reading a book and sipping from a glass of berry juice, perhaps with a few pinches of *iunipero infectus spiritus* (gin).

All day and night, the building is wrapped in smoke and cooking smells of onion, chives, garum, chicken, and fish (to name just a few). The staff must air the place out every day. Even at night, the taberna in the arcade below caters to the truckers, so to speak. A cargo master may come in the middle of the night and order a pitcher of watered down wine (the only kind most Romans drink). He might place an order of meals to go for his slaves. There is, by the way, very little beer to be had in Rome. Carbonated drinks are virtually unknown. Yet in some areas, for example the Eiffel not far from Augusta Treverorum, people commonly bathe in, as well as drink, naturally volcanically bubbly water. The taste is salty and mineral-rich, and still warm from the bowels of the earth. It has a kind of a health-enthusiast ambience that's not to everyone's taste. Spiced and masked with fruit flavors and honey, it could however be the world's first soft drink.

All day long, people have been tramping in and out, spilling wine or food, leaving muddy sandal or boot prints. There is no sudsy floor-washing apparatus, so slaves begin by collecting the sour, foul straw from the hallway floors. Out goes the straw, in comes clean sand. Slaves sweep the sand around, which scours the floors and gathers any stray bits of filth. They then sweep the sand up and take it away with the old straw. Now they strew fresh lavender, gardenia, and other fragrant dried herbs, followed by a layer of fresh straw. Balbus used to throw some cheap rugs in some of the rooms, but they had a habit of "walking away" with some of the shadier guests. Besides, many Roman travelers are accustomed to bring their own bedding and rugs (why not, if you have a slave to lug it?).

As we lie awake in an uncomfortable bed on fourth floor of the Balbi, we hear squirrels scratching about on the roof. Night birds come and go with flapping wings. It gets downright spooky up here, with the marsh winds blowing. Sometime during the night, we open our wooden shutters and lean out over the sill. As in a thousand similar moments, for an instant we think we might be in a modern motel. Then it occurs to us there is not a light switch to be touched. As we hear the soft hooting of a night owl, we inhale a huge draft of fresh, invigorating marsh air. Looking northeast, we see a glow under the sky that can only come from the hearth fires, torches, and oil lights of the million and more souls who inhabit the world's largest city.

Out on the river, the huge barges continue their endless processing. We hear a faint, distant pounding of drums. The wind blows the wrong way, and the slaves on board must row hard. The frontal sail has been trimmed, and the captains may even be considering throwing ropes from the main mast to a crew of slaves along shore. We can well imagine that the priests on board are just now burning extra incense to Tiber (the river god) and other deities. They want to assure a safe journey without beaching, collision, or fire these last several kilometers to the dock. As the broad, wet steering oars rise and fall like giant wooden ice cream spoons, we catch the gleam of river water, seen in the light of many yellow and reddish torches. We close the shutters, bolt them, and head for bed.

CHAPTER 4

LANTERNS IN
THE FOG

After a night spent tossing on a lumpy bed, we awaken blearily to a sound like rolling thunder. What now? We stagger to the window, toss open the shutters, and look outside. It's the loud rumbling of empty carts rushing back toward the port of Ostia with its docks and warehouses. They're competing to see who can be first in line at the most generous import companies, for the next night's cargo run. It's free enterprise, competition, the market system in operation.

Breakfast means a few figs and olives, a little cheese, and some bread. These are washed down with a cup of watery, honeyed fruit juice. The Romans have no coffee in the modern sense, so we'll not enjoy a caffeine jolt anytime soon. We could drink a hot chamomile tea.

Already the road is full of travelers. As the dust settles on the carts rushing west to Ostia, things grow a bit more settled. Again we see the striding professor and the cavalry officer on his clattering mount. The Etruscan diviner is holding a brass model of a sheep liver under one arm. The poor, and slave children are getting ready to offer cool drinks of water in the day's growing heat. Even a flock of those wild-eyed atheists who disbelieved in all of the many Roman and Mediterreanean gods and instead called themselves 'Christians' after their crucified leader are on the road.

A morning fog lies over the Tiber Valley. Towards Rome, it darkens with the sulfurous, yellowish-brown swath of smoke and pollution drifting from the city. Out here on the river, it masks the vast, bobbing hulks of the grain ships as if they were primordial beasts grazing amid fields of clouds. Occasionally a trumpet blares, elephant-like, as one ship warns another of its passage through the mist. The drums of the hortator (*hortor*, to urge) are quiet this morning. The large front and rear rudder-paddles glisten, and the vessels glide under sail like rounded phantoms. Men waving lanterns hang over the high decks, swinging their lights to warn pilots of other ships. Pole men stand ready to push away if another vessel gets too close. Others stand by with wooden blocks to throw between the boats if they are about to collide in the fog.

Closer to Rome, the water becomes shallower. One speaks of 'below the bridge' and 'above the bridge,' meaning the ancient Sublician Bridge, the city's oldest. The Tiber is no place for ocean-going ships. Here on the river, specially designed, blimp-like, shallow-draft barges do the trick. Even they must anchor downriver, within sight of the city. Their cargo is offloaded onto smaller boats, or directly onto land. For the time being, we lose sight of the river, since

Servian and Aurelian Walls: Bookends of Roman History. Rome is surrounded by two sprawling fortified walls dating to entirely different periods in this vast history.

The first wall is the Servian Wall, erected sometime in the murk of distant history. Some sources suggest it was built as early as the Sixth Century B.C. by King Servius Tullius, or as late as the Fourth Century. In any case, the wall signals to us across time that it was necessary to defend a young, growing Rome from outside attackers.

The second wall, the Aurelian, does not exist yet in the time we are walking in ancient Rome. For many centuries, it was unthinkable that Rome would ever be attacked by outside armies. Consequently, the Servian Wall fell into disrepair. Only its many gates remained as decaying but important landmarks. Rome moves through a long period of decline and unrest, until a strong emperor named Aurelian (*Restitutor Orbis*, Restorer of the World) arrives on the scene in 270 A.D. to restore order.

During the Third Century A.D., for the first time in over 600 years, outside forces invade northern Italy and actually threaten to move toward Rome. Though Emperor Aurelian temporarily defeats these invaders, a tribe called the Vandals, he decides to build a new wall around the city that will be known as the the Aurelian Wall.

the Tiber meanders away from us for some distance. The Ostia Road brings us to the Rauduscule Gate in the Servian Wall, and the excitement of the Aventine.

CHAPTER 5

SURREAL ARCHES

The sun has come out in full, and driven the morning fog away. As we approach the city, her size and power seem overwhelming. Her architecture is strangely modern yet at the same time almost alien.

Let's look at the panoramic view where we now stand. On our left, the Tiber meanders to the city. Across the Tiber from the main city lies Regio XIV (Augustan Sector 14), *Transtiberim* (*trans*, 'across' + *Tiberim*, 'the Tiber'). One day, that area will be known as Trastevere, and north of that will lie the Vatican State. At this time that area contains only outlying buildings including the infamous Circus of Nero and Gaius. This is where St. Peter was crucified upside down a century ago near the western *meta* or end post. Chariots now race through their turns here. We'll visit Transtiberim, the Ianiculum Hill, and the Vatican Hill later in our walk. For now, we confine ourselves to the right (eastern) bank, for almost the entire ancient city of Rome lies in the hills and marsh valleys on that side.

The Tiber flows by on our left, as we stand here with a slight wind ruffling our toga. The lower portions of the old Servian Wall are almost indistinguishably blended into a dense collage of walls, gates, doors, windows, columns, roofs, domes, and balconies. As the wind whispers in our ears, we hear the murmur of over a million souls busy at their daily lives. The urban sprawl here is both outward (past the old walls, into any dry or high spot in the surrounding fields) and upward. The open and black windows of huge insulae ('islands,' tenements, apartment blocks) gaze down on us like baleful eyes. Some of these insulae tower up to six stories high. It is easy to think we could squint one eye shut and be looking at a modern city, but just as easily we become aware of differences between this and our home town.

Aside from the haunting, glassless windows of high-rise tenements, an otherworldly feature of the Roman cityscape are the aqueducts that enter from various directions. These remarkable works of engineering have no exact parallel in the modern world. The closest might be if we imagine a city filled with overhead rail viaducts, set on stone and brick arches, rather than modern steelwork. They consist of arches set upon arches set upon arches. No train can turn such sharp corners. The city aqueducts run for a stretch in a perfectly straight line, then do a zig or a zag, and then run straight for another while. This pattern continues until the next hill, older monument, or sacred precinct forces another deviation. Often, an aqueduct follows one of the main, straight streets the Romans so devotedly built. Seen at night, by moonlight, with stars twinkling faintly in the smoking air, they lend an air of surrealism. We have truly come to a city that might occur in some uneasy dream.

Ancient Rome has been compared to modern hill-slums like those of Tijuana, Algiers, or Rio de Janeiro. This is not entirely valid, since a remarkable feature of Rome is her water system. The city has more bathing establishments today than all of Europe will have, until the late 1800s. The wealthy install lead plumbing (from *plumbum*, 'lead') from the dispensation stations to their palaces. The poor tap in illegally and secretly at night. There is a special department of police just to catch water thieves. Some streets even have reservoirs for shooting brief, planned floods along to clean the streets. The runoff goes underground through large manholes culminating in the huge drain of the Cloaca Maxima (Great Sewer or 'Main Drain,' so to speak). This empties from the Roman Forum out into the Tiber.

Still outside the city, looking toward the southernmost of the famed Seven Hills, the Aventine, we tear our gaze away from the cityscape. We walk across a great field with a mysterious mound in its center, that will one day be called *Monte Testaccio*. In its humble guts reside the trade secrets of Imperial Rome.

PART TWO

AVENTINE DISTRICT

(Regio XIII. Aventinus)

CHAPTER 6

HILL OF SHARDS

We cross the overpass where the stream Almo runs through an arch under the Ostian Road. We walk northward into a great triangular complex of warehouses. These are bounded on our left by the river, and behind us by the Ostia Road. Ahead, north, the complex touches the ancient city wall at the foot of the Aventine Hill. On our right, through trees and bushes, we see the gleaming tips of fantastic geometric shapes of lavish roadside tombs by the Appian Way (the Pyramid of Cestius, the huge cylinder of Cecelia Metella, and many statues and columns).

We come into the huge dusty lot with its granaries, warehouses, customs offices, and other buildings. Most of the warehouses are one or two-story buildings of a very utilitarian nature, with few frills. They are low, long, and have numerous loading docks on the outside. The buildings also have dry, clean storage rooms on the inside. We notice an abundance of the common house cat, *felix cat-*

> *Pomerium.* The roots of Roman religion are not polytheistic but animistic, and we'll explore their differences later. For now, it's important to understand that the animist lives in a dual world—one part material, the other spiritual. So, while it looks as though we're in Rome, we're really not yet in the city. To really be in the spiritual city founded by Romulus and ritually extended by later rulers, we must cross a supernatural border, a sort of spiritual membrane, called the Pomerium. During our walk in Rome, we'll cross the Pomerium once we cross the ancient Servian Wall and enter the Aventine Hill district.

tus. They are no doubt encouraged to prowl about and proliferate to keep down *rattus rattus* and *mus musculus* amid the *horrea* (grain storehouses). One day, this area will fall within the defensive perimeter of the Aurelian Wall, and with good reason. Though it is one of the most undistinguished places in all of greater Rome, it is an important distribution point for Rome's global commerce. Through her empire, Rome imports most of the essentials like olive oil and grain that keep her population alive and her prodigious mobs under control. Without this constant lifeline the masses would starve. The ensuing chaos would topple emperors and generals alike.

The sour smell comes from a mixture of various edible substances gone rancid. We detect the odors of: olive oil, cheese, the priceless fish sauce *garum,* and more. Mixed with that is powdered lime to minimize the stench.

From here to the other end of the city, where the old city port is at right and the Tiber Island in the middle of the bend, the right bank is one continuous series of docks. The present area is of prime importance, however, because not far away, around a bend, is the Sublician Bridge, near the ancient city harbor. The Sublician Bridge was built in the early Republic at one of the shallowest fording places on the river. It is also the end of the road for the deeper-draught barges. Shallower-draft, smaller vessels can travel further up the river, bringing fruits and vegetables to the markets around the old port. They might also carry special naval detachments assigned to duties at the Flavian Amphitheater (Colosseum) and *naumachia* (Gr 'sea battle') circuses. We see therefore the enormous importance of this staging area around the *Mons Testaceus* (Hill of Shards).

The day has grown full, and sunny, and we sweat as we stride over the flat, dry turf around the Hill of Shards. This is a manmade anomaly consisting entirely of the shards of about 53 million broken pieces of pottery. In its final days in the late Empire, it will reach a height of some 50 m (150 feet). Its circumference will span roughly a kilometer (meaning the diameter is about a third of a mile).

Unlike other Mediterranean people like the Greeks who were avid sailors, the Romans did not start out as first-class sailors. However, since Pompey swept the Mediterranean clear of pirates (before his partner in the First Triumvirate, Julius Caesar, swept Rome clean of Pompey), Roman ships have ruled the Mediterranean.

At the stone docks along the Tiber, huge grain ships are being unloaded. They are a government-contracted operation ongoing since Julius Caesar's time. These ships bring vast quantities of grain from the rich fields of the then-newly acquired province of Egypt. Likewise, corporate contractors (funded by venture capitalism) run fleets of large and small ships. They bring oceanic quantities of olive oil and wine from ports in Spain, North Africa, and coastal Gaul (future France).

Like ants, slaves swarm over the docks, gangplanks, decks, and around the customs houses. We break out in a sweat just watching them under the blue Mediterranean sky with its few patchy white clouds. The overseers don't brandish whips, contrary to modern lore. What you do notice is the prison-like guard stations quietly manned by soldiers with bows and arrows. Thousands of trained and disciplined soldiers and police are within a quick march of anyplace where this many slaves are together. The slaves themselves know the Romans have hard experience putting down insurrections. So, there is here a quiet sense of order, almost the illusion of contentment. The government also makes sure that citizens are kept on the dole and at the games to maintain public order. Private contractors delivering staples like grain or wine are exempt from the customs duties exacted on other goods passing through these docks.

We know from studies on human bones at Pompeii (which are exceptional, since the Romans invariably incinerate their dead leaving little for forensic archeologists) that most slaves are undernourished and overworked. It isn't so much that the Romans want to keep the slaves weak. More likely, it's that the large Roman underclass aren't much better off. Often, a half-fed slave is better off than a starving free citizen. We will continue bumping up against what seems to us odd or even sinister in Roman society, time and again at unexpected moments.

The container-ship of the time carries both dry and liquid bulk cargo in those odd pointy-ended *amphorae*. Now it appears that the economics of the amphora are as follows. It's not cheap to make an amphora, but the cargo it contains is more valuable. Thus, the container becomes an incidental expense. Furthermore, since Rome is a net importer of 'stuff,' most ships leave her harbors empty. It doesn't make much sense to load the amphorae back up. It's much easier to just leave them in Rome. Then the empty ship can go back for another load of 'stuff'. It's particularly undesirable to reuse jars that have held either olive oil or fish products like garum because the decay in the jars makes them highly unpleasant. What to do then with millions upon millions of jars sitting there on the dock?

First of all, each jar goes though a customs station, where an accountant uses a mallet to knock the handles off the jar. He then marks the ceramic piece with a pencil to indicate the importer. The broken handle stays on the table. At some point during the day, the tax accountants gather all the handles into separate piles depending on which contractor's name is on each, and count them. Next they assess the importer, and possibly the buyer, an import and a sales tax. The money for these transactions may be exchanged on the spot, depending on the size, or paper may change hands. Finally, the requisite amount stays in the bank in the form of a gold deposit. As in the modern world, the tax information can serve as verification for business partners. Bribery and corruption are illegal as in the modern world. There are, of course, cheaters. That's why the law courts over in the Roman Forum are busy day in and day out.

The jars themselves may be carried into the city, but this creates a disposal problem. Most of the buyers, if they are small fry, bring their own container to carry oil or garum away. There are thousands of individual stories, but they all add up to this. If a million jars go

So what's with these strange looking, awkward containers? Picture a rather typical open cargo ship of the time. Most do not have a deck. So the cargo lies directly on the inner surface of the hull. It is easy to understand that it's a bad idea to just dump tons of loose grain in there. The grain would be unprotected, and if the load shifts, as happens easily in a wind, the ship sinks, and the crew all drowns.

So why not have a sensible clay jar with a flat bottom? Based on millennia of bitter experience, captains learned that a jar with a pointed shape is the mathematically most effective way to load the most jars in the safest manner. This shape allows for a tightly stacked pile that is not going anywhere in a brisk wind or a rough sea.

> **Why Many Modern Banks Look Like Roman Temples.** Another oddity about Rome is that banks and temples are the same thing. The word 'bank,' in fact, comes from *banca*, 'table,' and refers to the money changing tables where pilgrims (depositors) bring their gifts to the god(s) of the temple. Priestly accountants charge a fee, which pays their salary and keeps the god in goat milk or candles or whatever that particular god relishes for sacrifice—usually, incense is also a staple, imported from Africa or Arabia. The most famous of Rome's temples is that of Juno Moneta (*moneta* here means 'she who minds/remembers/warns'). Juno is the wife of Zeus. Moneta means 'mint,' which is where our word 'money' comes from. Coins are actually struck in or for temples like that of Juno Moneta. Here the modern 'bank' has its origins, and it's all the more understandable why so many banks look like ancient Roman temples.

into Rome, a million jars must come out. Granted, some jars may be broken up if a homeowner needs an end cap for a drain pipe, or a shopkeeper needs a waste receptacle. We can imagine a thousand scenarios. Ultimately, though, most of the jars wind up smashed to bits and packed into the growing Mons Testaceus.

Building the hill of shards is, in itself, a sort of industrial process requiring dozens of workers. Engineers make sure the jars are broken up into small shards. Slaves with donkey carts carry baskets of the heavy shards up a ramp and onto the hill. The slaves (who wear boots to protect their feet from the jagged ceramic) evenly and systematically build up the hill one terrace at a time. While they do this, other slaves constantly throw in layers of white lime dust to absorb the smells of rotting fish and oil. The air is full of birds hunting for the little rodents that seek a morsel or two on the hill. Snakes and salamanders slither in and out, while squirrels dart about.

Before we take our leave of Mons Testaceus at the southern approach to Rome, we note that the great daily wait of the cargo wagons has begun at the gates. Wagon upon wagon is arriving from Ostia to enter the Rauduscule. Across the river, wagons are already lining up on the Port Road, which leads from the Claudio-Trajan Portus Novus (New Port) (across the river from Ostia) into Transtiberim.

CHAPTER 7

AVENTINE HILL

To enter the city proper, we pass through the crumbling Servian Wall. This is where we enter the sacred Pomerium, the ritual boundary of the city. We are in District 13 (Regio XIII) according to the redistricting of the city by Augustus about a century and a half ago.

We enter through a small street in the Servian Wall, near the large pyramidal tomb of Cestius. This is one of the more noteworthy of all the showy family tombs outside the city. It's some distance east of us, on the Port Road, near where one day the Port Gate of the Aurelian Wall will be built. We walk up a *clivus* (inclined street) rising sharply with the Aventine slope. On either side of us is a jumble of noisy, fetid lower class homes. Emanating from these dark cubicles and alleys comes a cacophony of children crying, mothers yelling, men laughing over wine and dice, and dogs barking. Smoke hangs in the air in a rancid mix of boiling laundry and stewing charcoal. We detect the odor of an indescribable mixture of fish soups and cheap sauces. Looming over the whole thing, on our eastern horizon above the rooftops, is the shadow of the Aqua Appia aqueduct.

Approaching the greater and lesser Armilustria neighborhoods, we have one of those magical moments that make our visit to Rome such a delight. Near here is a laurel grove, the Loretum, that forms a small grassy public park at the intersection of two *vici* (streets, neighborhoods). One is the Vicus Loreti Major on one side of the park, while on the other side is the Vicus Loreti Minor. The name refers to its laurel trees—there are still a few, but in the old days it was a small wood. For just a moment, we could be in a similar neighborhood in modern Rome. More importantly, we could be in a neigh-

42

borhood of a much older Republican Rome. Aristocratic trappings here are few, except in the mansions in the heights. Before long, much of this will be swept away under the vast Baths of Caracalla.

We hear the cries of children at play as a dozen ragged little boys and girls chase a ball across the dusty field. Nearby stand a cluster of elderly grannies in their long dresses, with veils over their heads. They gossip while keeping an eye on the children.

The Aventine is a mix of better and poorer housing. On its hillsides hang a variety of poor but not destitute neighborhoods. On top of the hill (as high as 65 meters above river level in places, or 213 ft) we see the high walls of palatial estates snaking among hillside olive trees and bushes. These are the equivalent of 21st Century U.S. gated estates. The floors up there are expansive and mosaic, and the halls full of statuary. The kitchens are full of exotic foods for important guests. Meanwhile, the working and poor people lead lives much simpler and in some ways truer to the archaic values of Rome. Most of the residents here still have some roots in the outlying villages. In fact, this area was until recently not enclosed within the Pomerium, or ritual city limits that coincided with the Servian Wall. It was considered *pagus,* or countryside.

Our path takes us to a shrine of Mars in a small park, or garden in the Vicus Armilustria. The neighborhood itself consists of workers, mostly poor Italians displaced from the Latium region. They are fortunate enough to have found work down along the docks, and housing up here in the hills. We have stepped into a teeming, noisy, smoky stack of tenements. We are given a foretaste of that ocean of humanity, the Subura, forming the east central region of Rome.

We walk past endless grain warehouses that feed the stomach of Rome. Since the population has grown to over a million, even the consolidated corporate plantations of Italy can't provide enough grain for the city's daily needs. In particular, the emperors need to keep the free dole and food handouts going to keep the city mobs in check. A large number of small farmers have been displaced by corporate buyouts (often forced, as farmers got into debt and lost their ancient homesteads). As a result, they had nowhere else to go. They were forced to join the unemployed and the homeless in the capital.

For now, we find a simple path of beaten earth that winds down into a cobblestone street. Like mountain goats, we hop from one boulder to the next until we emerge with wobbly knees a dizzying 30m (100 ft) below the Vicus Armilustria (whose name refers to a 'washing of weapons.' This is the custom of ritual cleansing. We follow winding, crowded streets with a tavern on every corner. At last we come upon the breathtaking sight of one of the largest shipping and shopping complexes built before the mid-20th Century.

CHAPTER 8

WORLD'S GREATEST SHOPPING MALL

Coming down from the Aventine toward the river, we walk along the continuous docks that line the city-side of the Tiber. From archaic times, there have been docks here for bringing supplies and market goods. Part of it is an especially fancy row of docks with offices and awnings, called the Emporium (from *emere*, to buy). The Emporium landing docks have square stone mooring protrusions, each capped by a lion's head and with a hole for tying up ships. The ships bring stone to the marble docks, and beyond that to the great river port. From the Mons Testaceus, it's about a kilometer (1000 m, or .6 mile) to our next stop, the Pons Sublicius. Before we go to the Cattle and Vegetable Markets, we must visit one of the world's largest shopping centers. There are other shops around here, including those of street vendors, but one building dominates. Let's go shopping.

We walk along, distracted by the hammer and bustle of work around the ships at the river on our left. Endless rows and files of warehouses seem stacked to our right, on the incline of the Aventine Hill. Near the river are remnants of the ancient Servian Wall. The incredibly long Porticus Aemilia dominates our view. We approach one of the largest shopping malls ever built before the mid-20th Century. At first glance, we see an endless straight row of lightly colored marble columns atop a low flight of steps. These are capped by three rows of barrel-vaulted roofs of poured concrete. At 487 m (1500 ft) long and 60 m (200 ft) wide, it is the first (and one of the largest) of many such buildings that we'll see in Rome. It is a *porticus* ('porch') imitating a popular Greek building style. We'll find that the Romans admire and copy much about Greek culture, while at heart being very queasy about what they consider Greek immorality.

From the Mons Testaceus to the river piers, we've seen almost exclusively men at work, whether free or slaves. Here, however, a profusion of women swarm around the Porticus Aemilia. They cling together in groups of three or four, or walk with a male relative. The women wear their best clothing and jewelry, and are excited about the outing.

Inside the Porticus Aemilia, which has at least three long arcades built on two stories, we find a riot of aromas, smells, sounds, and colors. Our eyes glaze over at the whirl of colors and noise, the smells and music. Thousands of shoppers mill about vendor booths lining the columns, aisles, and walls as far as the eye can see. As in a modern shopping mall, there is an open mezzanine on the second floor with more shops. There is no food court per se, but the air is pungent with the aromas of cooking delicacies. High up under the three long ceiling vaults, huge banner-like fans wave slowly back and forth to circulate the smoky air. Slaves standing along the walls operate pendular wooden shafts to keep the fans moving. Smoke and heat escape through vents in the eaves, while heavy clay roof tiles on the concrete roofs keep the building cool in the heat of day.

A young pickpocket snatches a purse and runs. Immediately, several agile young men in guard uniforms appear. They are the police, or urban *vigiles*. Some wear light, modified military-style armor, while yet others are detectives in plain white tunics. They dash after the boy, who sprints outside and down the steps, knocking over a nut-seller's basket. Shoppers briefly stop to look as the two men capture the teenager and beat him severely as dust rises around them. Shoppers shrug and turn back to their business, while more guards arrive carrying chains to take the young man to the local magistrate. The Romans have no jails to speak of—justice is swift, and often harsh. The pickpocket's victim, a stunned elderly woman, stands with her shopping bags at her feet. She holds her hands to her cheeks in shock, and is assisted by two shop girls supporting her shoulders. A manager arrives to take her name and address, as well as a statement to be read in court. The thief's case will most likely be heard in a day or so by a local magistrate, either in the harbor authority, or the nearby Aventine police court. Chances are, if it's a first offense, he may get a few months at hard labor. If he is a serious multiple offender, he might end up rowing a bireme for the rest of his life, or digging for salt. He might also find himself trying his luck with a sword in the arena against one of the third string, side-show gladiators. These men do nothing all day but kill inexperienced young street punks like this during half-time between serious matches.

As the crowd swirls around us, we get caught up in the dizzying frenzy of the marketplace. The richest of the rich may pretend not to shop here, but occasionally a jeweled and gilded litter gets carried through, accompanied by a retinue of guards and servants. We see one litter on the shoulders of four slaves, and walking before the litter is a herald carrying a standard of the imperial household. We see the shadows of two or three young princesses behind gauzy curtains as they excitedly point at this or that. One rug seller, a burly Syrian, tries to draw near to tell them about his pile of expensive Persian carpets, but two huge Nubian bodyguards shove him back so he sprawls onto his carpets. One doesn't approach imperial shoppers. They do the approaching if they are interested, or more likely have an agent do their talking for them. Sometimes, the wealthiest women, who officially wouldn't be caught dead in a common shop elsewhere, just come to watch. Window shopping and people-watching are favorite pastimes in any era.

An elderly patrician woman with a high hairdo leans from her litter to examine a pile of Persian carpets. No sooner have the four young, blond Germanic litter-bearers set her down, than Ennia Papiriae flies out from behind her curtains in a flutter of mauve silk edged with gilt. Her watery pale eyes have a hard look as she swoops in close to finger the matting and the fringes. The tip of her tongue protrudes, barely touching her upper lip, as she runs her palm over the thick, rich material. Behind her steps her accountant, the swarthy Egyptian-Greek slave Mettio, to dicker with the merchants. The rugs have come all the way from *Bactria* (Afghanistan). This surprises nobody here because her silk clothes have come from much farther, Hotan (in China), by way of the fabled Silk Road.

The Syrians who own the rugs cluster about—a father and his two sons—with nearly contemptuous defiance. Ennia is trying to

intimidate them, which only tells them she wants to buy. Since she
does not have a herald carrying official insignia, much less a *lictor*
bearing the *fasces* of power and authority, it's clear to the Syrians
that she is at best of minor nobility among the ancient families of
Rome. She is, more likely, just a newly wealthy show-off. The Syrians operate like wolves, separating Ennia from her accountant. The
handsomer of the sons kneels flatteringly beside the elderly woman.
He smiles radiantly into her lead-whitened face with its rouged lips
and pinked cheeks, its kohled eyes and penciled brows. He ignores
that her face still smells somewhat sourly of the milk-soaked bread
she had a slave girl rub patiently into her skin for an hour, to soften
the ravages of age. He ignores the musky warmth radiating from her
perfumed bosom. He can tell she is visibly softening under his flat-
tery. Meanwhile, the father and the other son engage Mettio in a dis-
tracting debate about carpets, import taxes, percentages, and other
numbers. Finally, somewhat weakly, Mettio and Ennia (she still on
her knees on the pile of rugs, he standing between the merchants)
call to each other for a decision. At Mettio's dubious nod, Ennia slaps
both hands on the rug, then rises. "I'll take this top one, and nothing more."

"Lady, you must have a matching set," her young flatterer says, rising with her.

"Two, you lumps. Nothing more."

"Ah, such stellar taste," say the Syrians altogether. They radiate with geniality, and open their arms as if Mettio and Ennia should jump into their embrace.

Mettio dourly says to the four blond boys: "Roll up the two rugs and get us out of here before they steal our clothes from us."

It's exhausting being around so many people, and we stop in a shady grove to eat. We buy honeyed fruit water, a bit of bread and goat cheese, some olives, some grapes, and a sweet juicy onion from a snack bar. Then we sit in deep, cool shade a little bit below ground level. Nature has considerately provided a huge oak to shade us, and we sit on its protruding roots. A stand of cypresses nearby blocks our view of the river, but provides more shade. As we eat, we watch the coming and going of people with their purchases. Every so often we catch a whiff of something not quite pleasant, rather sour, and we're not sure what. We also hear someone alternately singing and reciting poetry beyond that dark line of cypresses on the river side of our little picnic area. Then men working in the snack bar are harried, but friendly. It's a busy shopping day, and they have lots of customers for their wares. A specialty throughout Rome are little pungent bits of meat, which can be bought either with bread and wine, or wrapped Greek-style in cooked grape leaves, or on a stick.

When we are done eating we must follow nature's call, if only we knew where, and we inquire at the snack bar or taberna. Like most Roman shops, it's little more than a hole in the wall with a counter between the customer and the clerk. The thick-necked man with sweaty, curly black hair looks amused and points with a greasy finger to the cypresses. This is our real introduction to the Roman latrine, and what a marvel it is. This is actually a rather high-class exemplar, with a marble wall as its backdrop. It's an open-air potty for 20, with a slightly inclined clay-tile roof to shield from sun and rain. Other than that, it's more like a bus stop than a bathroom. It's simply a long marble bench with 20 openings cut into it, on which male and female Romans alike can wander in, hoist their tunics, and let the stench fill the bench, as it were. The unfortunate slaves who service this public function hasten back and forth with buckets full of fresh water. Wherever we are in Rome, there's always a major aqueduct someplace near, and this is no exception.

Here we are, amid a jarring Roman complacency about voiding in public, while two Greek poets take turns reciting from Attic classics. They intersperse these lines of verse with commercial messages, including singing odes to this or that gladiator of the Flavian Amphitheater (a.k.a. the Colosseum) or a charioteer at the Flaminian Circus nearby. That sets up a natural advertisement for the fighter's sponsor, who might be a wealthy baker seeking business, or a tribune seeking reelection. We get free entertainment with hidden messages that we should support Pindarus for aedile, or bury our dead in the Rauduscule Colombaria. We almost expect to be handed two-for-one coupons to the Circus Maximus (not far from here).

CHAPTER 9

BRIDGE TO
THE GODS

In a real sense, our next stop cuts to the heart of Roman history and religion. We'll visit the *Pons Sublicius* (Sublician Bridge), the oldest river bridge in Rome.

First, from the Porticus Aemilia, we walk through the Marmorata directly on the Tiber's edge. *Marmor* is marble.

The landings where we now stand specialize in handling sheets and blocks of marble for the city's temples and other public buildings. We pass through an area of docks specially configured for offloading heavy loads of marble from ships. We see huge wood and steel lifting cranes operated by block and tackle pulleys—powered by gangs of slaves walking in a large wooden drum-cage.

We stand at the pinpoint, the crux, of Roman history, on this very spot. Around the history of the Sublician Bridge cluster the earliest centers of archaic Roman civilization—the Roman Forum, the Capitoline Hill, and the Palatine Hill. This bridge, is where a small band of desperate marsh dwellers took their first step that would lead them to conquer half the world. Roman history is wrapped around this Sublician Bridge, along with the Via Salaria and the salt trade. The bridge lies innocuously before us, a dark blur of wood upon stone piles, while

Slave power short-circuits Rome from advancing to mechanized industry—because there is always a plentiful supply of human labor, the Romans aren't forced to rely on mechanized industry, with a few exceptions like, for example, the water wheels that drive giant grinding mills in Rome's largest bakeries, or in great silver mines like those in Lusitania, Spain.

the sand-colored Tiber churns and foams around its pilings with icy power. It is not the original bridge, which was swept away in 23 B.C. during one of the Tiber's occasional destructive floods, and again recently. During the reign of the current emperor, Antoninus Pius, the bridge had to again be totally rebuilt. More than any other place in Rome, this bridge has shaped the direction of our walk, and here we pause to understand why this is so.

Imagine the landscape around here as it must have been around 750 B.C. (900 years before our walk in 150 A.D.). Three peoples predominate: the Etruscans, the Latins, and the Greeks. Around 390 B.C over a million Gauls pour down through Italy and destroy the old balance of power, leaving Rome in a position to start grabbing power. The Carthaginians, a Phoenician colony, will then be Rome's last obstacle to becoming the dominant power in the Mediterranean.

North lies Etruria. We might spot the distant fires of Veii, the nearest Etruscan settlement ten miles northwest of Rome. Etruscan civilization itself is just starting to find its steam as the dark ages after the Bronze Age yielded to the Iron Age. The Etruscans stay north of the Tiber for the most part, though they will pick Rome like a ripe plum in the 600s. The Tarquin dynasty of Etruscan kings will rule until expelled in 519 B.C.

Archaic Rome lies on the other side of the Tiber because her founders are Latins, a separate people from the Etruscans. The very name *Latium* (flat) gives a sense of the terrain, which is bounded by distant mountains on three sides, and the Tyrrhenian (Etruscan) Sea to the west. The sky is drizzly and gray, with charcoal shadows under cold silvery clouds. Wind blows uneasily over ruffled marsh waters, bending tall reeds and making high grasses dance about in endless unease. Other Latium towns within a day or two walking included Alba Longa to the southeast, and Lavinium southwest near the coast. South of Latium, the newly awakened Greek city-states have sent colonists, but they have not yet forayed much beyond Neapolis (Naples) or Paestum.

Boat-shaped Tiber Island marks a big bend in the Rumo or Rumon (Tiber) River. Water rushes around that island, turns west, and flows through the marshes out to sea. In that turn, just downstream of the island, is the lowest and most fordable point in the Tiber. Anyone north of the Tiber, wishing to travel inland, must cross the river and is most likely to do so at that point. This becomes the defining element in early Roman power. For the moment, let's refer to the subjects of our study not as Romans or proto-Romans, but as Palatine Latins (even though they quickly merged with those Latins and possibly Sabines dwelling atop the nearby Capitoline and other hills).

The Etruscans had not yet spread beyond the Tiber, and in fact may have been reluctant to leave their lush highlands (so famous to moderns for the beautiful Tuscan landscape) to struggle with the Tiber delta. The Etruscans acquired highly developed civil engineering skills, which they would teach to their captive Roman population. During that century of breathing space before the Etruscan conquest, the Palatine Latins were able to exploit this river crossing as a choke point of trade. The escaped slaves, former bandits, and whoever else lived in the swamps of that region consolidated their own unique animist culture.

One story has it that a tribe of Latins called the Ramnes dominated this little region, hence *Romani*. Another story makes a connection to the nearby town of Tibur (east of the city), and that the Tiber gets its name from there. Yet another story has the river being called Rumo (which might be linguistically congruent with the little stream Almo, just south of Rome).

As the Palatine Latins consolidated their power locally, there was not yet a bridge. Most likely they provided ferry service back and forth. In that lawless part of Latium, it's likely that traders in salt and other goods were glad to pay for safe passage and also for protection. To protect their own backs, the Romans developed aggressive military skills and soon subdued their neighbors. Had the Palatine Latins been simply bandits, the kings all around would have sent soldiers to quell them. So, the Palatine Latins had to project confidence all around and a strong moral stance when they made alliances, contracts, and deals. That would not guarantee much in a treacherous environment, for we know they lived in constant fear of invasion (as we'll see when we get to the Capitoline Hill a little later in our walk). As long as the kings in the surrounding hill countries could rely on the Palatine Latins to protect salt traders and other merchants, to not gouge them excessively with tolls, and to keep order and stability in the region, it meant that the kings had something less to worry about beyond their small borders. In such a cocoon we imagine that the Palatine Latins flourished and grew.

For a long time, their territory was limited to the area immediately around their river crossing. In all, their territory probably was L-shaped. It included Tiber Island and the Janiculum Hill across the river as a bulwark against the Etruscans. Perhaps they controlled at best some 240 square miles (which sounds like a lot, but consists of a space about 20 × 12 miles). They probably had a boat or two, and ferried salt traders back and forth. Since they had to keep order in their territory anyway, they provided the traders a military escort to the border of the next kingdom, most likely for a price.

Legend has it that Ancus Marcius built a bridge from *sublicae*, wooden piles. This became the Pons Sublicius (Sublician Bridge). Its precise location within a few yards is in dispute. Italian civil engineers, in the late 1800s, explosively removed the last traces of the latest version of the bridge to clear the Tiber channel. In any case, the original Sublician Bridge crossed the Tiber somewhere below the Tiber Island, either in the turn or at its end, putting its eastern side at the Forum Boarium, the Cattle Market.

The Romans honored their past and were extremely scrupulous that every ritual and every public activity be done according to strict standards. Religion and the state were one, touching all aspects of daily life as in the animist past. The Romans appointed a college of pontiffs (singular *pontifex*, plural *pontifices*) meaning literally 'bridge-makers' (*pont-* 'bridge' + *fex-*, old Latin suffix 'maker') to oversee the maintenance of the bridge. Thus, the state of the bridge was a religious as well as civil matter, and anything really bad that happened to it was a *prodigium* (portent, sign, ominous event). Other offices of similar responsibility included curators (*curator*, one who cares for or about something, from *cura*, 'care'). Bridges, walls, temples, the river itself, all had curators who were responsible to the civil and religious authorities on the condition of their charge. If a prodigium or problem became evident, it was a matter for both

Out of Rome's animist past comes the definition of her future. For an overview of Roman history, see Appendix A. For a fuller appreciation of Roman state and religion, which were one, see Appendix B.

the civil engineers and the relevant college of priests. One not only solved the problem in the material world, but one also performed rituals to fix the problem which surely had to simultaneously have its manifestation in the supernatural world all around. That concept is a defining theme throughout Roman history.

The college of pontiffs developed its own system of auguries and similar system of religious rituals (pontifications). Several reasons are possible why the Romans were so adverse to using iron in the bridge, or in any public (therefore religious) structure, particularly temples. For one thing, since no iron was used the first time, in the Roman mind it would be sacrilege against the ancestors to use iron on buildings of religious importance in the future. Beyond that, iron was a curious metal associated with supernatural and stellar origins. It seems fair to think ancient people thought of comets when they saw how ferrous stones give off sparks when struck. The ancients also discovered that iron acts as a lightning rod during electrical discharges associated with thunder clouds and wet terrain. The Latin word *disaster* (*dis-* 'bad' + *astrum*, 'star') is a reference to sky gods. More than once a temple or other public structure containing iron was destroyed by lightning. The Romans concluded that using iron leads to disaster, and must therefore be evil in the eyes of the gods or spirits. Long after they adopted iron tools, roman priesthoods still disavowed the use of iron in temples or altars. If an iron object so much as touched a temple wall, the entire structure had to go through extensive purification rituals. Such deeply rooted, animistic thinking from the spirit-haunted marshes of the early Iron Age stayed at the core of Roman beliefs, long after polytheism and mystery religions wrapped themselves around the animist core, hiding it from view but never from power. That is the secret why Roman religion stayed robustly Roman while inundated with foreign people and ideas—and why the Romans could not accept Christianity without giving up their ancient identity.

As the bridge pontiffs grew in power and wealth, they remained among the most sacred of all Rome's institutions. As the Romans started becoming wealthy, they couldn't keep their coins and treasures down by the river, but had to move them to the best fortified spot in the area. That was the steep cliff at the northwestern edge of the Capitoline Hill. So, while keeping their racket going at the river crossing, they moved their money to the fortified Temple of Capitoline Jupiter. Throughout their history, the Romans would keep up the association between temples, money, mints, and the state. The Capitoline Hill became the religious nerve center of Rome. Remarkably, the chief priest of Rome was the Pontifex Maximus at the Temple of Capitoline Jupiter, a role that in later centuries would be given to (or taken by) Roman emperors. In time, the title of Supreme Pontiff would be carried into modern times by the Pope; all that, from a wooden bridge.

Leaving the Sublician Bridge and its cardinal role in Roman history, we walk on along the docks to the lively market places.

PART THREE

GREAT RACEWAY DISTRICT

(Regio XI. Circus Maximus)

CHAPTER 10

ANCIENT RIVER HARBOR

Every inch of available river front is occupied by docks, on both sides of the river. This includes a special naval detachment some distance upriver. They support *naumachia* or sea battles on several large artificial lakes. Near the Colosseum is the Misenum Barracks. The sailors stationed there are in charge of the rigging of a giant sail-like sunshield that covers the northern seats of the Colosseum.

As we leave the Sublician Bridge and walk along the big river curve on the east embankment, we come to a small harbor. We pass from the Aventine district (Regio XIII) into the Circus Maximus district (Regio XI). Indeed, the largest entertainment venue of all time (big enough to sponsor the 1968 Woodstock festival on a daily basis) lies just behind the harbor and markets we are about to visit.

Walking eastward on the docks, we see a stone groin in the water ahead in the turn of the river. This groin or break was built long ago to shield the area from flood waters. Anchored within the groin are a mass of small barges. Slaves noisily swarm around these vessels. We smell a mixture of vegetables and dung, as well as fish frying in little snack stands. Many of the vessels are simply flat transports on which cattle and pigs munch from feed bags while standing with their hooves in a mix of dirt and hay. The animals wear blinders to keep them from panicking, and they are tied to a wooden crossbar in each boat. Other boats are loaded with vegetables and fruit. We see the green globes of cabbages and yellower melons piled high. Here are baskets of apples, pears, and pomegranates. There are bushels of bright flowers, red and white and violet, as well as bunches of herbs (anise, saxifrage, lavender, and gardenia, as well as basil, thyme, parsley, sage, coriander, and many more). We notice small clay vats of honey to sweeten things at the household table, as well as little blocks of sea salt. Goats hop about, and sheep are never far away. The cobblestones are slippery with their droppings, and slaves rush after the scampering animals with buckets of water and brooms.

Above this little harbor are several markets conjoined by cobblestone walks. The vendors have tables set up, and most have *umbrellae* over them to guard against the midday sun. Even so, the wiry farm women working at the markets are sweaty and red-faced. Many are toothless, but their faces have a lean, attractive liveliness. Their eyes radiate saucy humor. They are expert hagglers who can figure a customer out in seconds. They are better at this than the indolent shopkeepers of the Porticus Aemilia. Many of them have walked all night from some outlying village. They sell their produce here, and then take the proceeds to their relatives in a Rome neighborhood.

In recent generations, large shopping centers and meat markets have opened in the eastern hills of the city, but the population explosion keeps this river port busy. Farmers and light shippers using the little port don't have to wait in the wilting sun until nightfall. It costs a bit more to use a river boat, but that cost is passed along to willing customers. Here you can buy a cow, a goat or pig, and have it slaughtered and salted in your neighborhood. This allows you to have something to tide you over to the next market day. You might even have sausages made with the casings, and pickle some pigs' feet. Nothing is wasted. You also find little wine stands here and there, in addition to *tabernae* and *cauponae*.

As we find at every turn in Rome, there is a temple or other religious shrine in the harbor and Cattle Market area. Among them is a small round one to Mercury, in a Greek style. Amid the several others in the Cattle Market is the Temple of Portunus. As the name indicates, Portunus is an ancient deity who personifies the main spirit of the port. This is in keeping with the animist practice of associating spirits with any place or object in the material world: from the hinges and locks on our doors to each small niche or phase in the agricultural cycle. To clarify: for moderns, 'deifying' is a loaded word, it can leads to argumentation, philosophy, justifications; none of which is necessary in an animist, pantheistic world. Every corner, every crossroads, every tumbled ruin in some wild place, or the wild place itself, every tree or rock or bush in it, has its own spirit (*genius*). In fact, a place may be inhabited by many such spirits. Eventually, when a spirit enters into the popular tongue, and stops being a nameless entity, it becomes a named god in the polytheist mode. Consequenty, all the spirits of the port became personified in the rather vague notion of a Portunus. That's not immediately the same as a full-fledged polytheistic deity like the 'Zeusified' Jupiter, with a whole body of mythological stories wrapped around him. Still, the spirit of the port must have his propitiations, and he gets them in this very old, Etruscan-style open temple. We'll see that style again in the massive Temple of Capitoline Jupiter when we climb up the Capitoline Hill shortly.

The portico of the Temple of Portunus is filled with the vibrant and colorful displays of dozens of flower sellers, for this is their special area. Sellers of charms and readers of fortunes abound, as do followers of various religions who want to proselytize. The gendarmerie *(vigiles)* are out in force, and pickpockets stand together in alleys, looking about with shifty eyes—one eye on the cops, the other trawling for likely victims. Like any market, this place has its daily cycle. It's early yet, and the cabbages still smell fresh. Every so often a wizened little man in a grayish tunic over here, or a young slave boy in a loincloth over there, pours a bucket of cool water over his wares and makes sure they are sheltered from the sun. Most of the booths along the warehouse walls have colorful awnings. We might as well make a big detour here into the valley between the Aventine and Palatine Hills, were the Circus Maximus spreads its enormous venue.

The Temple of Neptune pictured here is much like the Temple of Portunus. It stands a little distance upriver near the Pantheon and the Circus Flaminius.

CHAPTER 11

CIRCUS MAXIMUS

From the Cattle Market, we should head directly north to the Capitoline Hill. The logical progression of history would take us there from the Sublician Bridge. Since we are in the eleventh district, however, we can't resist first visiting one of the area's (and history's) great attractions. We continue walking east through the Cattle Market, and enter the valley between the Aventine and Palatine Hills. In archaic times, portions of this valley periodically flooded until the harbor was built up. We imagine a swampy area like the early Forum Romanum, north of the Palatine. Much of the water coming into Rome from underground springs was quite potable and sweet. In the early days, when the Circus Maximus had not yet attained this gigantic size, there was a shallow lake or series of ponds near here, said to be filled with nature spirits and water nymphs. One can imagine the Tiber in flood stage overflowing the eastern bank where the city port and markets are. One can picture yard-deep, swirling waters rushing through this valley, yellowed with disturbed sand. In the early days, a natural stream—probably the Marrana, which comes from outside the city along the Via Tusculana, then turns north into Regio I, Porta Capena, roughly parallel to the Via Appia—flowed through the circus grounds, and an archway was put in the *spina* to let the water get through. This was covered over in time, but indicates again the boggy nature of the lowlands around here. Eventually the stream finds its way into the Tiber by way of another cloaca, whose opening is about 100 meters (300 ft.) downstream from that of the Cloaca Maxima.

In the long valley between the Aventine and Palatine, we come upon the largest entertainment venue ever built. Even in modern times, the grassy outline of the Circus Maximus will overwhelm its surroundings. In 150 A.D., it is a breathtaking and colossal structure that looms before us. It is at least 28 meters (about 92 ft.) high, the equivalent of a nine-story building. The seating is in banks, totaling 30 meters (over 98 ft. wide) rising to the top of the wall. The lower parts of the structure are stone and concrete, and near the top are wooden bleachers. Inside and outside, it is faced with both common travertine and stretches of finer marbles.

Its overall dimensions are astounding. It is 621 meters (2037 ft, or .39 mile) long, and 118 meters (387.1 feet, or .075 mile) wide. Most astonishing, however, is its capacity: estimated at over a quarter million persons.

In shape, it is a long rectangle with rounded ends. That suits the intrinsic purpose of the *circus* ('circle' or 'roundway'), namely racing along a straight stretch and then going into a long turn at high speed (as on a horse or in a chariot). Down the middle is a dividing wall, or *spina* (spine). At each end of the spina is a turning post, or *meta*, 'goal.' At the eastern end of the *spina* stands an Egyptian obelisk brought by ship during the reign of Augustus, dating to 1280 B.C. On top of the *spina* are a series of *ova*, 'eggs,' to tick off the laps. In 55 B.C., when Pompey put on a show for the dedication of the temple of Venus Victrix (Venus Victorious), which was a part of the Theater of Pompey, he had 20 elephants fight. They trampled the iron railing separating the spectators from the sands. It is not entirely clear what happened when the elephants joined the spectators, but one can surmise the worst. Soon after, Caesar installed a moat before the stands. In 33 B.C., Augustus' great friend Agrippa installed seven bronze dolphins, whose mouths discharged water into a trough, from atop the spina. Two years later, a terrible fire raced through and destroyed much of the Circus. Augustus had it rebuilt, and put in place the Egyptian obelisk which, in modern times, will grace the Piazza del Popolo.

Starting gates for charioteers are staggered lane by lane, as in modern track events, to ensure each competitor an even beginning out of the chariot pens. Though these pens were originally built of sedimentary tufa stone, Emperor Claudius had them redone in marble, and the goal posts in gilded bronze.

As with all things Roman, the origins of the circus are religious—yet, its arcades are occupied by taverns and shops of every kind, including brothels. The games themselves may, in their primitive origins in the Iron Age kingdom, have represented some contest between good and evil, or more likely, between life and death.

During the Republic, the Circus Maximus was under the supervision of special magistrates *(censores)*. They not only saw to its upkeep, but made sure all the proper religious rituals were observed. These might include processions, sacrifices, auguries, and the like. Every public structure of any consequence had its dedicated public administrators. As to the Circus Maximus, Caesar, and after him every emperor, dedicates time and treasure to enhancing and repairing the great racing complex. When a fire broke out among some religious shrines on the wall facing the Aventine in 33, Caligula promptly had the wall rebuilt, and then spent considerable time and money on ceremonies to rededicate the shrines. Calamity befell Rome in 64 during the reign of Nero, when a vast fire destroyed parts of the city. During that and other fires, the circus was promptly rebuilt with great expense and ceremonies. We have hints that 13,000 perished in some disaster (crushed, perhaps, by collapsing arches) in the time of Domitian (ruled 81–96).

It seems that a fifth of Rome is here today. We hear the roar of a quarter million voices as we approach the stadium. Vendors do a brisk business from smoking snack stands; aromatic stands with fresh bread, garlic, onions, fish, and spiced meats. There are also specialty stands with wine and honeyed fruits. In the shadows of a tree grove, young male and female prostitutes ply their trade.

We pass through the stands, and glimpse an ocean of arms rising and falling, faces contorted with excitement, as teams of powerful chariots leave dust trails in yet another breakneck lap. In 150 A.D., few combats occur here. The chariot races actually compete with gladiatorial contests in the popular interest. We leave the Circus Maximus with a strange sense of oppression—hearts beating slower and harder, perhaps—because we find nothing here that brings any joy. Again, we wonder at how different the people of this time and place are, who passionately love all this brutal drama.

At the southward end of the long Circus Maximus, we stand at the northernmost end of the Appian Way inside the city. We are at a major crossroads of three streets: one coming northeast from Regio XII (Public Pool), one coming southwest from Regio II (Caelimontium), and a sort of minor continuations of the Appian Way, a street that runs between the northeast length of the Circus Maximus and the southwestern slope of the Palatine. The latter street is what we are going to take back to the city markets and harbor.

We take one more glance southward, to the high walls around the ruined Capena Gate in the old Servian Wall. The Appian Way runs through this gate on its way to Capua, Tarentum, and ultimately Brundisium which is on the Adriatic coast on the upper rear of the heel of the boot of Italy. We will be back here shortly. Over the brushy heaps remaining from the Capena Gate and the Servian Wall, we glimpse the temples and trees, as well as workshop and factory walls, of the Porta Capena District (Regio I), which we will visit soon.

We will now retrace our steps past the long, high walls of the Circus Maximus. We will go back through the Vegetable Market overlooking the Tiber near its bend and near the Sublician Bridge. Finally, we will pass through the Cattle Market slightly inland and up the slopes of the Capitoline Hill.

PART FOUR

ROMAN FORUM DISTRICT

(Regio VIII.
Forum Romanum)

CHAPTER 12

VELABRUM

The Capitoline Hill and the western half of the Forum Romanum are both in Regio VIII (District 8, called Roman Forum). To approach the Capitoline Hill from the Forum Boarium, we pass through one of Rome's busiest neighborhoods. Stop and look around for a moment. Behind us is the Tiber. Across the river, Transtiberim juts into the river bend like a small peninsula raised on stone blocks. Between this shore and the other, three major bridges allow traffic to pour in from Transtiberim and the New Port opposite Ostia. Looking downriver, we see the marble-docks and beyond that the great shopping complex of the Porticus Aemilia. Setting our sights upriver past the ancient Porta Flumentana (River Gate) in the Servian Wall, we spot the theater district of the Campus Martius, with its many historical and religious monuments. Among them are the Flaminian Circus, the Pantheon, the Baths of Nero, the Stadium of Domitian, and the Theaters of Pompey and Marcellus.

We come up from the city port, through the Velabrum, on one of Rome's busiest thoroughfares: *Vicus Tuscus,* or Etruscan Street (Neighborhood, what have you). It's also known as the *Vicus Turarius,* after the dealers in perfume and incense whose shops line the street levels of buildings. Nearby is also the Vicus Unguentarius (Street of Perfumers). Pickpockets, beggars, and all sorts of shady-looking characters abound. So do priests, scribes, merchants, middle-class women out shopping or strolling with their husbands, and officials hustling on government business. On every corner stands a stone shrine, and beside it a toga-clad priest tending to its incense and collections. We are within the Pomerium, the sacred boundary of the city, and the traditional gods of the archaic countryside are still the primary deities. Some of the shrines are those of the deified emperors.

Now, turning east, we enter the area known as the *Velabrum*. The origin of its name is lost in antiquity, but the Velabrum is simply the little valley between the Capitoline and Palatine Hills. This is where the runoff of the Forum Romanum drained into the Tiber since primordial times. Much of that runoff has been diverted through the Cloaca Maxima, and other drains, into the Tiber. The Velabrum is a densely built-up section with some seedy corners here and there, but overall we are heading into a region of immense wealth. The Velabrum's main street is the *Vicus Tuscus*. It's said to derive its name from the skilled Etruscans who lived and worked here in the early days of Rome. The street level is full of small shops, and the air is darker, noisier, among the tall buildings here. Most of the buildings house offices of the harbor authority, the warehouses, the tax collectors, and money lenders. Voices echo among the canyon-like streets, and we see children playing in dead-end courts off on either side. There are small courtyards with workbenches spilling out from tightly cramped shops. Makers of incense and religious goods cater to the religious trade, since this area is within the Pomerium and the old religion is strongest in this central region of Rome. Tucked in odd corners around here are the makers, menders, and cleaners of togas. Some shops specialize in the purple borders.

We would be hard-pressed to find any official temples of Isis or other foreign cults within the sacred Pomerium. As soon as we get past the Servian Wall in any direction, we may stumble right and left over temples of Isis, Serapis, and a dozen other cults—but not here. This is Rome proper, chugging along powerfully with the engine of her archaic animism wrapped in the later trappings of polytheism. Every little area or neighborhood in these precincts has some deep religious or historical importance going back a thousand years or more.

We come to a point where a street, the *Clivus Argentariorum* (incline of bankers and money lenders) goes north, left from our perspective, outside the Servian Wall (therefore outside the Pomerium) and into the Campus Martius, along the Tiber shore northwest of here. Let's go take a peek. The Clivus Argentariorum makes a bit of a dogleg going downhill, and lands at the edge of a vast, steaming stew of buildings. It's a mix of high-rise tenements of the poor, and expensive digs for the rich. We'll catch the Campus Martius toward the end of our walk, so we'll go no further here today. Later in our walk, we'll see the largest concentration of shops and tenements in the vast population stewpot of the Subura.

Part of the northern side of the Forum Romanum is in Regio IV, Temple of Peace, but that district is so large and vibrant, that we'll visit the entire Forum Romanum on this part of our walk. Regio VIII is filled with plenty of history, and lots to see, more than we

The Districts of Rome. Augustus, in remaking Rome as a necessary reapportionment to keep up with the realities of urban growth, increased the ancient number of districts within the Pomerium, or sacred city limits, from four to fourteen. The names of the 14 Augustan regions are not necessarily those officially assigned by the Roman authorities, although the numbers are authentic. The names (Circus Maximus, Porta Capena, etc.) were assigned by an unknown census taker or official tourist of the Fourth Century. He left a little laundry list of sites and statistics called the *Notitiae Regionum Urbis Romae* (Noteworthy Things in the Districts of the City of Rome). The list was transcribed about a century later, which copy came down through the centuries as the *Curiosum Urbis Romae* (Things Worth Looking Into in the City of Rome). Both documents disappeared in ancient times, and then reappeared in a private collection during the Renaissance. The documents, referred to as the Regionary Catalogs or Regionaries, are almost verbatim identical. For each region, they list not only the sights to see, but statistics on such things as the number of neighborhoods and their corresponding crossroad shrines, the number of the local police and fire brigade, the number of both tenements and palatial homes, the number of public water outlets from the aqueducts, and some measurement across the width at unknown points. Cryptic as the Regionaries are, they are a great help to anyone who wishes to figure out how many people lived in each district.

See *Appendix C: Our Itinerary* for more information about these fascinating ancient tour guides, the Regionary Catalogs.

can absorb without living here all of our lives. First let's pass through
the Velabrum, then up around the Capitoline Hill, and down into
the Roman Forum itself.

The name *Velabrum* may be of uncertain origin, but the geography is easy to understand. It's a long, narrow stretch of low ground
from the Tiber shore (just downstream from the Tiber Island, where
the river turns and the city port with its cattle and vegetable markets
lies) to the Roman Forum. It runs between the Capitoline and Palatine Hills. The Forum was originally a dismal area of rocks and thorns,
with swampy patches—a wasteland for the disposal of the dead,
whether in Latin cremation urns resembling the huts of the living,
or by Etruscan-style burial. The last burials occurred in the Sixth
Century B.C. as the necropolis was turned to uses of the living.

As a major drainage channel for the surrounding hills, the
Forum and the Velabrum were a sewer, in addition to being burial
grounds. The city begins with a curse on its head, because its founders built sacred altars and temples on ground already dedicated to
the dead. A good deal of ritual cleansing will go on around the Forum for the next thousand years. The Velabrum was very swampy in
antiquity, enough so to float small boats—probably for fishing and
hunting in flood season, or just to cross from one hill to the other.
Whenever the Tiber went into flood, the Velabrum went under water, especially before high stone embankments were built during
the Republic. One of the important early achievements of the Romans was to first channel, and then cover, the flow of effluent from
the Roman Forum and through the Velabrum. The drainage actually involved a larger area beyond the Forum, and a natural stream
flowed through there to the Tiber. The Tarquin dynasty began chan-
neling this stream between walls, as the city grew. Sometime during
the early empire, this channel was finally walled over, and the result was a major underground sewage outlet, a paved cylinder,
whose mouth opened upon the Tiber at a point near the Tiber Island. It will still be visible, and in use, in the 21st Century. At some
points it is 4.2 m (13.78 ft, or almost two standard modern eight
foot stories) high and 3.2 m (10.5 ft) wide. For centuries, the
Cloaca Maxima was considered a marvel of engineering.

As we become more acquainted with Roman religiosity, we are
not in the least surprised to learn that a local animist deity named

Cloacina started being revered very early around this vital urban public works project. Over time, Cloacina becomes identified with Venus, and thus assumes the title Venus Cloacina (one might say, 'Venus of the Sewer'). A shrine to her, in the form of a small round temple with a metal balustrade, existed in Republican times. This makes more sense when we reflect that Venus is associated not only with beauty, but also with healing. There has been a cult of the goddess *Febris* (Fever) a few hundred feet nearby on the Palatine since ancient times. Illness has always been a major issue and a mystery for the Romans, as for any urban dwellers. Regulating the flow of sewage was a clear victory for health and sanitation, one that would not be equaled by any modern city until the late 19th Century. By 150 A.D., we find the area is paved over, dry, and clean. The Velabrum is an important commercial and industrial center in its own right. It is a thoroughfare in and out of the central city. We are amazed at the throngs of shoppers, the smell of smoke and incense, the sounds of tambourines and flutes. We notice the entertainers—here a snake charmer, there a contortionist. Of course there are a hundred pickpockets to exploit those watching. There are religious processions mingling with official couriers and important-looking merchants and priests. The human parade here is dense, and endless. We see humble slaves and gorgeous courtesans. We see police (urban cohorts) on patrol in their relatively simple paramilitary uniforms, and Praetorian Guards in their resplendent ceremonial uniforms. We float inside the jugular vein of Antonine Rome.

Our path takes us through the Vicus Tuscus to the Roman Forum, to reach the Capitoline Hill.

The other main street or neighborhood in the Velabrum is the *Vicus Iugarius,* one of the most ancient streets in Rome. It dates to the archaic period of Iron Age salt traders, and the origin of its name is lost in the mists of time. The name suggests *iugum* (yoke) but probably does not represent there ever having been a quarter of makers and sellers of harnesses. Effectively, Vicus Tuscus runs along the southern edge of the Velabrum, at the foot of the Palatine Hill, from the Forum Boarium to the Forum Romanum. Vicus Iugarius follows a similar route along the northern edge of the Velabrum, so the Velabrum quarter lies between the two streets. The Capitoline Hill is directly north of the Vicus Iugarius. The Vicus Iugarius on its

Tiber-side curves around the foot of the Capitoline Hill, cuts through the Servian Wall near the Porta Flumentana (River Gate), and it enters the Campus Martius right near the ancient voting place (the Saepta). This is where Agrippa built the Pantheon. This is the Flaminian Circus district, which we'll visit later. On their Forum Romanum (eastern) ends, the Vicus Iugarius and the Vicus Tuscus arrive at the Forum at either end of the Basilica Iulia.

CHAPTER 13

CAPITOLINE HILL

We follow the Vicus Tuscus through the Velabrum until we arrive at the Roman Forum. At the intersection of the Via Sacra and the Vicus Tuscus, we pass the Temple of Castor on the right corner and the Basilica Iulia on the left corner. We will explore the Forum Romanum a bit later. At the moment, we merely pass through. We hasten through its impressive jungle of marble monuments to the northwestern end of the Forum Romanum. After passing the Vicus Iugarius on our left, we ascend the Capitoline Hill by way of the Clivus Capitolinus, a steeply curving ramp containing stairs.

The *Mons Capitolinus* is the religious and ritual epicenter of Rome. Its slope on the Tiber side is about 200 meters (656 ft) from the river. Tradition says the name derives from the find, during the excavation for the original Temple of Jupiter, of a large human head. According to hastily summoned Etruscan augurs, it was an omen that Rome would one day become *caput mundi*, 'head of the world.'

In modern times, the Capitoline is almost totally overwhelmed by the enormous monument to King Vittorio Emanuele, built 1885–1911. Many Romans consider it a monstrous confection of white marble, and give it various nicknames like 'the dentures' or 'the typewriter.' It obscures one's view looking toward the Capitoline Hill from the Campus Martius in the north. Other large structures include the Church of Santa Maria Aracoeli, the Piazza del Campidoglio, and the Palazzo dei Conservatori.

The Capitoline is the smallest[4] of the Seven Hills, being only about 460 m (1509 ft) long, and, on average, 180 m (591 ft) wide. It lies along a north-east, south-west axis. What made it a good defensive position was that it was surrounded by steep cliffs on all but the south-east side, where it descends into the Roman Forum, the heart of Rome. The Servian Wall enclosed the steep sides while inner defensive walls still somewhat separated the Capitolium from the Roman Forum in the city just below.

The Capitoline actually consists of three elements, which are the north (Arx) and south (Capitoline or Tarpaian) summits and the narrow connecting ridge (the Asylum) between them. While Lanciani cites an elevation of roughly 46m (151 ft) at the Temple of Juno, Plattner[5] offers 39m (128 ft) for the northern segment but 49m (161 ft) for the Arx itself, 38m (125 ft) for the southern (Capitoline or Tarpaian), and 30m (98 ft) for the connecting ridge (in ancient times the *Asylum* ('sanctuary,' 'refuge,' 'place of safety'); the modern Capitol Plaza, or Piazza del Campidoglio, begun with Michelangelo's design in the early 1500s as a Renaissance terrace overlooking the city).

In archaic times, the Sabines may have had a settlement on the Quirinal Hill, one kilometer from the Tiber and Tiber Island, and claimed ownership of the northern elevation of the Capitoline (the Arx). These are the same Sabines who did not fare well at the hands of the Romans Recall the legendary 'Rape of the Sabines,' in which the earliest settlers of the future Rome, who were probably escaped slaves and miscreants invited their neighbors over for a feast, filled them with wine and song, killed the men, and kept the women as their wives. While this story may horrify us, it is proudly recalled by the Romans throughout their history. The Romans absorbed the Sabines, and all of their other neighbors as they seized the hills of Rome.

Back in the Eighth Century B.C., when the college of pontiffs (the first magistrates of the river crossing) moved their treasury, they chose the highest point on the Capitoline, which is has its back to the cliffs on the north side. There, they broke ground for the Arx ('fortress' or 'citadel') amid great religious ceremony. Around this time, nearby, they also founded the Temple of Juno (wife of Jupiter, goddess of fertility and the sanctity of marriage). A famous

One of the earliest elective bodies in Rome, was the *comitia*. When the Palatine Latins expanded their rule across to the Capitoline Hill, they did their voting on neutral ground in between—in what would become the Roman Forum. When that was flooded during rainy season, they would meet in the Campus Martius just north of the Capitoline, in an area called the Saepta that was enclosed by walls. (We'll walk by there later when we walk through the lower Campus Martius in District 9.) When the people and their leaders gathered in the Campus Martius below the Arx to hold elections, they were vulnerable to attack and slaughter. Accordingly, the early military posted sentinels on the Arx, and along the Asylum, as well as on the Ianiculum Hill across the Tiber. Signals could be made by trumpet or at night by fire. They could also signal danger in the daytime by waving the proverbial *vexillum russi coloris* (red flag). If a threat came from the sea, the Ianiculum watchers could signal to the Capitoline watchers to warn the people below to retreat to safety on their hills.

story has it that one night in 390 B.C., Gauls tried to storm the citadel. The guard dogs failed to bark, but the alarm raised by nearby geese alerted the defenders, who fought off the invaders. What follows is a story that sounds both absurd and horrible to modern ears: The geese became sacred temple animals, maintained in the finest circumstances at state expense (again, as part of the overall machinery of propitiating the gods). Ever after, every year on the anniversary of the attack, a number of dogs are horribly crucified as a reminder of the failure of the temple dogs on that long-ago night. The sacred geese are paraded around town in a procession by the priests, on litters with special cushions of gilt and purple signifying the highest state honors accorded only to emperors.

On the Arx is a grassy open space called the *Auraculum*, where augurs gather to interpret omens. From the Auraculum one has a clear view to the Alban Hills, where Monte Cavo stands 27 km (17 miles) southeast of the city.

The Asylum, a depressed ridge between the two crests of the Capitoline, is so named because here Romulus welcomed refugees to his new settlement. Vediovis has a small temple at the northern edge of the Asylum. He is also Veiovis, one of the many archaic deities hanging around in Rome. He may be of Etruscan origin. His name (*ve-?* + Iovis, or Jupiter) is taken to mean 'little Jupiter' or even 'destructive Jupiter.' One cannot help speculating if it is a contraction of *vetus Iovis*, 'ancient Jove.' Another possibility is that the prefix *ve-* comes from *ave*, 'welcome.' All is speculation. Veiovis' grumbling thunder was preceded by mysteriously flashing lightning. To archaic people, this must have seemed a sure sign of divine power: the ability to time flashes of lighting with slower oncoming rumbles of scary and deafening thunder. Though associated with the Roman sky-god, Veiovis is also thought to be associated with the Etruscan lower world (not necessarily the same as the Roman

Every inch of the Roman and Latin landscape is encrusted with religion—the old nature worship, overlaid with Etruscan and Latin deities, later with the Olympian deities of the conquered Greek peninsula, still later with the Middle Eastern corn and rebirth deities from Persia and the Indus Valley and the rich images and ideas from Egypt. One can understand how it would have seemed to a Roman that the Christian 'atheists' wanted to replace all of that with what seemed like a light-weight cult whose only god was powerless to prevent his own death at the hands of a provincial Roman governor.

Add the fact that every charlatan of antiquity (like Simon Magus, or Simon the Magician, mentioned in the New Testament) had figured out how to perform seeming miracles. Stories of virgin birth dated back at least to the Bronze Age, often used to save the reputation of a girl who'd gotten in trouble, and a foolproof way for a guy to prove he was of divine origin (if his mother was a virgin). There seemed little new in all this to convince the average Roman, and a lot to make him contemptuous, if not frightened for the safety of the state and therefore of his family, his ancestors, and himself. Rumors were rife that Christians were cannibals and ate babies. The persecutors played on these fears and made the term 'Christian' about as fearsome and loathsome to contemporaries as Christians later would regard the dreaded 'paganism.' See Appendix B for more about Roman religion.

underworld, or *inferno*). In their inimitable fashion, if there was a deity, the Romans went on worshiping it. If the shrine wore out, they replaced it with the same exact materials and figurations.

Crossing the Asylum to the other side of the Capitoline Hill, we see that the sides of the cliffs on the north side have been integrated into the ancient Servian Wall, which surrounds the city of Rome proper. We can look north and see the jug-handle shape of the Campus Martius (Circus Flaminius, Regio IX), bordered by the curving Tiber nearby on the left (west) and about 1.7 km (1 mile) north. The so-called Martial Field is where Republican generals were constrained to hold their triumphal marches. They were not allowed to enter the city with their armies. By 150 A.D., as we look out across the Ninth District, we see a staggering array of closely packed buildings. Some of them quite magnificent—among them, the Baths of Agrippa, the Pantheon, and the Circus Flaminius.

From this vantage point, we pause to look out and see how the Servian Wall stretches around the city. The earliest city defenses were earthen ramparts from the early Fifth Century B.C.E. The wall of Servius Tullius was probably built and rebuilt over many years starting in the Fourth Century B.C. Already in 150 it is half a millennium old, and crumbling in places. Here and there, in modern times, a gate is still standing, including one arching 3.3m (12 Roman feet) across, so one must imagine it had to be about half again as high (pure speculation, 18 feet) and therefore the wall enclosing that gate had to have at least one upper story, possibly two, making it anywhere from 9–12m (30–40 feet) high. By comparison, the much more extensive Aurelian Wall (280 A.D. onward, started by Aurelian and completed by Probus) will be 4m (13 ft) thick at the base, and 6.4m (21 ft) high. The Aurelian Wall will have a perimeter of over 12 miles, and will be doubled by Maxentius (306–312) to over 40m (131 ft). Portions of the Servian Wall will survive into modern times because the Romans put upper courses on the obsolete structure—a relatively cheap way to extend an aqueduct.

The Servian city had spread to include the Palatine, Quirinal, Capitoline, Aventine, and Caelian Hills within defensive earthworks rather than stone walls. Servius Tullius enclosed those hills, plus the Esquilae and Viminal Hills, within his stone wall. That adds up to seven hills plus the low areas among them (the Velabrum and the Roman Forum, for example). Typical blocks, capable of with-standing the siege-craft of the invading Celts as well as the Etrus-cans, the Greeks, and the Samnites further inland, averaged roughly 0.2m–0.3m (8–12 in.) high, 0.55–0.66m (22–26 in.) wide, and 0.75–0.90m (30–35 in.) long. These were generally quarried from tufa, which is plentiful in the region, and relatively easy to work.

The 'saddle' of the Asylum has at various times been buttressed by massive stone work (the *Tabularium*) to support added structures on the side toward the Forum. By contrast, on the side facing the Campus Martius, around the Servian Wall, were jammed various five story *insulae* or apartment blocks.

We cross over to the south end of the Capitoline Hill, to the temple complex of Jupiter, Juno, and Minerva. This part of the Capitoline was at one time called the Saturnian. Now it is often called the *Mons Tarpeius*, after the Tarpeian Rock. This is a cliff over-looking a steep drop at the southwest corner, where in antiquity certain types of prisoners were flung to their deaths below.

Largest of its type ever built, the Temple of Capitoline Jupiter, dated to the Sixth Century B.C. The Tarquins built it on a gigantic scale in the archaic style of Etruscan temples. Its base was a rectan-gular stone platform with steps leading up in front. On top of this, massive columns formed a porticus or porch all around. Set back in the interior against the back wall were three *cellae* or enclosures. The temple actually contained the three deities of the Capitoline Triad, one in each enclosure from left to right: Juno, Jupiter, and Minerva. There were shrines to various archaic deities, all of whom allowed themselves to be dispossessed by the proper religious rites, except Terminus and Iuventas. The Etruscan rulers incorporated the shrines of these deities into their great new edifice. The statue of Jupiter, sitting in the central cella holding a thunderbolt, was the work of Vulca of Veii, and the priests painted its face red on festival days, according to Ovid. Each deity had an altar in its cella, plus statues, trophies, and other arcana. The temple's façade famously bore the chiseled legend *Iuppiter Opt. Max.*, for *Iuppiter Optimus et Maximus*, 'Jupiter the Best and Greatest.'

509 B.C. was a seminal moment in the history of Rome, coin-ciding with the expulsion of the Etruscan (Tarquin) Dynasty and the founding of the Republic of Rome. Some of the wealthiest and

most powerful citizens had homes on the Capitoline until 384 B.C., when the Senate decreed no patrician should live on the hill henceforth. That removed the likes of M. Manlius Capitolinus from the Arx, and on the latter's home site was then erected the Temple of Juno Moneta, Juno being the wife of Jupiter, and Moneta being a reference to the bank and mint. This deity, echoing older animist custom, sprang up to fill a local need. Moneta became a new manifestation of a very old deity (congruent with the Greek Zeus' wife Hera). There were other shrines and temples on the Capitoline—on our walk, we find there is never any lack of them on every corner, under every tree, by every roadside—including the Temple of Concord (dedicated 217 B.C.), and possible Vediovis; and Honos et Virtus (Honor and Virtue). Other shrines and monuments include the Temple of *Fides* (Trust), and toward the Forum, the Temple of *Ops*, a Saturnian goddess of abundance.

The Temple of Capitoline Jupiter, or Jove the Best and Greatest, has a fascinating history all of its own. Legend has it that, in Etruscan times, an elderly woman approached King Tarquin the Proud (last of the Etruscan kings) and offered to sell him nine books of prophecies. In the books, she told him, was written the entire future of Rome, blow by blow, the good and the bad. The king, who was a cheapskate, balked at her high price and sent her away. She returned some time later (and we can imagine this with darkness, blowing wind, howling spirits, and spooky eyes filled with flashes of lightning) telling the king she had burned three of the books, but had returned to sell him the remaining six at the same high price. He laughed and sent her packing again. When she returned a third time, she told him she had burned another three books, and now had only three left. She still demanded the same high price. The king, having learned she was probably the Sybil of Cumae, one of the greatest soothsayers of the ancient world (a sister of the famous Delphic Oracle. Their method was to sit in an underground chamber, become intoxicated with divine exhalations from inside the earth, and then in a trembling swoon write cryptic words on oak or laurel leaves—such leaves the Sybil at Cumae had bound together into books. Now terrified and regretful, the king paid the price. He was soon overthrown in a coup by the Romans, who established their Republic. The precious Sibylline books were kept in a special case in the Temple of Jove the Best and Greatest, until they were destroyed by lightning and fire in 83 B.C. The special priesthood dedicated to the books soon managed to find other sets of prophecies (or they'd go out of business), and it's not clear exactly what the augurs made of the cryptic writings at any given time, during any given crisis when the books had to be consulted. Rome had its share of ups and downs during her long history. She suffered some terrible defeats and humiliations in her rise to the top. The Romans tended to learn from their mistakes, sometimes the hard way.

CHAPTER 14

PONTIFEX

Today is a special day of worship, and His Majesty the Emperor, Antoninus Pius, is about to arrive at the Capitoline. We watch from a spot on the Arx overlooking the Roman Forum with the Temple of Jupiter Capitolinus behind us. Antoninus preaches restraint in all things. Consequently we don't see quite the enormous pomp and circumstance that might have accompanied other emperors. His Majesty is almost apologetic in not wishing to disrupt people's work or cause them expense by his movements. Still, a resplendant sight lies before us. From our high vantage point, we can see the large purple carriage coming up the Via Sacra (Sacred Way), drawn by several white horses. Mounted Praetorians with plumed helmets and wind-filled capes canter in front of and behind the coach. The full troop of 24 lictors bearing the fasces on their left shoulders walk ahead in a single file.

Trumpeters run ahead to warn of the emperor's passage. The coach stops for a time, and a stillness fills the air on this sunny day. We feel a pleasant breeze, sweet with blossoms from the gardens around us, as we look out over the Roman Forum and toward the Palatine. What is going on? Ah! Now we see the crowd pushed apart by Praetorian foot guards. They are making way for a slow, dignified procession of women wearing long white gowns. All six Vestal Virgins, some carrying flowers, others pots in which flickers the sacred hearth fire, walk out from their convent by the Temple of Vesta. Passing before His Majesty's coach, they nod slightly in his direction, then turn and walk toward the Capitoline Hill. They do not avert their gaze again or lower their faces. The fate of Rome, the

The fasces is a bundle of sticks tied together with a red ribbon, and symbolizing the fact that one of the elm or birch rods can be broken, but together the people, like a bundle of sticks, are unbreakable. Under the Etruscan kings, there was an ax embedded in the fasces, symbolizing the life and death power of the king. When the Romans in 509 B.C. expelled the last Etruscan king and created a republic of checks and balances, they removed the axe. Ceremonially, the fasces is carried by a lictor (usually a freedman) on his left shoulder to precede important official. In the hierarchy, a priest of most official cults is preceded by one lictor. Legates were preceded by five lictors; praetors by six; consuls, by 12; and emperors 12. Domitian (81–96 A.D.) raised the number for emperors to 24. When one ceremonial procession involving lictors passes that of a higher office, the lictors of the lesser official lower their fasces in salute.

In modern times, Mussolini's nationalist socialist party in the 1930s will style themselves *fascisti*. In the U.S. House of Representatives, two fasces complete with ax stand behind the podium of the Speaker. The fasces is featured in many modern symbologies relating to law and authority.

survival of the city and empire, depends on the perfect execution of all ancient rites. Every significant milestone in these rituals is minutely choreographed from centuries of unvarying tradition.

Soldiers of the Praetorian Guard have blocked off the route. This is our first glimpse of the Praetorians, and we are surprised to note that they do not carry typical field armor or weapons. Every Republican general had one of these bodyguards. Augustus established a permanent Praetorian Guard of nine cohorts to protect Italy where no one was stationed. These particular troops are outfitted in the antique style of white leather armor and helmet with capes with gilt trim. Instead iron spears, javelins, and large rectangular shields like field soldiers, each guard carries a smaller, round shield of leather, a bronze gladius (short thrusting sword), and a dagger. These weapons are better suited to thwarting surprise attacks by seasoned street ruffians or even gangs of gladiators in the close quarters of narrow streets, palace hallways, or colonnaded porticoes.

From our high vantage point, we see dark shapes moving on top of temples and other buildings. They are expert marksmen of the Praetorian guard, who use short, powerful bows and perfectly balanced and feathered wooden arrows with bronze tips. Roman religion of old has proscriptions against iron, and these men may have to fight inside sacred precincts that would be ritually defamed if touched with iron.

The procession of Vestal Virgins moves among the temples, basilicas, and monuments of the Forum, followed by the Emperor and his guards. The imperial litter stops, and His Majesty steps forth. He is immediately surrounded by praetors, priests, quaestors, curule aediles, and other officials. Closest to him, however, walk a half dozen younger men in plain white togas. We are puzzled about them, until a fellow gawker explains. Those are the plain-clothes Praetorian Guards, usually young officers of high family. They wear togas instead of military uniforms. Close at hand are swords and daggers so they can protect his majesty. The lesson of various assassinations— like Galba's in this Forum, Julius Caesar's in the Curia of Pompey's Theater, Caligula's in a tunnel near the Circus Maximus—have been all too well learned.

The emperor arrives at the foot of the Capitoline Hill, at the Arch of Tiberius. The Via Sacra ends a narrower paved way called the *Clivus* (incline) Capitolinus, which turns into a stairway leading up to the saddle between the two hills, where we stand. We thus get a close view of the Vestals and the lictors, as well as the Praetorian Guards, as His Majesty ascends the stairway. Our ears are shattered by blasts of trumpets and rolls of drums. There is a constant tinkling of bells from various nearby temple priests who have come out to honor His Majesty. Antoninus, robust and dignified at 60, makes the climb with little effort.

The procession pauses when His Majesty reaches the saddle of the Asylum. We can see sweat on his jowls, and rolling down his beard, as he grasps his purple toga around himself. He turns toward the other hump, the Arx, and there, in a grassy area called the *auguraculum*, stands a wild looking figure. He is an Etruscan diviner, or augur. The man is naked, except for a loincloth, and has come out of a primitive hut preserved like its predecessors since archaic times at that spot. It is the Little Place of Augurs. A dozen or more of these Etruscan throwbacks surround their chief as he tells His Majesty in ritual sing-song that the auguries for today are favorable. His Majesty, in a surprisingly clear, loud singing voice, offers back his thanks. As they lead, the Vestals and other onlookers chant the appropriate *responsoria*. Never far from the soul of Rome are the archaic augurs who learn much from the flight of birds or the entrails of a sacrificed animal. In response, His Majesty does what a Roman does at any moment of emotional or ritual importance: he flips the end of his toga over his head to cover it, as a gesture of piety toward the gods.

Toga-clad priests of the true and ancient Roman state religion swing open the great bronze doors. The Temple of Jupiter Best and Greatest stands ready to receive the Emperor. A thick gout of charcoal smoke rises from a travertine-topped altar before the temple steps. The smell somehow reminds us of when this land was inhabited by very few humans, and very many faceless numina. It is a smell of autumn and mystery. Saying prayers to Father God, to Deified Rome, to the hearth goddess Vesta, and the other great deities, the priests bring forth several prime-quality farm animals for ritual sacrifice. Among them are a sheep and two lambs, a ram, and a goat. All the animals are decked out in festive ribbons and marked with sacred symbols. His Majesty moves forward eager to begin the sacred ceremonies. He raises his hands, *primus inter pares* (first among equals) with the pontiffs or bridge-maker priests. All the priests, and all men and women present, cover their heads with the ends of their togas. Two strong young priests produce bronze knives and expertly slaughter the first of the animals. An Etruscan *haruspix* stands by, distinguishable from the Romans primarily by his crookstaff. The entrails are taken to a separate marble altar, where Etruscan and Roman priests will read them for portents. Meanwhile, the young Jovian priests expertly carve up the animals and place them on a grill above the fire to cook. After sacrificing and praying inside, the Imperial party will return outside, and the ritual meal will be eaten by all the officials present.

His Majesty and the Vestals now walk up the steps into the huge temple. Only they and the senior temple priests will enter; the rest of the crowd must wait outside. The only exception are two young toga-clad Praetorian officers who never leave His Majesty's side.

This temple stands upon the ground where its predecessors stood. For many centuries, this location has been especially prone to lightning strikes. The original temple was destroyed by lightning and fire on 6 July 83 B.C. It had since archaic times been dedicated to the Capitoline Triad of Jupiter, Juno, and Minerva. The Tarquins—Etruscan kings of early Rome—built the structure among shrines and altars dating to the primitive Iron Age. It is likely that some of these predated even the Latins, and may have belonged to the primordial inhabitants during the Bronze Age. The Etruscan kings scrupulously and patiently consulted their diviners, horoscope makers, augurs, and other priests. With many rituals and propitiations, almost all the resident numina and deities were either driven off or relocated. The only exceptions were the shrines of Terminus and Iuventas, who would not let their shrines be moved. This is hardly surprising, since Terminus is the ancient Latin god of boundary stones, and his particular stone is right there. Every boundary stone in animist Latium has its own local deity, and the Romans continue to collectively worship these Termini in an annual ritual (the Terminalia) on 23 February. Iuventas (Youth) is associated with the offering long ago made by Roman boys as they assumed the *toga virilis* (man's toga) during their transition to manhood—a ceremony now performed at a shrine in the Circus Maximus. Thus, the shrines of Terminus and Iuventas were incorporated into the Capitoline Temple. As is customary in temples for multiple deities, each occupies a *cella* or apartment. Originally, the cella of Iuppiter contained a terra cotta statue, made by Vulca of Veii, of the god holding a thunderbolt in his right hand. The priests painted the statue's face red on festivals. A cella to the right of Jupiter's was that of Etruscan Menrva or Latin Minerva, the Italian goddess of trade and crafts, who assumed the martial aspects of Greek Athena Promachos (champion). She became associated with war (as we find Athena to have been during the Bronze Age, per Homer's *The Iliad*). Minerva also has a shrine on the Caelian Hill and a temple on the Aventine. She has no less than three festivals each year, in March, June, and September.

A cella to the left of Jupiter's is that of Juno, which illustrates an important point about the polytheistic deities. While maintaining a fundamental identity, they easily morph as Roman civilization embraces new geographical areas. Juno is a prime example of this, blending with mother goddesses everywhere. She fulfills many needs of women in Rome itself. Juno is Jupiter's wife, corresponding to the Etruscan Uni or the Greek Hera. Daughter of Chronus and Rhea, she is both sister and wife of Zeus in the tangled web of mythology. As with all important polytheistic deities, Juno has various attributes, signified by epithets. For example, Juno Lucina is a goddess of childbirth, whose festival, the Matronalia, is celebrated March 1. Another childbirth manifestation is Juno Opigena. Juno Caprotina is goddess of fertility, honored in the Feast of Serving Women in July (held by the Vestals in their temple. No men are allowed, and the multitudes of women who come from all over Rome must come barefoot). Juno Sospita was Juno the Savior. Juno Moneta (Rememberer) has an important temple also in the Forum, which is the main Roman mint and, like many wealthy temples, a bank. Juno Populonia is the protector of the Roman people in war, while Juno Curitis is the protector of spearmen (festival 7 October), and Juno Sispes protects the state always. Juno Sororia is the protector of girls at puberty (festival October 1). Most importantly for our purposes today, Juno Regina (Queen) is the manifestation who dwells in her cella in the Capitoline Temple.

The temple has been destroyed several times by fire and lightning. Each time it has been magnificently and lovingly rebuilt by the consuls and later emperors amid precise ritual propitiations.

His Majesty and the Vestals move into the temple itself, and the great doors swing shut. Inside, a lighter, grayer smoke lingers through the air, and we smell the cloying sweetness of incense. This is the most sacred space in all of Rome, save the fireplace in the Temple of Vesta. From high, small windows in this ancient house of the father god, rays of soft orange light shine down on the Deified Antoninus and the Vestal nuns. They approach the central altar, where flowers and incense are among the gifts laid before *Deus Pater, Iovis, Iuppiter,* 'Father God.' The walls and columns all around are richly hung with all manner of gifts. Many wealthy families have donated fabulous treasures to the temple, including statuary, paintings, jewelry, and ornamented weapons. Some gifts are trophies of victories presented by great generals. Donated books and scrolls may also be found in the great Bibliotheca Capitolina, housed in a

separate building nearby. In a stone box in the cella of Jupiter, under strict lock and key, are a collection of Sibylline Prophecies about
the fate of Rome. These are not the originals, which were destroyed
in the great fire of 83 B.C., but replacements gathered carefully from
the proper sources. The most mysterious feature of the temple are
the entrances to underground tunnels and caverns. There, the
priests have over the centuries collected all manner of treasures and
relics. For example, every time lightning strikes and knocks down
some statue or other ornament, that is carefully gathered and
stored down below. Much of the temple treasure is stored in the
tunnels of the Capitoline.

A dreadful story illustrates how even this holy place is not safe
from the ravages of human affairs. During the Year of Three Emperors (69), before Sejanus restored order and helped install the Flavian Dynasty, the defeated forces of Vitellius (reigned three
months) went on a rampage. The future emperor Domitian, son of
Sejanus, and brother of the future emperor Titus, came to the Capitoline for refuge along with his uncle Sabinus and their entire family. During a violent battle, the Vitellian supporters managed to
fight their way into the sacred precincts. Domitian and most of his
family disguised themselves and barely escaped, but the prominent
Sabinus was hacked to death and his headless body dragged
through the streets. During this struggle, the Temple of the Capitoline Triad burned to the ground. Sejanus rebuilt it, and subsequent
emperors have restored it in the glory of its gifts.

His Majesty completes the rituals and prayers inside the Temple of Jupiter Best and Greatest. Antoninus and the Vestals walk
back outside to lead the sacrificial feast. We, however, must walk
on now, down the steps into the Roman Forum. On our way, we'll
pause atop the Arx for a splendid overview of the city.

CHAPTER 15

LOOKING NORTH FROM THE ARX

It seems puzzling at first that the Notitiae and the Curiosum tell us Regio VIII was jam-packed with insulae and domus, and hordes of people. How can this be? Nobody has been allowed to dwell in the sacred precincts for centuries (except the Vestals cooped up in their nunnery, and maybe that old Etruscan in his hut on the Capitoline Hill). Then we realize: the district includes a portion of land north of the Servian Wall, toward the Campus Martius and the Hortulorum (Small Gardens) Hill. From the wealthy homes close to the Capitolium, along with some insulae that have sneaked their way into a few available crevices, an entire city section radiates outward. We'll pass by there later as we complete our circle of the thirteen regions of Rome proper, before crossing the river to finish our walk in the 14th.

Standing on the Arx now let's stop a moment and look out across the northern half of the city. It is afternoon on a lightly damp, hazy day. The massed ranks of tall buildings swim in a faintly bluish-gray tint, and it looks like a picture that someone with a thousand tiny paint brushes has daubed with dots of silvery light. In places the light of so many oil lamps, stoves, lanterns, braziers, street lights, torches, and coach lamps looks like a gilded rain dribbling among the alleys. It looks as if that same pensive painter daubed every one of myriad open windows with a brush of molten gold-dust. The northern districts are long, and they radiate away from the Arx as if their imaginary borders were spokes in a wheel.

On our left, toward the Tiber, is Regio IX (District 9, Circus Flaminius, named after a major race track just north of the Capitoline Hill). The area's historical name is *Campus Martius* (Military

Field), and the Tiber flows south along its western and northern shores. It's so called because, when the Romans expelled their kings and formed a Republic with safeguards to prevent any one person from ever assuming power again, one of the things they did was to forbid any general to enter the city with his army. Triumphal processions led from the Campus Martius into Rome's city centre; they were the one occasion when soldiers were allowed to cross the pomerium. A triumph was typically a huge free-for-all party: a parade, with lots of wine for all, with captured kings, queens, and generals being paraded in chains like common criminals before they go to the Tullianum for execution. In the center is a long, narrow district, Regio VII (District 7, *Via Lata* or Broad Street). Since the Via Lata is actually in the Campus Martius, this is a bit confusing, until we realize that it's the Via Flaminia, coming into District 9 from the north, and then angling straight into District 7. As it does so, it becomes (as the name suggests) Rome's Broadway, with monuments, shopping, and toward the lower end the theater district. That's where the Clivus Argentariorum curves down from the Forum region.

To the right is Regio VI (District 6, *Alta Semita* or High Lane). That's a street that follows the ridge of the Quirinal Hill toward the Praetorian Guard area. The Alta Semita itself passes eastward through the Porta Collina in the Servian Wall and becomes the Via Nomentana, eventually heading to Nomentum 14 miles from Rome.

We see a pool of darkness toward the northeastern corner of the city as we look over the densely packed insulae, warehouses, and homes. Far off, between the distant mansions and gardens to the left on the slopes of the Pincian Hill bordering the city on the north, and more to the right the high, curving thread of the Alta Semita, that pool of darkness is a valley containing the fabled Gardens of Sallust, a wealthy historian from the Republican era.

That's a view of the entire northern half of the city. The laws of real estate are the same in all places and times. Property along the Tiber is fabulously valuable, and most of it reserved for government and large commercial purposes, mainly the movement of goods and entertainment for the masses. High ground is far more valuable than low ground, which is why the valleys between the hills are filled with the housing of the middle, working, and impoverished classes. Immediately before us, sprawling below and away from the Arx is a nearly unbroken sea of five and six-story buildings like massed dominoes standing upright. If we are to believe the Regionary catalogs (see Appendix C), these three districts alone contain about 2,000 high rise buildings distributed in and around some 67 *vici* (parts of town, neighborhoods, settlements, each with its own central square and shrine). There are also over 370 rich private residences spread among these three districts, some distributed here and there where we can see their marble facings and gardens with high surrounding walls, but most of them in a ring toward the more sparsely settled regions as one approaches the Pincian Hill.

For now, we are going to go back down through the Forum Romanum, past the Colosseum, and up the Palatine Hill to resume our walk through the southern areas of the city. We'll go counterclockwise from there, coming north along the east side. We'll make a few side trips, one of which brings us back through the center of Rome, before we march east into Subura and then north.

Trajan's Forum, Basilica, and Column are not to be confused with monuments in the Forum Romanum, which lies behind us. These works of Trajan are in the northern end of the Imperial Fora. Just as the works of Agrippa and Augustus dominate the Campus Martius, so the works of Trajan dominate the area immediately northeast from the Capitoline Hill.

Trajan's Market is one of the great commercial centers of the city, a recent addition to the nearby markets we have already explored (the Vegetable and Cattle Markets) down in the old city harbor. Trajan's Market, and in fact this entire complex including Trajan's Basilica and Trajan's Column, are a spill-over from the fora behind us and to our right, which include the original Forum Romanum and then the added-on Imperial Fora (those of Caesar, of Augustus, of Vespasian, of Nerva, and finally of Trajan). Trajan's Forum includes one of those huge shopping malls like the one we already saw in the Porticus Aemilia. Trajan's Market is remarkable in its own right because it has galleries several stories high. Like a modern shopping mall, it includes shops, offices, storage areas, schools, and just about everything imaginable.

The Basilica of Trajan (Basilica Ulpia) is another of those vast and imposing halls where the business and religion of empire get done, including law courts. The complex includes a great *biblio-theka*, or library.

Trajan's column has a remarkable story all its own. Trajan, one of the Good Emperors, extended the borders of the Roman Empire briefly to their greatest extent, so that on the easternmost border one stood looking across the Arabian Gulf toward Persia. Trajan brought home much booty from his wars, in particularly against the Dacians (in modern Romania). The complex of buildings here were built by the great master architect Apollodorus of Damascus. Apollodorus removed or leveled an estimated thirty million tons of earth, removing the ridge (similar to the Asylum) that connected the Arx to the Quirinal Hill northeast of the Capitoline. It's said that the height of this Doric column offers a measure of this great work, showing the depth of earth and rocks removed—the pillar is about 38 m (125 feet) high and wide enough to contain a spiral staircase leading to an observation ring on top. Trajan wrote a series of Commentaries on his Dacian Wars. It's been suggested that the continuous spiral of reliefs (200 m or 800 ft long, and 1.2 m or 4 feet high) stretching around and around the outside represents a gigantic copy of the papyrus scroll of Trajan's. Modern historians glean much information about the fine details of life from the near-photographic realism of the reliefs. Trajan must have felt the column was the dot on the 'i' of his reign, since he had his ashes immured in the base.

CHAPTER 16

FORUM ROMANUM

Rome has a number of *fora* or civic plazas, but none nearly so historic or special as the Forum Romanum. The northern side of the Forum, and the Colosseum Valley southeast from that, are actually in Regio IV (Temple of Peace). The central districts of the city all seem to meet at an area near the Flavian Amphitheater, or Colosseum. The Colosseum sits on a low drainage site, associated with a *stagnum* (pool) of Nero's Golden House.

Nobody is quite sure where the word *forum* originates amid the mosaic of languages and *patoix* spoken in archaic Latium. The field is open to speculation, but a simple guess would be that *forum* comes from a family of irregular verb forms surrounding the root *for*, 'to speak.' Alternatively, a sense of 'outdoors' has been traced to the Indo-European root 'dwhor,' from which we get the English word door, from the German *Tür* or *Tor*, and so forth backward in the linguistic branches. In any case, this vital word *forum* carries with it underlying democratic concepts about free speech, assembly, and other key freedoms moderns deem essential to good government.

We enter the great plaza that contains the 'Navel of the World,' and many other great monuments. As imposing as they all are, our eye catches the Flavian Amphitheater or Colosseum looming over the southeastern end of the Forum. There, every day of the year, about 50,000 spectators roar as the spectacle of violent death soaks the sands with blood and littered body parts. The Colosseum was dedicated in 79 A.D. (just 81 years ago) by Vespasian. We'll visit there soon, but first we'll sort out what is possible for us to absorb in the jumbled theme park of bronze and marble that is the Forum Romanum.

The Forum Romanum is an uneven, roughly rectangular area about one Roman mile long. Today, in 150, it is one vast marble monument to the power, glory, and history of Rome. It is simultaneously also a place of law courts, of important religious priesthoods, and most importantly a place where huge corporate financial transactions take place. There are too many fine details here to understand in one walk, so we'll look at some of the most important.

In archaic times, this was a forsaken swamp full of brambles and brackish pools. Early on, at the far end away from the Seventh and Sixth Century settlements, lay a burial ground or *Sepulcretum*. In this overgrown wilderness, haunted by wolves and foxes as well as the occasional human brigand, were both the urn-burials of cremated Latin remains and the interred remains of Etrurian type. By a stroke of fortune, the early Latins were in the habit of burying these ashes in urns modeled after the homes of the living. As a result, moderns have a good image of the little four-cornered huts that stood upon the Palatine in archaic times. The Forum down below was a burial ground and refuse dump for people living on the surrounding hills. In fact, throughout the future history of Rome, extra care and propitiatory sacrifices had to be made because it was fundamentally sacrilegious and defiling to create a sacred Pomerium containing a burial ground. During the early centuries, the Forum Romanum was a sort of rude, Wild West town center. Where today stand 100-foot high marble walls of the Basilica Iulia along the western side, and the Basilica Paulli (Aemilia) on the eastern side, stood rows of wooden shops. In this square, the early Romans all gathered more or less democratically to vote on important issues. When rained out (as was often the case, since this forum drained much of the Seven Hills area) they would meet over on the Campus Martius instead. Until the late Republic, Romans held gladiatorial games in the Forum.

By the Sixth Century, under the Tarquins, the Forum was turning into a market place. On either side was a row of *tabernae*, 'taverns.' The older establishments ran along the south side, with their backs to the sun. Later, there was only room to build along the north side, and newer establishments popped up. As Rome grew into a settlement of thousands, the Forum became the center of public life. Gladiatorial contests, races—all the public entertainments that had their origins in Etruscan funeral games—were held here.

In archaic times, a stream ran through the Forum on its way to the Tiber. This stream is thought to have formed one of the defensive barriers protecting the earliest Palatine Latins, separating them from people on the Capitol and Quirinal Hills. The stream began to pick up a dangerous plume of human waste and refuse, contributing cholera to the already rife malaria of the swamps. Rome will be associated with malaria and fever into modern times (e.g., as in *Daisy Miller* by Henry James). Eventually, the stream was bricked into a course, and then totally enclosed.

Until sometime in the late Republic, in the middle of the Forum was an irregularly shaped pond about 30m (98 ft.) across at most, called the Lacus Curtius. As with so many ancient features, several stories as to its origin have come down. According to one story, a fissure opened mysteriously in the Forum. Soothsayers said that the chasm would only close when it received what Rome valued most. People threw in all sorts of their precious things, with-

Julius Caesar, the last of Rome's occasional 'emergency' dictators, ruled 46–44 B.C. and was murdered at the Curia of Pompey's Theater. After a brief civil war, Augustus became the first emperor (31 B.C. to 14 A.D.). Augustus was the greatest of the otherwise pretty mediocre Julio-Claudian dynasty. This included Tiberius (14–37) who presided during the time of Pontius Pilate in Judaea; Caligula, a madman who ruled 37–41 and was murdered; Claudius (41–54); and Nero (54–68), another cruel madman. The Year 69 A.D. was one of civil war, with Galba, Otho, and Vitellius. These were followed by the Flavian dynasty, consisting of Vespasian (69–79), one of the great emperors; Titus (79–81), famous for his destruction of Jerusalem, and remembered in a triumphal arch here in the Forum; and Domitian (81–96). These eleven men, the first emperors, foreshadowed both the dark and light eras to come. Collectively, they represent the best and worst of Roman government, in particular the problems of succession that led to so many empiricides, and would dog the empire to its closing days.

out result. A soldier named Curtius figured that the prophecy must refer to the courage of Rome's soldiers, and so sacrificed himself by riding into on his horse, whereupon the gap closed over him. The Lacus Curtius was a dry depression by the time of Augustus. This pond or *lacus* was the scene of an emperor's murder.

The year 69 A.D. was a dreadful interlude in the Golden Age, and an omen of things that would much later come after the death of Marcus Aurelius in 180 A.D. It was the turbulent 'year of three emperors,' Galba, Otho, and Vitellius. Galba was 70 when he succeeded Nero. At first, the reaction to Nero was so virulent that Galba was welcomed for his courage and ambition in seeking the supreme office. The Senate proclaimed Galba emperor on June 8, 68. He was a thrifty, severe little old man, and he made the mistake of playing the troops wrong. Nero had run up enormous debts and nearly bankrupted the state. Galba wanted to unburden the state of that debt, and tried to stiff the army commanders their customary bribes. He told the commanders he did not want to buy troops, but levy them. He further irritated the Senate by appointing all sorts of corrupt individuals to whom he owed favors for getting him into office. Within a few months, the rebellion against Galba began.

Nero's governor of Lusitania in Spain, Otho, conspired to seize power. On the morning of 15 January 69, while Galba performed the required sacrificial rites in the Temple of Apollo on the Palatine, Otho had himself proclaimed emperor at the camp of the Praetorian Guard, in the northeastern part of the city. Galba returned to the palace and began to hear rumors of a coup. Seizing the initiative, he ordered slaves to carry him in a litter to the Forum. He was accompanied by Piso, a 30-year-old man of good family, whom he had adopted as his successor. In the Forum, by the Lacus Curtius, Otho's agents swooped down on horses. They tipped the litter over, spilling Galba on the ground while his slaves and retainers fled, sensing an overwhelming force. A soldier named Camurius, of the 15th Legion, stabbed the emperor in the neck. Piso, his successor in waiting, escaped to the Temple of Vesta, but was dragged out and killed. The army and the mob combined in a frenzy, cutting off their heads and parading them on poles. Galba's remains were ultimately recovered by his steward Argivus, and buried lovingly in the emperor's garden at his estate in the Via Aurelia. His successor, the vain and slinky Otho, lasted about three months. He died in April during an uprising that put the third emperor of the year in power, Vitellius. He was another admirer of Nero, with a sordid reputation even in the debauched later years of Tiberius (when Vitellius was known as a *spintria*, 'male prostitute'). He was simply in the right place at the right time. His reign was short, lasting only until July 69, when forces known as the Flavian faction loyal to Vespasian finished him off. He was found hiding in a doorkeeper's closet in the palace, hauled off to the Forum, tortured, killed, and thrown into the Tiber. Some of the rage against him probably stemmed from he fact that, because of his political weakness, the temple of Jupiter Best and Greatest on the Capitoline was burned to the ground during an attempted coup by his faction.

The most important temple in the Roman Forum is that of Vesta, goddess of the hearth. In this small, round, archaic temple, the priestesses of Vesta tend the eternal flame of the state, just as in every household burns the hearth with a similar flame dedicated to the heart of the family. Near the temple is the House of the Vestals, a more modern rectangular building several stories high, with every imaginable luxury for its virginal inhabitants. No other aspect of Roman life or religion commands so central an importance for the survival of Rome (the people, the state, the culture) as the eternal flame of Vesta, and the purity of Vesta's nuns.

We pass the Arch of Titus, whose triumphal reliefs include images from his sack of Jerusalem. We see images of the seven-armed candelabrum, taken by soldiers from the Jewish Temple and carried to Rome with other spoils of war.

At the southeastern end of the Roman Forum stands the colossal statue erected by Nero, which now has a radiant head of Sol Invictus instead of Nero's visage. Among the many temples here is that of Divine Faustina, late wife of the current emperor. Also nearby is the Meta Sudans, or Sweating Fountain, a rounded cone taller than a man, from whose top issues a dribble of water. People like to sit on the marble rim built around it and chat, or wash their feet in its basin.

Filling one's view, at the southeastern end of the Roman Forum, hovers the great bulk of the Flavian Amphitheater—the Colosseum, as it will be remembered through the ages. Near that is a great tri-

umphal arch of Trajan (which one day Constantine will upgrade
and call his own).

We will revisit the Colosseum and its surroundings a little later
in our trip, coming down the Esquiline Hill at the border between
Regio III (Isis & Serapis) and Regio IV (Temple of Peace).

We arrive at a covered flight of stairs that will take us up onto
the Palatine Hill (Region XI).

PART FIVE

PALATINE HILL DISTRICT

(Regio X. Palatium)

CHAPTER 17

SWAMP
TO PALACE

We walk to the Palatine Hill from whose prominence we can look down toward the Circus Maximus on the southwest. From the Via Sacra, we begin ascending along the Clivus Palatinus, a street leading uphill to the Palatine.

At one of Domitian's quadrifontal (four-sided, four-legged) arches along the way, we stop and look back. We see the Capitoline Hill on our left beyond the smoke and noise of the Velabrum directly below us. The Forum Romanum is a little more to the right of that with the Temple of Rome and Venus. The massive Colosseum is directly below us with its surrounding buildings (to which we shall return later). To our right are the Baths of Titus and Trajan in the Isis & Serapis District. To our extreme right, looking southeast, we glimpse the famous Appian Way coming toward us from the Capena Gate. Looking as best we can, farther east around the bulk of the Colosseum, we catch some of the smoke and tangle of Subura, with its spread of buildings and city lights. Here is also a great central vantage point to see the dozen or so great aqueducts and their spurs coming into the city.

Today, the Palatine is no longer a collection of old neighborhoods mixed with rich palaces. Starting with Vespasian, each successive emperor—Titus, Domitian, Nerva, Trajan, Hadrian, now Antoninus—has added to the dazzling wealth of the imperial residences atop the Palatine. One legacy of this hill is the word 'palace' to describe a wealthy home of royal proportions and pretensions.

Around 36 B.C., Octavian, before he even was emperor, sold his expensive house down in the Forum Romanum and moved into the *Clivus Victoriae* (Victory Neighborhood) on the northeast cor-

ner of the Palatine. As Augustus, he furthered the cults of Victory
and also of Palatine Apollo. It is thought that his intention in moving here was to portray himself as the new Romulus of a newly imperial city. His successors added more buildings, and by the time of
Domitian, at the end of the 1st Century A.D., the top of the Palatine was reserved for Imperial palaces. An extension of the Aqua
Claudia delivers copious fresh water for the baths and fountains,
pools and gardens, that cover the entire hill. The *Aula Regia,* or Hall of
Rulership, is bigger than the *Regia* of the Senate down in the Forum
Romanum. We see great gardens, marble libraries, a nymphaeum,
and temples honoring Apollo Palatinus and Cybele.

Legend has it that Romulus had his hut on the Palatine, and
kept his *lituus* (traditional crook or staff of an augur or diviner) in
the temple of the Salian Palatine priests. Romulus made his divina-
tions regarding where and how to found a city, from an *auguraculum* here. Yet another auguraculum (the Remoria, after 'Remus') is
associated with the murdered brother of Romulus, variously said to
have been downriver outside of town, or in the eastern slope of the
Aventine overlooking Regio XII.

The Palatine Hill is the very spot on which the Roman nation
was born. The hill rises 32m (105 ft.) to 43m (141 ft.) above Tiber
level. It is an irregular square, roughly 2km (1.25 mile) across, covering about 25 acres. This hill has two prominences, the Palatium
and the Cermalus, but is otherwise flat. Originally, during the dark
ages leading up to the Eight Century B.C., the settlement consisted
of a few mud huts in which huddled some grim but determined

The name of the world's ritziest address may have originated, in
archaic times, from the word *palus,* meaning 'swamp.' The hill
would thus have been called the *Paludine* or *Palutine,* which over
time morphed into *Palatine.* (Other suggested etymologies include
balatium, from a word for the bleating of sheep—which paints a sug-
gestive image of the early settlement; and *pa-{?} + latini,* Latins, possibly Marsh Latins, or Shepherd Latins, or even Apollo Latins, since a
significant temple of Apollo exists here and for all we know may have
archaic precedents—all guesswork).

families. They were scared of the elements, of their neighbors, and of the fevers bred in the marshes all around. It's possible that the first settlement was actually two clusters of huts, one on each high point, with grazing and farming land in between. During these times, the people living in near isolation in the central western lowlands of Italy developed their

> For a broader historical background of Rome, see Appendix A. For important information about Roman religion, and its foundations in an archaic animism with striking resemblances to Japanese Shinto, see Appendix B.

own local animist belief system. These were similar to animist faiths found elsewhere in the world and in time. The embellished tales passed from generation to generation by grandparents, village elders, and shamans, tend to lack the layers of abstraction found in civilizations where specialized priesthoods have the time and the means to think at length about good and evil. In the Latin villages, deities were capricious and local. A spirit *(genius)* might dwell in a particular grove, on a bend in a stream, or in a cave. These were not polytheistic gods and goddesses with long, interlocking mythological biographies, but *numina*—spirits. Every object had its own spirit. Inside the household, the specialized spirits were the *Lares* and the *Penates*.

One morning in 753 B.C., according to Roman legend, a Palatine Latin man named Romulus performed the religious ceremony in the Etruscan rite for founding a settlement. His story has become woven into the history of our world for all time. Given that the date coincides very closely with modern archeological discoveries, it seems likely that at least some small part of the story is true.

The story begins in the legendary city called Alba Longa in the Alban Hills. Its king and queen were Numitor and Rhea Silvia. Before these two had offspring, a younger brother named Amulius deposed Numitor. Amulius made himself king, and forced Rhea Silvia to become a Vestal Virgin. The vow of chastity she had to take would ensure that she would not have children that could threaten Amulius' rights to the throne. Mars comes along and impregnates Rhea Silvia who bears twins. This virgin birth didn't violate her vow. Amulius had the infants put in a basket, and they floated down the

Tiber. They drifted ashore, possibly where one day Rome's river port would be. A she-wolf and a woodpecker, both totemic animals sacred to Mars, cared for them. A shepherd named Faustulus, and his wife Acca Larentia, found them and raised the two boys. They eventually figured out their origins, killed Amulius, and restored Numitor to the throne. For some reason they then wandered off and became simple shepherds on the Palatine Hill. Shrouded in austerity and simple virtues, they raised sheep and managed to stay out of trouble—for a while. Apparently, both young men had the ambition to start their own realm. So they consulted Etruscan augurs about the best way to do this, and that's how trouble came their way.

The animistic world[6] is really two parallel worlds—the material world of the living, and a spirit world. The supernatural other-world is not 'over there' or 'out there' as in polytheistic sky-religions and monotheism or even 'under here' as in earth goddess religions. The supernatural is 'right here' all around us at all times, in all the objects we see, in all the things we do, in the changes of seasons, and in all stages of a human life. Boundaries have both material and spiritual reality. By creating a bona fide settlement with a Pomerium (spiritual boundary), rather than just putting up a fence, an animist believes he increases his blessings within the border, and decreases the ability of evil spirits to cross over and harm him.

The first part of the ritual was easy. The twins dug a pit, called the mundus, or world, and put sacrifices into it relating to the birth and death of crops. They then covered this pit. For the next thousand years, three times a year on specific feast days, priests would open this mundus so that the spirits of the earth (perhaps animist genii, perhaps plutonian underworld deities) could come out and roam the world before returning to their infernal realm. Now came the hard part: Romulus and Remus must determine the spiritual boundaries.

The brothers went off, and separately performed auguries to find out where and how to create the borders of their tiny realm atop the Palatine. The Etruscans were masters at speculation, or looking. This involved the arts of bird-watching, star-gazing, and entrail-reading. Problem was, the boys came up with different results. Apparently Romulus was quite a hot-head, and Remus may

have been something of a whiner. Romulus hitched his plow to a
pair of cattle—a bull and a cow—and started cutting the furrow in
the soil that would determine the future city walls. The furrow was
not just a material cut, but a spiritual division. Meanwhile, Remus
stood by arguing about which way they line should run. Romulus
was at that moment trying to say the appropriate prayers and
chants to make it all good with the deities whose haunts he was
stirring up with his plow. In frustration, he gave his brother a whack
and Remus fell down dead. Romulus probably felt bad about it, but
he was stuck in mid-ceremony and had to keep plowing. We know
that Etruscan law required a settlement to have a minimum of three
gates, so at the appropriate places as determined by his auguries,
Romulus lifted the plow and walked the exact number of paces required, holding it, before setting it down again to continue cutting
the soil. This way, he laid out the initial Pomerium. Had Remus
had his way, the city would quite likely be known to history as Remoria. Meanwhile, Romulus now was the ruler of a bona fide spiritual as well as physical domain he named after himself—Rome.

He invited runaway slaves and other roaming refugees to join
his band. When they needed women, they invited the nearby
Sabines over for a feast, killed all the men, and kept their women
to be their wives. The women were apparently so happy with their
new husbands that they put in a good word for the Romans with
the Sabine King Titus Tatius. Romulus and Titus Tatius became co-
rulers for a time. Titus Tatius died, and Romulus disappeared into
a storm, probably of divine origin ('went to heaven'). His descendants and their subjects deified him as the god Quirinus, whom the
Romans would honor through almost their entire history.

As Rome acquired wealth and power, the first families became
famous as the founding clans, and their homes became bigger and
more opulent. The first *domus* (palace) must have appeared by the
middle Republic, and later, the emperors would build their *palatia*
here. Deities worshipped on the Palatine included Volupia (sensual
pleasure); Aius Locutius or Loquens (a mysterious voice out of
nowhere, who spoke one night around 390 B.C., warned of approaching Gauls, and saved the people); Dea Viriplaca (Goddess
Husband-pleaser); Febris (Fever); Fides (Faith); Fortuna (Fortune);
Iuno Sospita (Juno Savior); Luna Noctiluca (Moon who brightens

the night); and others. Only a few sanctuaries have been actually located, and all date to the later Republic. These include Victoria (Victory); Iuppiter Victor (Jupiter the Victorious); and the Magna Mater (Great Mother, an early adaptation of the foreign Cybele cult). This brief roster is from among a profusion of Latin deities (who have started becoming anthropomorphic or human-like) gives a good flavor for the imaginative manner in which animist and polytheist (anthropomorphic) ideas powerfully intertwine.

Most of the wealthy Republican homes, and the streets among them on top of the Palatine, have been blotted out by imperial and aristocratic palaces during the empire. The *aedes Romuli,* or House of Romulus, was a thatched hut next to the houses of Augustus and Livia. Ostensibly it had survived from early times, and Romulus was supposed to have lived there. It often burned down and was restored or replaced. It will last until the 4th century A.D. Modern archaeologists have found the post-holes of such huts on the Palantine.

In the time of Constantine (307–337 A.D.), the Palatine gradually reverts to private residences—albeit there will long be an imperial residence here, and the homes in general are extremely upscale. Emperors still come to the Palatine when 'in residence,' but for many of them that is rare. The imperial capitals will be at Constantinople, Ravenna, Trier, Split, and elsewhere after 300.

CHAPTER 18

EMPEROR

His Majesty the Emperor, Antoninus Pius (Titus Aelius Caesar Hadrianus Antoninus Augustus Pius) was born 19 September 86 A.D. at Lanuvium, which is about 33 km (20 miles) south of Rome. His full name at birth was Titus Aurelius Fulvus Boionius Arrius Antoninus. He followed the normal *cursus honorum* (moderns would call this 'ticket punching') through the ranks of service as a patrician. His services included those of quaestor and praetor, followed by a stint as consul. He served as governor of the province of Asia, in western Asia Minor, 135–6. Serving as a Senator at Rome, he was adopted by Hadrian as his successor, on 24 January 138. He received the agnomen Aelius from Hadrian's family. The adoption was formalized on 25 February. He acceded to the throne 10 July 138 at age 52, receiving the name Pius and the title *Pater Patriae* (Father of the Nation). Upon accession, the Senate awarded him the Tribunician and Consular powers several times, and also the title *Pontifex Maximus* (Supreme Bridge-Making Priest). He married Annia Galeria Faustina, who died 140. They had two sons, Marcus

Antoninus Pius will die of natural causes, aged 74, at Lorium 7 March 161. He will be deified by a grateful Senate, and interred in the Mausoleum of Hadrian. His wife, who preceded him in deification, shares her temple in the Forum Romanum with him.

His will have reigned longer (138-161, or 23 years) than either of his great predecessors, the Deified Trajan (98-117, or 19 years) and the Deified Hadrian (117-138, or 21 years).

Aurelius and Marcus Galerius. They had two daughters, Aurelia Fadilla and Annia Galeria Faustina (the Younger).

His Majesty Antoninus is a remarkable man in appearance, demeanor, and modesty. Contrasted with some of his earlier predecessors, the likes of Caligula, Claudius, and Nero, he is a true Pater Patriae. In appearance, Antoninus is contemplatively good looking, as if his thoughts are in some distant and philosophical realm. He exudes an air of quiet strength and competence. Even more importantly, he is the supremely gifted leader. He is confident, sympathetic, fatherly without being overbearing, and always reserved in the most highly admired quality of the Classic Greeks. Antoninus is a great administrator who rules wisely and fairly what has been entrusted to him.

His own family came from Nemausus in Gaul (modern Nîmes, France), but had long been a leading family of Imperial Rome. They own rich country estates in Etruria.

During his rule, he has successfully coped with defensive military requirements. He has abandoned Hadrian's Wall in Britain, and has erected a newer Antonine Wall some miles north of there against Pictish tribesmen (Scots). He has suppressed rebellions in Germany, Mauretania, Egypt, Judaea, and Greece. He has subdued Dacian and Alan tribes of barbarians threatening the Danube provinces. He continues to arbitrate many international disputes among kings within his empire, including a near war between the Parthians and the Armenians. He is slow to offer battle, and relies upon his formidable speaking and persuasive powers to bring peace rather than forcing peace by violent means.

Antoninus rules wisely and modestly. He leaves no major monuments, aside from that relatively modest Temple of Antoninus and Faustina in the Roman Forum. He gives his citizens the best gifts of all, peace and prosperity and safety.

All the peace accrued in the years of Antoninus seems to shatter during the less fortunate years of Marcus Aurelius (161–180), as the last of the good emperors is forced to spend his entire imperium fighting defensive wars while nurturing his failing health. In the end, he is replaced by his own son, one of the notorious monsters of Roman history: Commodus.

PART SIX

PUBLIC POOL DISTRICT

(Regio XII. Piscina Public)

CHAPTER 19

PUBLIC POOL

From the Palatine, going downhill, we walk south-southeast to a place we visited earlier: the southern end of the Circus Maximus. Several major roads intersect there, including the city terminus of the Appian Way. We cross this intersection, skirting the southern edge of the Aventine, and enter the Public Pool District. This is an area of poorer neighborhoods and many workshops. In particular, a lot of the small industries in this section on the edges of the city are concerned with commerce coming in and out on major roads. The primary road coming into this section is the Ostian Way.

On our right, above the rooftops and trees, we see a significant hill called the Aventine Minor. It's connected by a ridge to the larger Aventine Major looming beyond it.

We come down to the ancient Servian Wall that still defines the sacred Pomerium of the city. The major gate in the Servian Wall for this district is the Porta Raudusculanae. The origins of this name are lost in history, like those of so many other names in this 800-year-old city, but it's possible there is a connection to *raudus*, copper coin, or *raudusculum*, a minuscule debt, as of a few pennies. Nobody knows to what antique story this may relate. Perhaps a comedy play that was popular in the theaters of the middle Republic, or a small tax long ago to bring goods in this way.

In this district is the private house of Hadrian, not far from the Aventine. It is the house where he lived before his adoption as Trajan's heir. The current emperor, Antoninus Pius lived in the house before his adoption as Hadrian's heir.

Pilgrims come to the Temple of *Bona Dea Subsaxana*, 'Good Goddess Under The Rock.' Bona Dea Fauna is the female counter-

The most famous building in this district in modern times is not yet standing in 150 A.D., but it soon will be. Caracalla, a brutal tyrant, will consolidate his power in 211 by murdering his brother Geta. He will leave behind the breathtaking *Thermae Antoninianae* (Antonine Baths) better remembered as the Baths of Caracalla.

part (sister, wife, or daughter) of Faunus, protective deity of agriculture and of shepherds, grandson of Saturn, and father of Latinus. After the conquest of Greece, the Latins morph him into Pan, and later as a multiple manifestation of the Greek Satyrs. Roman piety out the window, Greek lechery in the door. Fauna (also *Fatua, Oma*) is regarded as a chaste and prophetic divinity. She reveals her oracles solely to women, while Faunus prophecies only to men. Vestals celebrate her rites on May 1, usually in a consul's home, and only women may attend. Bona Dea Subsaxana is a goddess of healing, and in her temple snakes move about freely without fearing harm; also, the temple contains fragrant herbs of every kind.

Subsaxana refers to a rock in the eastern Aventine slope, overlooking Regio XII. The temple is *sub saxum*, 'below the rock,' or on lower ground. According to legend, there was an *auguraculum* here, an observation point, the *Remoria*, at which Remus, brother of Romulus made his own calculations and observations about where to found the city,

We walk along the Clivus Delphini on our way from the Via Nova to the Via Ardeatina. Along the way, we pass through a quarter dedicated to wool workers, or *lanarii*. Long ago, sheep were kept on the Palatine, and throughout the future city. Nowadays, the sheep are in the countryside far from the city. The little farmers are long gone, replaced by corporations using thousands of slaves to operate huge plantations or *latifundia*. The corporations bought out the farmers during economic hard times. It's one of the classic differences between the Republic and the Empire. The little guy has taken it on the nose, while the rich get richer. All the timeless clichés apply. The farmers were displaced by years of civil war and disaster during the last decades of the Republic. They had to sell their ancestral homes for a song and left for the only other place they could think of—the city. There, they couldn't compete in the labor market, which was filled substantially by slaves. As a result, they began a generational spiral into joblessness and crime.

Speaking of law and disorder, we are about to meet one of the city's Finest.

CHAPTER 20

POLICEMAN

The police detective Publicolus is 40 but looks ten or fifteen years older. At first glance, we're not sure if he's more cop or more crook. He is of medium height, but looks bigger. Around his neck is a leather thong, on which dangles a medallion of Matuta. His hair is white and curly, cut short around the top, but plastered around his sweaty, wrinkled neck. He wears a small gold earring on each earlobe, and we smell garlic around his mouth and a sort of honey-sweet pomade around the curls on his brown neck. His arms are long and brawny. His hands, which are taffy-colored, seem more delicate, as if he has not had to do any physical work or fighting in many years. His mouth is wide and expressive, with a kind of grim humor accented by grape-colored lips. In his jowly face, which seems to be raining tiny chocolate-colored freckles, the most prominent feature are his large, dark-green eyes. These eyes are incisive, cynical, but still somehow kind and accepting. He will give us a tour of the police station.

To keep public order in the Public Pool district, there is the barracks of the Fourth Cohort (*Cohors* IV) of the *vigiles* (watch).

Publicolus meets us near Barracks IV, which serves both the Piscina Publica and the Aventinus districts from a location on the Aventine. It is late afternoon, and it is getting dark. Already, the lamplighters are going about lighting oil lamps inside glass lanterns on street corners. The wind has a little bit of a bite, both because of a chill in the air, and a dusty grit that stings the cheeks at odd moments. People hurry by, wrapped in cloaks. Publicolus walks with us, hands behind his back in the folds of his toga. He looks pensive, ready to help us, yet from long habit suspicious and

116

When Augustus reorganized the city from the ancient four to the modern 14 *regiones* (districts), he created one *statio* (station, precinct; pl. *stationes*;) of police and firemen to serve every two districts. The emperors also established 14 smaller posts or *excubitoria* around the city for better coverage and quicker response times.

The barracks were numbered, but the numbers did not coincide with the district numbers. Thus, Barracks I was on the east side of the Via Lata in Regio IV. Barracks II was on the Esquiline. Barracks III was in Regio IV, covering the Subura, from a spot near the Porta Viminalis of the Servian Wall (from which a minor connecting road leads out of the city along the southern edge of the Praetorian Camp). Barracks IV was on the Aventine. Barracks V is on the Caelian, near the Macellum Magnum (Big Butcher Market). Barracks VI is in Regio VIII, Roman Forum. Barracks VII is in Regio XIV, Cross-Tiber.

observant of all who pass. "This will be a quiet night for the vigiles," Publicolus tells us with quiet confidence. "I know, because I walked this beat and others in my youth."

"Were you a uniformed officer?" we ask.

"I started as a thief and a forger," he tells us without shame. "My parents abandoned me, and—"

"How awful!" we interrupt. "Why?"

He gives us a look that says *you really don't know much, do you.* "Exposed me," he says with a trace of bitterness. "I believe they were very poor, displaced from a family farm somewhere near Tibur. I know almost nothing of them, and maybe that is best. They could not support another child, and so left me out for the wolves." He winks darkly. "What wolves they were, who took me in. Left like so many infants by a public road, at a shrine, or some other remote civic place, I might have been eaten by animals, or taken as a slave, or worse. I was lucky, because an elderly man named Noventus and his wife took me along. They had lost all their children, but still had a small house outside the southeast city wall. They were old and had almost nothing, but they managed to grow their radishes and turnips to trade at the market for bread. They found me in the weeds beside a shrine of Matuta." He fingers his medallion for a moment. "My adoptive parents were good people," he says in a voice grown thick with emotion for just a fleeting second. After a pause, he continues, "they did give me an auspicious start. Matuta is the goddess of dawn, and harbors, and the sea, but also a patron of infants. Thank you, Mother Matuta," he says choking, and stops a moment with his eyes closed. Despite his shifty eyes and constant air of sly insinuation, we do not doubt the genuine emotion of this moment. He kisses the medallion and tucks it close to his chest, out of sight, as if protecting it. "So I had a very happy childhood with these old grandparents. I played among the pigs and crawled in the mud looking for a berry to eat. Then, when I was a young boy, they died of fever during a particularly warm, rainy winter. Soldiers came from a wealthy corporation and took their farm to put up a bakery, which still stands today under the arches of a high aqueduct." He points a beefy finger at his chest. "In my heart, I treasure the memory of simpler and better times." It is a common sentiment among urban Romans, who cherish the distant cultural memories of an idyllic past.

"Then you feel Rome has grown too much, too fast?" we ask, to make conversation as we cross a little square of cobblestones among sharp-edged buildings pointing from several *vici*, or small streets. We smell cabbage and onions steaming on a stove. Somewhere, a blacksmith continues hammering on his anvil in a forge lit by dancing firelight. The first wagons start to roll into the city in a constant stream that won't abate until morning, and we can hear the river of voices coming with the traffic on nearby roads (the Raudusculana, the Appia, the Ardeatina). At times, from our height, we glimpse a train of torches downhill, when we can see through spaces between trees and house walls.

"It is no longer Roman," he declares. "All the riffraff of the Mare Nostrum wash up here. I should know. After Noventus died, I was taken in by an unscrupulous man named Pella, who sodomized me and beat me until I ran away. I was an angry kid, and ran with a gang down in Subura. We thought nothing of stealing our food or lying in the gutters drunk. When we wanted something, we took it. If we had to, we hit someone over the head or knocked an old lady down for her purse. We were proud of how fast we could run, and we got away with anything. Then, one day, a friend of mine made the mistake of borrowing a sum of money from a money-lender named Farsus. I'll make a long story short. My friend didn't pay the money back in time, though the rest of us took up a collection and urged him to be sensible. He drank our money away. We were young men almost of early military age by then (15). My friend was found floating among the marble docks by the Emporium with his eyes gouged out. Farsus even sent two sicarii to try and extort the money from me and my friends. That's when I wised up. A detective named Patronicus came by and convinced me to help bust Farsus and his cronies. I received a small sum of money and was given a chance to join the vigiles, because I was physically very strong and, if I may say, a fairly brainy fellow." He grins and points to his forehead.

We come to an archway in a masonry wall, the entrance to the precinct house. On either side of the door, on the rather ugly brown stucco wall whose cracks reveal the underlying brick, are guttering oil lamps within little glass lantern panes. The wooden doors are open, as they are most of the time, since there is a constant stream of policemen, firemen, prisoners, magistrates, and others. Along the high wall to our left, looking down the block, we hear men hollering in a constant din, a sort of sewer of human voices clogged with brutish laughter and violent shouting. "That's the lockup," Publicolus explains as we walk on the cobblestones under the archway. We note the heavy wooden doors with their iron studs, made to resist an attacking mob if need be. We enter a cobblestone inner courtyard that is most likely a small mustering point for each shift as they go on duty. At the moment, it is empty except for a few toga-clad officials hurrying by on errands. A statue of Mercury stands to one side, and one of Neptune to the other. Neptune, the water god, is the patron of fire-fighters. Around it on a narrow ledge or altar are small offerings. A ring of oil lights covers the walls all around. About half the windows are bolted closed for the night, and dark behind wooden shutters. The other windows all seem to be open, and throwing out lantern light. A smell of cabbage and vinegar (more likely, cheap state-brewed fish sauce) drifts over from the lockup where drunks and pickpockets sit among knifemen and rapists. Some of the smaller criminals will be out by noon, while the more serious get shipped to a gladiator school or even crucified outside the city.

Rome does not have jails in the modern sense. There is no sense of punitive, much less corrective, imprisonment. In general, the Romans do not keep prisoners, except briefly while awaiting trial, execution, or binding over to the arena or a gladiator school. Aside from the casual lockup, Rome possesses only one prison, and that consists of two openings in a cistern above the Great Sewer: the Tullianum, located at the foot of the Capitol Hill near the new Curia. It was known in Medieval times as the Mamertine Prison.

Publicolus takes us on a tour of the Fourth Precinct station. It is a surprisingly large building, two stories tall, with its own baths, dormitory, and kitchens. Except for the latrine, the halls and rooms are immaculately clean. Slaves sweep, wash floors, and do dishes. Off-duty vigiles sit in the workshops, maintaining fire and police equipment. There is a latrine in a small courtyard, with a mossy brick overhang, and the dozen holes in its travertine bench emit a strong reek of urine. "We sell the piss to a fuller shop," Publicolus explains. "We use half the money they pay us to keep candles burning at the shrine of Mercury, our patron. The other half we use to run a betting pool on the Circus Maximus." Fulling is the last step in creating wool or cloth blankets and garments. A fullers's slaves stir the garments in a solution of decayed urine to dissolve dirt and grease before a final washing. It's one of those things toga salesmen don't mention, even if asked.

The *vigiles* sound confident and professional, with plentiful rough and ready humor. They talk passionately about sports—the races at the circus, and the fights at the stadium. At the moment, a gladiator named Whale seems to be the unstoppable tank, but two Thracians named Meat Hook and Glory Boy are up and comers, and there is excitement all over the city about an upset in tomorrow's games. We also look in on the infirmary, where injured policemen and firemen are recovering from wounds. One policeman lies unconscious after being stabbed in the abdomen while trying to arrest a thief. Two others sit together nursing broken arms and watching over their comrade. A fireman hobbles in to get the dressings on a burned arm changed. He is in a lot of pain and smells of wine and medications.

Publicolus says: "I'll take you on a tour of the streets. Better here than in Subura, I'll tell you that much." Several policeman lounging over dice at a table nearby laugh knowingly. Subura at night is the Fort Apache of their trade. In the previous century, one might even encounter a Nero or a Caligula out for the night with his fellow murderers, rapists, and drunks; it was an arrest one avoided trying to make, and these seasoned veterans of the street marvel at what their predecessors had to handle.

CHAPTER 21

VICUS HORSE HEAD

"I'll show you a real Roman neighborhood," Publicolus declares as we walk out the back gate of the barracks. We head for the eastern slope of the Aventine. The Vicus Capitis Canteri is a lower middle class to working poor area that just barely avoids being downright poor. We wonder if it's dangerous. "Not as dangerous as many other places," Publicolus says with an annoyed sniff. "I adopted this place, or it adopted me."

"This is the real Rome," Publicolus tells us proudly. "What's left of it." Approaching along a series of narrow, zigzag streets, we smell a variety of enticing cooking smells. "Ain't it grand?" Publicolus says holding his arms out and smiling with his eyes closed, as if taking a shower in the affections of his neighborhood. After a moment's reverie, he resumes his forward march. "When I made detective, I got a slight raise. It isn't much, but it gives me an edge. I worked a bunch of down-home neighborhoods, and this is the one I chose to live in ten years ago. I've never regretted it."

We come to a crossroads of three narrow, cobbled streets. Rome doesn't have cars, so its streets follow a different set of instincts than moderns are used to. Rome has some main streets, usually thought of as *via* this or *clivus* that, and they generally run straight for some distance. Many of them traceable out into the countryside like the Via Appia. The truly characteristic street of Rome, however, is the *vicus*, which translates not only into 'small street,' but also neighborhood. But it's more than that. It's a safe place, a sanctuary, a world unto itself. If you are lucky enough to be part of a good vicus, you have a relatively safe retreat from the urban chaos and danger. The vicus actually has a sacred history, like all else about Rome.

It always centers on a *compita*, or crossroads. Here we are again at the animistic core of Rome, the religious fundament of the *numina*. We may be in the heart of the world's greatest urban sprawl, a la 150 A.D., but people see themselves somehow still as farmers, rustics, *pagani* (country boys, from *pagus*, 'country') at heart.

The Horse's Head Neighborhood is probably named after a tavern that stood where a fountain now splashes beside a shrine in a small square in 150 A.D.

The noise all around us sounds generally happy. Children run in packs, chasing a ball or spinning a top. Several girls stand with wooden dolls in arm, chatting about imaginary married lives in their future. An elderly granny sits looking out of a window at first floor level. An elderly man sits in a doorway, whittling a piece of wood into a duck. A mother leans out to call her son Marcus in from play. Two laborers are just arriving from work outside the Capena Gate; they look sweaty and dirty from a day's work hoeing a communal vegetable garden. One has a bag full of cabbages, while the other carries their hoes in one hand and a dead rabbit in the other hand. We catch glimpses of the interiors of the houses,

Many modern urban centers consist of ancient villages that were swallowed up by a growing metropolis. This is true, for example, of London and Tokyo, as well as New York City. Where the modern Empire State Building stands, a farmer used to have his field, and the waters that rose to irrigate that field still occasionally flood the basements.

Tokyo is a modern urban sprawl that can be parsed into neighborhoods. They in turn can be parsed into the separate villages that they once formed.

In London, one can walk down a street (in Westminster, for example) and be surprised by the number of Anglican churches every so many blocks. Centuries ago, many of those churches served separate village parishes.

It is no different in the Rome of 150 A.D. It's been centuries since the vici (plural of vicus) were absorbed into the greater urbs, but each vicus retains a certain original historical flavor.

each a tiny brick cubicle of one or two rooms and no running water. A makeshift stove under an open window serves as the cooking
stove for the family's one pot. One or two little wooden pallets covered with straw serve as beds, but if there are more children, they'll
sleep on a reed mat on the floor. If they are lucky, they have a good
blanket to cover themselves. Publicolus greets the man carving the
duck, and the man shouts a toothless wisecrack. The granny in the
window gives the detective a good natured ribbing about being too
old to chase criminals. She teases that maybe he'd give a lady of her
age a run for it. He replies that her imagination is too feeble to lead
her to do anything bad enough to make a cop chase her. The children run in circles around us and then disappear like a flight of
sparrows, only to reappear seconds later out of a courtyard entrance
half a block down the street. We pass the community bath, which
is a small neighborhood tap on a nearby water reservoir (*castellum*,
or receiving tank). The reservoir draws water from one of Rome's
extension aqueducts, the Antoniniana Iovis, which is a branch of
the Aqua Marcia (one of the ten major aqueducts entering the city
from afar).

"Look," someone says pointing up to one side. For a moment,
it seems as if there are children running on the rooftops.

"No," Publicolus explains, "they run up and down on those
narrow paths to play with children up on the hill behind us in another vicus. Don't worry, it's perfectly safe. It's another working
class neighborhood where people take care of each other, because
nobody else will watch out for them." He puffs a bit as we walk, obviously no longer the sprightly young beat cop he was long ago.

As night fully descends, the air grows chilly. We are lucky to be
underneath a full moon that hovers among the arches of a nearby
aqueduct. There is dampness in the air, and the moon looks large
and amber. We stop at one of many little open shops to get a bite
to eat. This is in the very heart of the vicus, where the ancient crossroads meet. There, in the center of a tiny cobblestone plaza, stands
a simple shrine with small altar. Flickering in a stone depression on
top is a wooden torch; cool blue flames lick around its pitch head,
between bursts of a yellowish flame that gutters back down as soon
as it erupts. The light casts dancing shadows among the reliefs carved
on the eight-foot-tall travertine slab of a little shrine and altar to

the nameless numina, the community lares and penates, the genii of the neighborhood. We spot a few little offerings left by children and the poor: a strip of cloth, a flower, a smooth piece of broken brick-red ceramic with religious symbols drawn in charcoal. For a moment we wonder who left the torch on top of the fountain, but we quickly learn why. Several doors open, and residents come out with greetings. Two tired figures are trudging up the street from the direction of the Appian Way. They are Sylvia and Marcia, two sturdy older women who have trudged many miles pulling a little wagon filled with farm produce. Publicolus explains: "Many of the better poor living in these neighborhoods still have connections to the old farm villages in Latium. They went bankrupt long ago and had to sell, but some still have contact with old neighbors. Thus, we send all sorts of little manufactured items—door knobs, brooches, hair pins, cosmetics, things that they don't have in the villages. They send our people back with fresh fruits and vegetables. Many of these people are on the dole, but tell me you wouldn't rather have fresh *fraga* (strawberries) or a nice shiny red *malum* (apple) once in a while instead of always the same government *frumentum* (grain) from Egypt." For a few minutes, the toothless women glow as they receive a few copper coins. They are happy because they know the pleasure they bring. They have walked the entire day. They slept the night in a tiny ancestral village, visiting with cousins. They had to wake at first light and wend their way back to the Horse Head Neighborhood.

The shopkeepers are ready to close their wooden shutters and bed down for the night. These little one and two room boxes are their shops by day, and their homes by night. The air is filled with the richness of salty, onion-spicy cooking, the slightly sour tang of smoking wood or charcoal, and the bite of roasting chestnuts. Children can still be heard yelling as they run in their games, but a woman's voice can be heard: *Marce! Priscilla! Huc agunto! Nunc, et statim! Aut papam agam, Mihercle iuro!* ("Marcus! Priscilla! Get over here! Now, and immediately! Or I'll send your father, I swear to you, Hercules!"). We hear a final swish of clothing and running of feet, the slam of a door, and no more children yelling. Each of these vici is a tiny world in itself. Some vici dead-end in a hillside or blind alley, and the crossing shrine is little more than a turnaround.

Other vici are thoroughfares in the winding spider web of streets that varicose all through residential Rome in hundreds of little fits and turns. Though this vicus is quieter than many, sound carries all too well. We hear a dog barking, a man yelling at the dog, a woman yelling at the man, children yelling at the woman and the man, a neighbor yelling at the family, other neighbors yelling for them all to be quiet. Meanwhile some drunks are singing loudly, and somewhere a horse trudges over cobblestones on clattering hooves. "It's a good little corner to live out my years," Publicolus says. "Before we go to sleep, we really need to make a stop and relax a bit."

We walk down a curving alley. All around us, we hear the sing-song of conversation. People here have very little, but they sound contented as they count their blessings. Somehow, they have survived another day, and their children are healthy. Death and illness lurk at every corner, as the whims of myriad nameless and capricious deities dictate. Even the poorest family has some sort of shrine, even if it's only a shaky rendering of Minerva or Juno Sospita in charcoal on the crumbling whitewash. Most families have at last a small brick oven for heating water or soup in a single dented pot. For the very poorest of these families, their only source of running water is the *castellum* or neighborhood reservoir.

CHAPTER 22

BALNEUM

Publicolus introduces us to a remarkably Roman institution, the neighborhood bath house. To get there, we must go to a neighboring compita, where the streets of several vici meet. From there we go down a rather industrial looking little alley with trees and a canyon on the left, and a dark brick building on the right. As in modern Tokyo, every vicus has at least one of these institutions. Many vici like the Horse Head will vanish in the future as Caracalla's Antonine Thermae (giant baths) destroy old neighborhoods. Rome has nearly 1,000 *balnea* (plural of *balneum*) scattered through every part of town. Most are known after their owner's name, but this one is called *Balneum Fortunae Tentatae* (bath house of Trusting Good Fortune, a credible slogan for the very poor but honest residents of the area). We smell the wood burning, and see the smoke curling from a brick chimney above, from the fire of its *caldarium* (hot bath). The building itself is long and low, about the size of a modern four-bay auto mechanic shop. With Publicolus in the lead, we enter by a simple wooden door at one end. The structure has only high, wooden shutters for venting. There are no windows. The entire building smells surprisingly clean and refreshing. For a moment, we are enveloped by a blast of steam coming from the ruddy gloom. Only oil lamps, glassed lanterns, and the occasional openly crackling torch provide light. We welcome the moist warmth. There are several rooms in a row, separated from one another by a thin brick wall with a narrow doorway. Coming into the building, we offer our coins to a swarthy, curly-haired dwarf who shakes hands, smiling, with Publicolus. "Hey, detective, whom are you after tonight?"

Publicolus shakes the slave by one shoulder. "Let me look into your face, you Arab, and see the guilt written there. Ah, you scoundrel. You are too dark to see."

"I'll blame it all on Calla and Hymettus," the slave says, working diligently even while joking. He pushes clean towels across a work-worn wooden table. He has named some of his fellow slaves who maintain the bath house. Laughter rises as old friends greet each other. Publicolus walks around shaking hands with a half-dozen gray-haired men who sit on wall-benches in the first room chatting. They have finished their baths and sit with towels loosely draped over their loins.

We walk through the series of doorways into thickening steam, until we come to the caldarium or hot pool. Three men are just emerging from its oily looking depths. The water is not chlorinated. Small amounts of salt or vinegar may be added to the water, along with herbs like lavender and gardenia. This gives the entire building a fresh and pleasant smell that makes customers want to return. The poorest baths in Subura may have a mixture of olive oil and wood ash thrown into the hot water to act as a primitive emulsifier or soap. The better balnea, including this one, have a true soap. One legend attributes the invention of soap to the fact that priests on Mount *Sapo*, upriver from Rome, would allow rainwater to wash their altars clean of the ashes and fat after sacrifices. The residue flowed into the Tiber and mingled with the clothing of washerwomen on the Tiber banks, who noticed that both they and the clothing became cleaner. Another legend attributes the invention to the Celts and even more ancient peoples. The modern English 'soap,' German *Seife*, and Latin *sapo* all reflect an Indo-European root *seib*, meaning to trickle or run out. Some plants produce vegetable tallow (Latin *sebum*, from that same primordial *seib-* root).

Before Publicolus steps his naked, olive-colored bulk into the caldarium, he first removes his toga. The dwarf comes by and grabs the toga to give it a quick rinse (a full wash requires special handling at the fuller's). Publicolus squats on a little tile surface near a dripping hot water spigot. There, he rubs himself in a mixture of olive oil, ash, and sand. He rinses himself with hot water, especially his thick and well-oiled hair. The worst of his street dust and other effluvia drain away down a tiled ditch in the floor, running along the wall. Almost all the water of Rome runs along under gravity's pressure, rather than by pumps. Water flows to the back of the balneum from the castellum or neighborhood reservoir slightly uphill. Some goes directly to the *frigidarium*, or cold tub. The rest goes to the heating tank, which is a stone reservoir heated by the hypocaust under the floor. The slaves Calla and Hymettus spend their hours shoveling charcoal, firewood, and even cattle dung rich with straw into the furnace pit to make the water in the caldarium hot enough while not parboiling its occupants. Keeping the temperature even is quite an art, and the two slaves are adept at moving in slow motion, doing just enough to keep the balneum functioning without straining themselves. Even at that, their work is long and hard. They divert themselves by endlessly chattering about the horse races and arena games with customers. The trick, if you're a slave, is you hear all the gossip of the vicus. You hear the latest predictions about how Whale will be trounced in the arena, and what the emperor's and the mayor's police are up to so everyone can avoid problems with the law. Publicolus himself is adept at siding with the people whenever possible. Sometimes he passes colorful but inaccurate information to the many police spies. After all, this is a tyranny, however benevolent the current His Majesty may be. As one saw with the change from Vespasian and Titus to Domitian, benevolence and caprice can replace each other with Janus-like suddenness. The dwarf and the other two bath slaves, therefore, are respected and beloved fixtures in the balneum and the vicus. Their job security is better than that of many a freeborn. Rumor has it that the dwarf, in fact, has been building up a nest egg from all the little bribes he has collected over the years. He plans eventually to buy his freedom, marry a certain tall Nubian woman he sees during his rare free hours at the large *thermae* of Trajan. He hopes that they will sail off into the sunset to a villa in Syria, his homeland. Dreams abound; the bitter reality is that, with his first few gray hairs already worming their way out, he will probably live a few more years and then end up in a common pit among other slaves. At best, his savings will buy him a fine burial shroud, but no tomb along the Appian Way. Perhaps his owner, a wealthy merchant whose agent comes by once or twice a day to supervise that all is going well, may inter the dwarf's cremated remains in an inferior niche in the family tomb. It is doubtful he and his lovely friend, whom he cannot legally marry, will see that splendid sunset, but hope keeps the spirits up. One never knows what miracle some as yet unsuspected divine intervention may bring about. Praise be to the Mater Matuta and other good deities.

Publicolus emerges from the hot bath, wringing water from the leather thong that holds his holy medal around his neck. He doesn't part with the medal even for a moment. The dwarf uses a *strigil* or scraping stick (looks like a sort of ivory razor) to squeegee water off the larger man, who presses a coin in the other's palm. Without any great haste, the detective saunters into the middle room, or tepidarium. He joins several cronies who are pickling themselves in a lukewarm pool. In many baths, the tepidarium is simply a warmish room for cooling off. Eventually, Publicolus will grow weary of the conversation and wander into the frigidarium for a final brisk plunge. Then he may decide to sit with his cronies a while on the bench. Instead he may wander off for a final cup of wine, maybe a few olives, grapes, cheese, and little chunk of bread, and then off to sleep.

For those who desire sex (our Publicolus is too tired tonight), three or four shadowy women in shroud-like togas always appear on the street along the balneum wall. Their service can be consummated for a few coppers and little time, in a niche of packed earth behind the balneum amid wild olive trees. The women are of sturdy stock, and know how to take care of themselves. A man left in the bushes to sleep it off isn't hurting anyone, except perhaps himself, especially if he has a purse under his belt. That can be lightened and divided among the girls. The men know enough to go easy, because the women have a pimp. That's Materius, a Thracian ex-boxer hired by the balneum for general security. Materius takes a small cut of the action, in return for providing law and order. What he does to you depends on what you try to do to him, which in turn depends on how drunk you are. Word of advice: he packs a wicked left hook that comes out of nowhere like the wings of Mercury or the kick of a horse. When it connects with your temple you won't be whistling for at least a week after you wake up.

Where we'll spend the night is a short walk down through a winding path amid a grove of palms and stunted oaks. Publicolus leads us, feeling his way in the dark. The house of Publicolus is slightly better than that of some of his neighbors. Located at the edge of the Horse Head where it obtrudes on a slightly more middle-class vicus, his house has two stories. It's a small house, with a foot-print no larger than 360 square feet (about 19 × 19 ft, or slightly over 6m, each side) which is roughly doubled by the addition of a second story. We learn that Publicolus is a bit hard to get along with. His wife of ten years died of fever, and he has had a succession of concubines, but there's always been a reason why the women left. Sometimes it was for a man with more money, sometimes for a man with less volatile temperament. At the moment, Publicolus is living the bachelor life, and being picky about who the next woman in his life may be. "I'm near the end of my years and I have no children," he tells us, "so what do I care? The dwarf enjoys the pleasure of a statuesque Venus to whom he pays every last obol of his money, and my sleuthing tells me she has one or two other dunces on the hook. Why, then, should I not simply purchase for myself the most beau-tiful young slave woman who stands terrified in the cattle market and have my pleasure, get my toga cleaned, and the hell with what people say? Don't try to dissuade me—I'm on the verge of driving home the deal. All I need to find is the right girl, and this will be happy home. It's simple. I grant her a will, stating that when I die—provided she doesn't kill me to hasten the moment—she will be manumitted officially by a lawyer friend of mine and will inherit this little house and my few possessions. What better bargain could there be?"

Like the dwarf, Publicolus has his dream. Eventually, we all have our dreams as we lie upon our beds; those being piles of straw on the floor, with a spare toga thrown over them. We are too tired to care.

What a strange place this is! The smell of the baker's bread starts to waft through the air, mingling with the nitrous and bloody arts of the sausage maker. We hear the distant rumbling of wagons on cobblestones. and, yes, the songs of a dozen drunken sailors who tomorrow will hang in the shrouds above the Colosseum, pulling the giant shade-sail over the crowd's head to shield them from the sun.

Publicolus has retreated upstairs. In a corner of his lower room is a wooden ladder leading rather steeply up into a hole, from where he reaches his second floor bedroom. He does have a regular Roman bed with wooden frame, and cross-laced canvas straps to support the straw-filled pillow or mattress on which he sleeps. He rolls up his toga for a pillow, and keeps a ceramic cup of water on the night table. He has a cupboard up there with an upper compartment that is his lararium or shrine. Like the vast majority of Romans, he has no death masks. In fact he has no real idea who his ancestors may have been. Still though, he closes his eyes and hopes rather grandiosely they were genuine ancient Romans. He hopes that they were not upstarts from Carthage or Palaestina, to name just two possible fountains of his *gens*. We will leave Publicolus in the morning. He returns to his duties as a semi-retired, consulting detective at the IV Cohort, Urban Vigiles. We will press on in our walk through the ancient city. Through ordinary citizens like Publicolus and his neighbors, we continue to see from one moment to the next how similar life here is to ours in the modern world. Yet, in the absence of certain technologies, and in some fundamental ideas that seem strange to us, we realize how alien their world is. Then again, by understanding the Roman soul a bit better, that which seems alien may become a little more understandable.

A night wind stirs through cracks in the wooden shutters over glassless windows, and the dangling oil lamps gutter out one by one. We get goose bumps looking at the figures stamped on them, some are tragic and comedic masks from bawdy Plautine theater. Others show hulking gladiators meant to look scary, still others depict sexual grotesques. The mask-lamps swing back and forth, spinning, as the masks regard us with huge eyes and stick out their tongues. *Welcome*, they seem say, *now die of fright. Ha ha ha . . .*

PART SEVEN

CAPENA GATE DISTRICT

(Regio I. Porta Capena)

CHAPTER 23

APPIAN WAY

The most ancient of Rome's great highways, the Appian Way, stretches from Brundisium (modern Brindisi), an Adriatic port on the upper rear of the heel of the Italian boot, across to Tarentum (Taranto) in the arch of the boot, and then northwest diagonally across Italy, via Capua, to enter Rome from the south at the Capena Gate. The Appian Way continues about .75 kilometer within the city, ending just before the southern end of the Circus Maximus. At that point, three streets converge: one coming northwest from the Public Pool District (Regio XII), one coming southeast from the Colosseum, and one running southeast alongside the Circus Maximus.

The Porta Capena District is irregularly shaped. It is the eastern of three regions whose southern borders form the southern edge of the city of Rome. Regio I also has a long, narrow section that runs, never more than 150m (492 ft.) wide, to the southeast side of the Palatine, while being bounded on the north by a long run of Regio II (Caelimontium, or Caelian Hill) and on the south by Regio XII (Public Pool).

As the Appian Way approaches the city, it crosses the Almo Stream, which forms the southern boundary of Regio I now that the city has overgrown its limits within the Servian Wall. The Almo is effectively now the southern boundary of the city at Regions XIII (Aventine), XII (Piscina Publica), and I (Porta Capena). The Almo is notable for its fresh, clear water. Like all else in Rome, the stream is steeped in history and religion. Here, since time immemorial, devotees of Cybele have performed an annual ceremony of washing her statues in the Almo. Cybele, the *Magna Mater* or Great Mother, is derived from Greek, and before that, the Cretan Rhea, goddess of the Earth, wife of Cronos (Saturn). She is identified with Kybele, and far earlier with the Hittite Kubaba. She originated in the late Bronze Age, as best we know, as a minor goddess and then grew into a major deity during the dark ages (c. 1150–750 B.C.).

We stood near here earlier in our trip when we walked around the Circus Maximus. This time we have come over the top of the Palatine, and down its southeastern slope. We have walked down a clivus, or sloping street, and now we stand once more at the triple crossroads below the Circus Maximus.

This time we walk southeast on the Appian Way, the short extension of it inside the Servian Wall. The broken archway of the Capena Gate was rebuilt by Domitian (ruled 81–96). Not that a defensive wall was needed, but parts of the Servian Wall were restored at various times to serve as convenient supports for the still-growing system of aqueducts. Domitian's engineers extended the Aqua Marcia aqueduct over the Caelian. That required building a *rivus*, or branch, called the Herculanean. The Porta Capena now has an extra level of arches across its top. In fact the insides of the main gate arch are black with moss and streaming fresh water from a leak that never seems to get fixed. The Romans are efficient, to be sure, but the government has become a huge bureaucracy dominated by political and religious interests. There is, in an imperial public works *aula* (hall), a scroll on which some engineer maintains a list of works. These are to be done in the order in which the city censors decree they shall be done. Antoninus is a rare exception to the rule that Roman emperors must outdo each other (and the leading patricians) in creating vast public works for the people's benefit (and thereby their own fame). The great offender in this game was Nero, who built the largest palace in human history. People weren't so much offended by its absurd grandeur, as they were by two violations of fundamental principle. The palace took possession of just about the entire Palatine and the valley near it. This meant Nero hogged a good section of downtown real estate. More importantly, nothing about the *Domus Aureus* (Golden House) in any way served the people. It was all a lot of selfishness by one of Rome's craziest and most heartless rulers. Not a soul batted an eyelash when the Roman equivalent of steamrollers (slaves and pack animals carrying huge loads of rubble and sand) covered the entire obscene mess over and created parks, temples, and other public buildings a Roman citizen could enjoy. Of course, that meant burying tons of priceless statuary and wall paintings for medieval popes and renaissance princes to loot. It also gave a few new words to the world's dictionaries, including 'grottesque,' from the Italian *grotteschi* (things in a grotto), which referred to the many fabulous statuary groups illustrating themes from Classic mythology. Nero ordered them built into artificial underground caverns or grottoes in his huge palace.

To understand why the Romans did what they did, it is important to understand the notion of *munificentia*. The *ficia* part is easy: it means 'doing' or 'deeds,' from the same root as, for example, *fact-* in manufacture (manus 'hand' + *factus* 'made'). The *muni-* part is a little more complicated, since it involves several notions: *munus*, an office or duty; but also generosity. The same root even extends to the protection of the state (*munimentum*, 'defense'). Ultimately that ties in with Roman religion, the nation, and the place of man in the universe. Roman social order for a long time flirted with democracy, and many surprisingly modern institutions were voted in. Things took a turn for the worst with the murders of the patrician Gracchi brothers in the Second Century B.C. Rome had a long history of internal struggle between the people in general, and the patrician (from *pater*, 'father') aristocracy. Through a number of hard-won struggles, the common people *(plebs)* won some basic democratic rights over the centuries of the Republic. The Republic had many safeguards built in so that no one man could seize power for himself. This is precisely what happened when the Republic turned into first a dictatorship (Marius, Sulla, Julius Caesar) and finally into an Empire.

Tiberius and Gaius Gracchus were two noblemen of ancient lineage (the Sempronia *gens* or 'tribe') who tried to push through reforms that would have given the common people greater freedoms and rights. Instead, they were murdered by their patrician peers, and in the late Republic, the vast wealth of Rome became consolidated as the property of about 300 of the most powerful families. Augustus was arguable the greatest con man of all time. He sold these 300 craven plutocrats on the idea that he would restore the Republic if only they gave him absolute power *(imperium)*. The boldness and rapaciousness of their earlier generations sapped, many sought merely to hold on to what they had. They trembled at the financial losses that disorder would bring them, and welcomed the arrival of a strong man to take charge of the state. It helped that Octavian was the adoptee of Julius Caesar and could claim to represent the ancient Julian clan. Augustus played this theme to the hilt in commissioning Virgil to cement his alleged Bronze Age family links to the Trojan War figures Aeneas and Anchises. It is perhaps the most splendid piece of propaganda in history. Augustus had the patricians wrapped around his finger, and had no intention of restoring the moribund democracy of his forebears. What makes him memorable, at the same time, is that Augustus was not only the first, but the greatest and most innovative of Roman emperors. The success of his reign defined the future of Rome, and in many ways of the world.

Rome was already an empire in all but name, centuries before Augustus put the final stamp on it. To succeed, society demanded that the fabulously wealthy make lavish donations to the public good, continuing Republican notions of public piety. Patronage at all levels was the scaffolding that maintained social order. People did not riot, because it was easier to get something they needed through the orderly system. It might be a street tough getting his dosage of free wine, bread, and circus games (in exchange for his vote for the politician who spent the most in a campaign). Perhaps a humble middle class artisan, needing a loan, attended court at his wealthy patron's morning audience. A senator, needing a state favor, might use his closeness to the Imperial bureaucracy or the emperor himself to bribe or wheedle.

The Gracchi, in some sense, were the assassinated Kennedys of the Republic. Had the Gracchi lived and succeeded in their reforms, there is no telling how much closer to the ideal modern democracy the ancient Romans might have come. In many ways, the cards of the future empire were already dealt in late Republican times. Instead of a system of checks and balances that the Roman founders had carefully crafted, the long struggle eventually went to the wealthy and aristocratic. Bit by bit, the worth of the common man (to say nothing of his wife and children, who had little legal standing) slipped away. Wealthy corporations would buy up all that they could of a good year's wheat crop, store it, and then sell it to the very people who had grown it at exorbitant prices during a year of poor crops. The farmers had no choice but to borrow money to buy the wheat to stay alive, and thus got deeply into debt. As soon as they inevitably defaulted, the corporations were there to foreclose. The ancient family farms disappeared, replaced by huge *latifundia* owned by wealthy corporations. These were farmed with slave labor, in a system that foreshadowed the feudal system of the Middle Ages.

The tiny minority of vastly wealthy families who turned Rome from a Republic into their own private property, in effect, gambled that the system they had created during the final centuries of the Republic, and which Augustus finalized for them, would hold up despite its inequities. There are a lot of reasons for this. Among them is that life was always hard, and for most people, the improvements or munificentia of the patricians and the emperor actually made things more tolerable. Under the veneer of imperial, aristocratic, and religious blessing, the most depraved can sate their endless blood thirst in the Colosseum day in, day out. They lived on the dole and presumably stayed drunk all night. More likely, the vast majority of Roman citizens spent their days working hard just to survive. Out of some 1.2 million Romans, many of whom were slaves, probably never more than five or ten percent actually wasted their lives watching the daily games. The Circuses, for all their size, were only full on specific holidays. There was a strict hierarchy of seating in all these venues—usually nobles sat low and close to the action, male citizens and possibly freedmen sat in the upper and back rows, women and slaves sat at the far top. How often slaves were given a few hours off to watch the games is not clear, but we can guess it is not very often. These are but some of the ruminations that cross our minds as we continue on our walk.

Just outside the Porta Capena stands a Temple of Honor and Virtue *(Aedes Honos et Virtus)*, not to be confused with a temple of the same name in the Roman Forum. The original temple of Honor dates to 234 B.C., built after a successful war with the Ligurians. In 208 B.C., after taking Syracuse (222), M. Claudius Marcellus restored the old Temple of Honor, and his son, in 205, rededicated the temple to both gods together. Nearby, still outside the Porta Capena, is the Fountain of Prometheus.

Also nearby is a large bath house with the name Torquatus in large, beautiful lettering on a wooden board above the entrance portico. Nearby is a little park dedicated to Apollo, with gardens and footpaths. Near the Porta Capena and we find more bath houses including those of Abascantus and Mamertinus—no surprise, here by the Via Nova of the Appian Way. Travelers have come far, and their first thought is of a long, hot soak with a cup of wine and some good hometown conversation.

We walk through the *vicus vitrarium* (street of the glaziers). Most Roman houses do not have glass windows. More and more, the idea of a glass window is catching on as imperial Rome during its golden age acquires broader wealth. It is similar to the proliferation of inventions such as the telephone, automobile, or refrigerator in the early Twentieth Century. The Romans have become expert glaziers, and craftsmen in all sorts of glass. We pass by dazzling arrays of pottery in every bright color imaginable—ranging from sharp white to the darkest blue, blacks and maroons. We see drinking glasses, mixing bowls, ointment jars, medicinal vials, and little statues. We find glass blowers at work, throwing round vases at the end of long tubes with air blown in by mouth. We also see men carefully pouring clean sheets of window glass into smooth metal frames.

We walk through the *area pannaria* (area of the rug makers). Here we see many colorful rugs being made of wool. We see imitations of Persian and Afghan models being woven on looms operated by slave women and children.

We pass by the Mutatorium Caesaris, on the east side of the Via Appia, opposite where one day soon the Baths of Caracalla will stand near the southeastern tip of the pseudo-Aventine. This is a temple of the nymph Muta (mute), whose tongue Jupiter cut out because she talked so much (more on this story elsewhere).

We see a Temple of Minerva here, and over there a famous temple of Temple of Tempestas, a weather goddess. Lucius Cornelius Scipio, while nearly drowning in a storm at sea off Corsica in 259 B.C., promised to build this temple if he were saved. Nearby is the Manalis Lapis, a rough mass of stone identified with the early animist religion of the Latins, who said prayers for rain here. On the Appian Way, just north of its juncture with the Via Latina, stands a magnificent triumphal Arch of Divine Drusus. It was erected by the Senate after 9 B.C. in honor of the elder Drusus. Also known as the Arch of Remembrance, it is coated in marble and adorned with trophies. The surrounding neighborhood is called Vicus Drusianus.

The most important feature around here is a great Temple of Mars that we'll come to shortly.

CHAPTER 24

VETERAN

We meet him by chance, a gray-eyed man with the lower half of his left leg gone. It has been replaced by a wooden peg strapped to his thigh by a leather sleeve. He is still, for his graying hair and scarred jaws, a brawny and energetic sort. His tunic looks a bit frayed and dusty, but he carries a money pouch on his leather belt with a pointed dagger in its sheath next to that like a warning. He accosts us as we wander down the Via Tecta, or paved street. This is the repaved section of the Appian Way from the intersection near the Circus Maximus to the incline just outside what will one day be the Aurelian Wall.

Out the Capena Gate we go, with its dripping arch, and out among the sprawl of Regio I. This is the fabulous section of the wealthiest tombs outside the city limits. Here we see the urns of the cremated dead stacked in wall *colombaria* (dovecotes, from *columba*, 'dove;' wall-tombs where the middle class can immure the ashes of their dead). Rich show-offs have left pyramid shapes, cylinders, and all manner of shrines. More so than anywhere else, this is where wealthy Romans compete among each other to impress passers-by. For miles, this priceless real estate is lined with marble memorials squeezed elbow to elbow. Beyond this funerary row, we glimpse the more mundane. What looks like a row of garages is really a series of small factories. They make everything from gloves to buckets, from glassware to carpets, and we gaze with interest on the white-washed brick walls.

Like most parts of Rome, the streets and shadows teem with people. Some have legitimate occupations, and many are slaves hurrying on errands. Many others are jobless and looking for any possible scam to earn enough copper coins to buy their next jug of wine or get a ticket to the races. There are the usual beggars and prostitutes. Child slaves compete with poor free children to offer water, juice, cold washcloths, bread, honey, fruit, or a few morsels of squid dipped in *garum*. Most noticeable in this area are the veterans.

We are by the *clivus* of Mars, next to a famous temple to that same god of war. A clivus is a changing grade in a street, and this is one of Rome's most famous. Records indicate that this part of the Appian Way was paved in 296 B.C. and again in 189 B.C. At that time, Republican Rome built a porticus along the roadside. This is the Mars sector *(Regio Martis)* where a statue of the helmeted war god throws its shadow over the southern extreme of the city. Most famous is the Temple of Mars, which has long been the staging area for armies marching out to war. Already, at this hour, the traffic of wagons rumbling out of the city is lessening. New carts are lining up to be first into the city after dusk this evening. The cargo-masters may sell their waiting slaves' free time to local artisans, or just let the slaves sleep in the shade under the wagons since they've worked and walked half the night. That's time for the mechanics from a nearby carriage shop to offer their repair skills. We see men in leather aprons with steel tools climbing around one large wagon whose iron-shod wheels are cracking under the strain of a mass of stone heading to a building site.

We encounter Marcus, the gray-eyed soldier. He has spotted us as likely prey in his survival game, and sidles off a roadside boulder to hobble quickly into our path. *"Magistri,"* he says brusquely while holding up his palm like a beggar. Somehow, his posture makes clear it is not a simple *as* (coin) he begs. "Masters, let Marcus help you, for I see that you are strangers here. Rome is not a place to look innocent or lost, as you do." While he speaks, he has an odd way of rolling his eyes up in an arc from the left and down again to the right. "I can help you."

Receiving a small coin, he clasps it in his gnarled fist, close to his heart, and murmurs thanks. Then he hollers over his shoulder: *Martina! Age huc!* ("Martina, get over here!"). A minute later, a girl of about ten comes skipping around a corner. She is a pretty child, but dusty, with skinned knees shining wet and pink in otherwise olive-complected skin. Her eyes are large and animated, almost dark-blue. Given Marcus' gray eyes, we imagine the girl's mother, a lost, dark-eyed beauty. Martina's hair is thrown back in a ragged ponytail that spins halfway down her back. She wears a patched tunic that looks a few sizes too big on her. It may be an older brother's hand-me-down. *Ago, papa. Quid accidis?* "I'm coming, pop. What are you hacking at?"

"You must forgive my daughter," Marcus says. "Her mother passed away when she was small, and her aunt, my sister, is raising her along with five others. I do what I can to help feed them." He rolls his eyes again in that odd motion, and launches into a recitation of his woes: "I am a native born Roman, unlike so many dogs now unmanning the army. I went away in Hadrian's time, and taught those blue Picts a thing or two. Left many of my dear friends lying face down in those wild heaths, too. I looked forward to getting a farm somewhere near Londinium, maybe a red-haired English girl or two to keep me warm in their soggy climate. Fate decreed otherwise. I took a whack on the head that left me blind for weeks. My eyes still roll around in my skull like loose marbles, which I can't help. Luckily I am still of sound mind, I hasten to tell you. So the doctors patched me up at a field hospital and discharged me from the service with a few months' pay. What misfortune! I lost my chance to retire and own some land, and fate threw me back ashore in my home town to become a beggar at the same gate where once I proudly marched away. I do have this child, who is a good girl, and for a fee she will conduct you through the neighborhood."

"Only if I get a piece of the action," Martina says. She stands with her hands behind her back and makes herself thin as a show of defiance.

"The hell you say," he bellows at her. He turns instantly purple, and shows his few remaining large yellow teeth. She stands her ground, rocking her entire body in "no" and "uh-uh" motions the way one shakes one's head. He softens immediately. "All right, I'll give you money to buy some ribbons."

"And a honey cake."

"There will be nothing left for me."

"Two honey cakes, if you insist."

"This girl will leave me broke in my old age."

"You can have a bite. A small bite. And a lick of honey."

"Yes, yes, get out of my sight and give a tour worthy of your an-
cestry, before I fall dead from apoplexy. Take your brother."

"Yes, papa." She turns our way. "Follow me." We have to run to
keep up with her skipping figure. A tall boy, Lucius, joins us, aged
about 14. He has a slight forward stoop of the back and neck, and
a hooded look. He resembles her in complexion and eye color, but
his thick black hair is short-cropped. He accosts us with his hand
outstretched, and it is clear he will negotiate the fee. It's not too
painful, and he runs back up the street to give the money to Marcus, then rejoins us.

Martina waits for us at a row of particularly garish marble tombs.
There is some logic to keeping the martial presence around this important temple of Mars, even if it's mostly destitute and crippled
veterans. They may earn a few much-needed coppers to patrol the
tombs to prevent the tombs from being looted of precious marble
and metals. Despoiling tombs is a particularly serious capital offense, but the poor are hungry and desperate. Many freeborn end
up selling themselves into slavery if they can't make it as free persons. They feel their lives are worthless. Such people are dejected
shadows who feel it's better to be a well-maintained piece of property than to be a starving free person. If nothing else, Marcus and
his children are exemplars of cunning and free enterprise.

Martina is loquacious and intelligent, while Lucius bumbles
along—he's the muscle of the operation. He's already done half his
job, extorting our money. Now he's doing the other half-protecting
his sister from the many obvious dangers. There are not only child
molesters who might pull her into a dark corner in some shop, but
actually child stealers who might sell her into slavery in some distant city. It is possible that they would even cut her tongue out so
she can't tell her story.

Martina leads us between the tombs, past crippled veterans who
share a wine flask and eye us suspiciously. We follow her through a
hedge, down a goat path among dense trees and bushes, and down
into a grove that opens into a blind vicus. As we emerge on the cobblestone street by the compita, with its shrine and fountain, we
find ourselves assaulted by smoke, noise, and mingled stenches.
Hammers clang, metal rings, saws rip. Men whistle and laugh while
others tell jokes and one man yells in pain over a tapped thumb.

There are plenty of reasons why this vicus of small factories is located here. For one thing, wagons can come and go at all hours, since it's technically outside the Servian Wall and at the edge of the city. For another thing, the Appian Way is a major commercial artery, and business here is good. Rents are high for commercial real estate, but factory owners generally earn a good return provided their bookkeeping slaves keep honest books, and the owner knows how to run a business. It's in many ways a *laissez-faire* system of free enterprise geared to the utter benefit of the entrepreneur

It's not that this ancient society is entirely lacking in social net, but that the availability of protections and services is spotty by modern standards. The police are there initially to provide protection to property owners, though of course this means providing for general law and order. The law initially exists not so much to punish and reform, as to protect the hierarchy of owners. It is also there to protect the state from those who would religiously profane its underpinnings. Eventually, it evolves toward a rudimentary justice system, in which monetary reparation takes the place of violent revenge among parties.

CHAPTER 25

ENTERPRISE

As Martina informs us in a piping voice, each trade or craft is centered in its own street. We quickly see that some, like the glove makers, own a few adjacent shops, while others occupy an entire area or neighborhood.

The biggest business of all in this part of town are the transportation trades. Martina and Lucius lead us to a long sort of open field. A gritty wind blows among the sparse vegetation. This might have been a grassy area but the soil has been worn to dust and sand. Dozens, even hundreds, of carriages of all sizes and shapes are parked here under the watchful eye of private guards. All around this square, or *area*, are garages that either manufacture or repair rolling stock. We see everything from a huge four-wheeled *carrus*, resembling a Conestoga wagon, to various types of two-wheeled carts and chariots. We see large *carruca dormitoria* (sleeping cars), and even a sort of tanker wagon for carrying liquids like wine, water, or olive oil. Examining one of these tankers, we note it's a modified four-wheel carriage. It is lined with a copper tub covered with a hooped canvas top with a round, high-necked filling orifice on top. Spigot plates are bolted to the sides with petcocks for drainage.

At one end of this square are several nice looking hotels in which travelers may spend the night if they are too tired to continue through the often unsafe city streets. We recall our stay at the Hotel Balbi, and recognize the shops with their awnings and counters along the bottom floors. Many of the windows have articulated wooden awnings similar to those of modern Rome. Persons who arrive by day may not take their carriages into the city. Instead they'll leave them here in the care of paid parking attendants. Some of the transports have had a rough haul, and need to go into one of the dozens of mechanics' shops for maintenance. Nothing like a good grease job on the wheels, having nuts and bolts tightened, or getting cracked wooden members replaced by a carpenter. An owner or his wife may tire of having a green wagon, and hire men to paint it blue. We also see the state administration building, which regulates transportation and collects taxes. A special college of priests have their temple here, given that travel and roads are key ingredients in Rome's religious life.

Further down, we find a huge section for the care of animals, and for trading in them. By now we are not surprised to see there is also a small slave market nearby. We are surprised to note that not only can one buy an ox, a horse, a donkey, a mule, or a slave, but small numbers of camels and elephants are available. The Romans remember the devastation rained down on Italy by Hannibal and Hasdrubal with their war elephants during the Punic Wars. They don't like the idea of these huge and occasionally belligerent beasts tromping around the countryside. The Romans have provinces in which elephants and camels do much of the heavy work, but in Italy the elephant mainly remains an attraction in the controlled environment of the games. Still, the occasional wealthy show-off must have one, or feel diminished in social standing.

This Porta Capena district is not only at the heart of the Appian Way, but it's not far from the Tiber with its river traffic, and the area around the Hill of Shards (Mons Testaceus) where sea-borne jars are smashed and discarded. We are in the little valley of the Almo stream, where draft animals obtain drinking water, and crews of slaves wash down dusty carriages arriving from journeys. The transportation trade, huge as it is, spins off many ancillary business needs. For example, there is a square of rug making shops (*area pannaria*), and a street of glass makers (vicus vitrarius). There is an administrative center for the olive oil industry, including some press factories where olives are processed. Nowadays, most of the olive oil is imported from overseas, however.

It's a long walk, and we are as tired as Martina and Lucius by the time we return to her aunt's (his mother's) house. As we climb the little hill back up to the Via Appia, we hear loud singing. About a dozen men are bellowing forth marching songs and bawdy barracks ditties about the girls in Britannia. We hear a woman's voice, and look over just in time to see Martina run away toward a wooden fence at the back of a seamstress shop. There is a handsome woman in her mid-30s, holding up yellow and green silk ribbons and a pair of honey cakes. Lucius and Martina favor us with one quick departing wave as they hurry to receive their reward. We continue on to the street itself. There, among the gleaming red, green, and black marble shrines, are a bunch of old veterans. Foremost among them old Marcus. He has already spent his money, and just now hands the last coin to a young lad who has brought a glass jar of wine. They are singing a song about a recent emperor (who remains unnamed in case there are spies about, but Hadrian comes to mind) famous for his sexual inclination. The song has a repetitious two-line refrain in which the first line ends in Castra Praetoria, while the concluding line ends in 'Casta Praetoria' (*castra* means camp, *casta* means chaste). We can still hear the growling, singing, and 'Cas-*ta* Prae-*to*-ria!' a quarter kilometer away as we head toward the Caelian Hill (Regio II).

PART EIGHT

CAELIAN HILL DISTRICT

(Regio II. Caelimontium)

CHAPTER 26

CAELIAN HILL DISTRICT

The Caelian Hill District (Regio II) includes most of the Caelian Hill. It is bounded by the Porta Capena District (Regio I) to the south; the Palatine District (Regio X) to the west; Regiones III (Isis et Serapis) and V (Esquiliae) to the north; and the Servian Wall to the east. The district is also defined by a straight street running from the Colosseum to the *Porta Caelimontana* in the Servian Wall.

As we walk up the Caelian Hill from the Valley of the Camenae (nymphs) and the Porta Capena, we pass a grotto called the *Antrum* (Cave) of the Cyclops. This is a scenic little bushy grove in a rocky cleft amid the built-up neighborhoods that cling to every bit of flat ground amid the major commercial and administrative structures of the Caelian. The grove gives its name to the street, Vicus Cyclopis. At the northern end of the street, as we pass by, we see the gray barracks walls of the precinct house of the Urban Vigiles, Cohors V.

We stroll along a street famous for its brothels. Women of all ages stand about, each eager to lure customers to her particular establishment, or *lupanar*. The term for these women, *lupa*, literally means 'she-wolf.' The Latin-derived word 'prostitute' means to stand before, or step in front of.

The Caput Africae, a paedagogium for the training of imperial pages, is located in this district. The unusual name (literally 'Head of Africa') comes from the name of the nearby vicus that runs from the Colosseum to the Macellum Magnum. As in the rest of our tour, we won't mention all the many streets, neighborhoods, compitales, and so forth that we pass—for example, *Arbor Sancta* (Sacred Wood), which must have had religious significance in far simpler, long ago times.

There is also an important military administrative headquarters, the Castra Peregrina. *Peregrinus* means pilgrim or traveler. This barracks houses soldiers and centurions of provincial armies who have been detached for special duty here in Rome. Most numerous are the *frumentarii*, or supply soldiers (from *frumentum*, grain). However, some of these are military couriers dating to the times of Augustus. Thus, the Peregrina provides a combination of various modern services, including adjutant general, signals, and logistics. Rather poignantly to any soldier, in any era, who has ever served far from home, the barracks contains a shrine to *Iuppiter Redux* ('Father God who brings us home'). The shrine expresses a soldier's longing for home, almost as if in exile. More chillingly, under Hadrian the corps of frumentarii (particularly the officers and noncommissioned officers) began acting as special police and spies. Even as far back as Augustus, the type of police state familiar in modern times was not far off. Our friend Publicolus back in the Cohors IV is but a mild and innocuous form. He is tinged with a little corruption, perhaps, but well known in his district, and an upholder of the general public confidence—precisely because he sees himself as, and is seen as, more of the people than of the state. One obvious advantage of using peregrini is that increasingly many of them are not Roman. This means that they can mingle unnoticed in any crowd. The emperor's greatest fear actually is not the mob, which is in itself pretty fearsome but easily controlled with the bread and games of the Circus. He is most afraid of the army and his own Praetorians. At least one emperor is said to have worn body armor under his toga, and sheathed the halls of his palace in highly reflective marble, so that he could see anyone trying to sneak up behind him. It is expedient for the Imperial office to maintain a corps of spies within the military.

Nearby is the Temple of Divine Claudius, originally built by Agrippina. This structure, like so much north of here, was gobbled up by Nero's Golden House. In turn, when Vespasian destroyed Nero's palace, he also restored the Temple of Deified Claudius.

The dominant structure in this part of the Caelian Hill is the *Macellum Magnum* (Great Market). Built by Nero, it is crowned with a large dome, somewhat reminiscent of the even larger Pantheon across town. It doesn't have the permanence of the Pantheon, and will vanish by Medieval times. Like the Porticus Aemilia on the other side of town, this is a central commercial building amid a huge portico of shops and bazaars. It's located near a main city gate in the old Servian Wall, and we can see the arches of several aqueducts above the ruined wall. The Macellum Magnum includes a two-storied circular colonnade of 22 columns. Curving around hehind it are two porticos, two stories high, open with columns in the front and enclosed by rear walls.

The region is a thriving commercial center, with plenty of supporting businesses for the macellum. The area toward the Via Tuscolana (east) and the Via Metronia-Via Latina (south) is rife with the smells of dung and rotting blood. To walk among the tiled walls of those streets is to be in a great abattoir, a sluice of blood. Much of the blood from the animals is actually used in preparing various dishes. A lot of it simply runs off and hardens to black tar in the drains, so that the air on most days is black with flies. The Romans are not so fond of beef, for most cattle are working animals that are lean and sinewy. Cows are milked until old age. Romans do like their pork (except for the pious Jews, who have their own slaughterhouses in the Transtiberim, and whose priests enforce special dietary regulations). Meat is best fresh, from cattle who have been herded to the slaughterhouses near the macellum. Likewise, there is a constant stream of sheep, goats, and lambs being herded along in a bouncing, jumping wave of wool and fur. By night from the other direction, down by the old Forum Boarium and the Tiber port, come wagon loads of fish. By day, slaves carry bundles of fresh fish that must be rushed to market. Large quantities end up being pickled and salted in special packing plants for distribution to the city's tabernae and cauponae (restaurants and taverns).

A mix of interesting smells greets us as we approach the macellum amid the insanely noisy, babbling throngs that crowd the streets here every day. Pretty soon, we recognize the smell of burning pine cones. Here it serves to mask the strong odors of fish and meat. When we wander among the stalls in the porticoes, however, we also enjoy a variety of utterly delightful aromas, from every imaginable herb, nicely cured leather, perfumes and ointments, fragranced soaps, and of course the usual cooking food and freely flowing wine and fruit juice *(sucus)*. Perhaps the best aroma, though, comes from a huge bakery and sandwich shop called the *Mica Aurea* (Golden Grain), where one can buy golden wheat. Crowds stop and stare with hypnotic fascination, the way one watches flowing water. They look up as slaves on a stage above hear the shouted requests of customers holding up empty household containers. The slaves pour grain from their measuring scoops, as if pouring little golden waterfalls.

This complex of buildings reminds us of the market we first saw by the river. The flow of faces and lives here is fascinating, a cross-section of city life.

CHAPTER 27

BEAUTY

A carriage chances past us as we walk amid the thick, cloying aromas of sweet figs, jasmine blossoms, and ripe pears. All eyes turn, with a few hard stares from both men and women at the odd couple carried in a double chaise. They are in a special sort of *lectica* or litter, with two seats rather than a couch to lie upon. Six black Nubian men carry the pair. At first glance, we think the occupants are two beautiful girls. Upon a closer look, we find that the front occupant of this two-seater is a delicate-featured young man of about 18 named Marcus Julius. He is dressed as a young priest of the *Dea Syria* (variously: Syrian Goddess, Cybele, or the *Magna Mater*, Great Mother). There is an almost audible shudder all around us, for all that the boy's nature says about the beautiful young woman behind him. Bystanders tell us their story in whispers, shaking their heads over the fate of Rome as it is becoming invaded by foreign cults.

She is Metroönia, a freed slave aged 25. Her mother, Danae, was a Greek from Asia Minor who was known for her beauty as well as her singing voice. Sold into slavery at Ephesus by her dissolute and drunken husband to pay off his debts, Danae became a prostitute and actress for a few months. Then she was purchased by a Carthaginian merchant of great wealth, Sergius. It is said they were so in love that he freed her, and legally married her. For about two years they lived happily in a villa on the North African sea coast, overlooking the Mediterranean. They had a daughter, Sergia. Disaster struck when her husband drowned on a sea voyage. He had a lot invested in that trip. When his ship sank so did a chest of gold he had borrowed from investors. He had planned to purchase a cargo of priceless sables at Alexandria, for resale in Rome. With the loss of her husband, Danae was beset by both creditors and suitors. She lost her home and wealth. She was forced to marry an elderly and lecherous wine merchant who took her to Ostia. There, she lived in misery with his family, who hated her. His sisters would pull her hair, and his grown children, who were older than she, would fondle her while the old man grew feeble and demented. As the old man neared death, someone—perhaps one of the sons, Laertius, who was a drunkard and debauched—took Danae to the Tiber on some pretext. He drowned her in the dark of a moonless night in winter. Her cries carried over the frigid water, but were lost in fog and in the clamor of slaves working the big grain and wine barges. Her body washed up on the Lido south of Ostia days later. It was half eaten by fish and recognizable only by a brass and carnelian bracelet on her right wrist. Sergia, meanwhile, had fortunately been betrothed to a handsome young cavalry officer of the Gens Julia. They married and lived in a splendid villa on the Caelian. It overlooked the mountains beyond Rome to one side, and the smoky inferno of Subura on the other. Sergia and Caius had a child, who then died in infancy from fever. Sergia was a pale beauty with large dark eyes and long black hair wrapped in a thick crown so that she resembled a princess. She acquired the sad, stony look we see today. Caius died with a barbarian spear tip in his spine on the far pale of Britain, where Hadrian had built a wall to protect the imperial province. Sergia began to spend all of her time at the temples of Febris, and Venus, and Mars, praying and sacrificing.

Some years passed. Caius' younger brother Marcus came of age and inherited the entire estate of his ancient family, since his parents had passed away. Now he was, at 15, master of a considerable household (over 100 slaves at the city estate alone, plus over 1,000 at a *latifundia* near Puteoli). What to do then, with the terribly sad and magnificently beautiful widow of his brother? Marcus has always been a quietly, profoundly spiritual individual. He was raised in the traditional religion of Rome, but seems to be seeking something more. He devotes two years of his life to studying the Greek philosophers in a search for truth.

Sergia, meanwhile, is fending off a host of unsuitable suitors. She knows well the experience of her mother in Ostia. She would rather die than be married off to some aging, cruel lecher. Somehow, by an intersection perhaps of her guile and Marcus' studious sincerity, she and the teenager become lovers. Aging by Roman standards, the then-23 year old woman agrees to wed the 17 year old boy. Soon, they produce a daughter, who sadly dies not yet named, within a week of her birth. This tragedy, though common enough in a world of premature death, pushes Sergia in to a state of hopelessness. It also pushes her young husband into a different realm. He announces to her that he will become a *gallus*, a priest of Cybele, and henceforth be celibate.

Cybele was, in mythology, born a hermaphrodite, both male and female, but was castrated by the gods. Nana, daughter of a river god, conceived Attis, who became the consort of Cybele. Nana impregnated herself by gathering the blossoms of an almond tree that grew from Cybele's buried male organs. Cybele fell in love with Attis, but he did not love her, so she drove him mad, and he castrated himself and died under a pine tree. Guilds of laymen that worship Cybele, called (in Greek) *dendrophori*, or tree bearers, offer their services as burial societies, reflecting the elements of death and resurrection in their cultus. The *Megalesia*, Cybele's main festival, is held from April 4th to 10th, and constitutes the cult's new year. It consists of a period of mourning at the end of the old year, followed by days of rejoicing as the religious new year starts. Aside from self-flagellation and castration (in imitation of Attis), the most dramatic rites of the Cult of Cybele revolve around the *taurobolium* (*taur-*, 'bull) and the *criobolium* (*crio-*, 'ram'). In either situation, the priest stands in a pit underground. Over his head is a grill or slatted floor. The bull or ram is sacrificed, and the priest below is drenched in an explosion of its blood and gore.

Marcus tells Sergia of his decision, on a balcony of their palace. It looks from afar toward the Temple of Capitoline Jupiter, which glistens distantly in the fading rays of a foreboding copper-colored sun. Sergia cannot understand how this foreign cult could destroy her life. She falls unconscious. She is carried to bed by slaves, and revives soon after. She spends the night sobbing uncontrollably at the thought of her lost children, her lost youth, her fading though still formidable beauty. In the ripeness of full womanhood, she is full-breasted, but otherwise tall and pale, with huge, exotic eyes and a lush mouth. Rome has long become a melting pot of empire, and miscegenation is nothing unusual. Even by that standard her Mediterranean, hybrid beauty (Egyptian, Turkish, Syrian, Roman) is stunning. Still, no respectable aristocratic family would have her, knowing her mother's background and her own unusual history. More than one aristocrat inquired about making her a mistress, even after her marriage to Marcus. The offers died down at first, but with the latest developments, the offers have been arriving again by surreptitious means.

Marcus sealed the fate of their childless marriage by undergoing ritual castration at the Temple of Dea Syria. He has now, in the eyes of his priesthood, become a woman. In the eyes of Roman law, he is a eunuch. He loves his wife, but the call of his divine office became more irresistible than her pleas to try for a normal marriage. She wants to have another child. Now her choices are too stark to contemplate. He even orders her to change her name to Metroönia, which means Altar of Cybele. She cannot decently remarry, even if she divorces Marcus. If she does not stay with him, she faces the likelihood of eventually ending up in a brothel. She might even be forced into slavery as she ages and her only asset, her beauty, diminishes into a faded memory of itself. So, she remains married to a eunuch, and is the talk of Rome. Her face, as she passes by us, is a haunting, tragic mask. Her eyes look leaden and dead. Her hand, resting on the edge of the bier as she passes, looks pale and delicate, and we can easily see that she could not survive on her own. The two are carried away in a flash, whisked into the unreality of their own little world with its clanging bells and rising incense.

CHAPTER 28

LATERAN

On the southern edge of the Caelian Hill, between the Street of the Cyclops and barracks of Cohort V of police westward, and the Via Tusculana eastward, lies a property that was once owned by the Laterani family. Plautius Lateranus was executed by Nero for complicity in the Piso conspiracy. After the Great Fire (83 A.D.), Nero was widely hated and suspected of, at worst, of having started the fire or, at best, pretending to offer aid, while secretly overjoyed at the opportunity to rebuild the city as he wished. This went against the grain for many reasons. Chief among them was the feeling that it might affect the great works of Augustus. Also, many people died or lost everything, so there was much bitterness. Nero tried to deflect blame on the Christians. Few citizens believed this, not so much because they liked the Christians, but because they hated Nero.

Nero started a police roundup of prominent citizens, particularly those he suspected of being his enemies. As was so often the case during the Empire, there was resentment against the emperor from the senatorial faction who had long been the main property owners and conservative ruling class. When Nero turned on them, rounding them and their families and allies up for execution, a group allied with Caius Calpurnius Piso schemed to assassinate Nero during the circus games 12–15 April 65. Nero's police rounded up dozens of prominent citizens, of whom at least 19 died and 13 were sent into exile. The following year, 66, he barely managed to squash another conspiracy of distinguished senators and Praetorian Guard officers, led by General Gnaeus Domitius Corbulo. In 67, a revolt in Gaul spread through the empire, resulting in Nero's suicide and the accession of Galba.

During the Piso affair in 66, after Plautius Lateranus was executed, his considerable estates were seized. The estate seems to be given to a Lucius Lusus Petellinus (likely a confrere of Nero), then reverts back to the Laterani under Severus. The estate, known as the *Domus* (House) *Laterani*, ends up in imperial hands again.

In 313 A.D. Constantine gives it to African Pope Melchiades or Miltiades in fulfillment of a vow that he will give the Christian church munificia in exchange for victory. This becomes the Lateran estate.

The Lateran Basilica will be inaugurated in 327 A.D. when Constantine is emperor and Sylvester I is pope. The Laterani Domus becomes the official papal residence for centuries. In 800, Pope Leo III adds a lavish banquet hall to celebrate the accession of Charlemagne whom he crowns Christian emperor. After the popes take up residence at Avignon, in Provence, the domus deteriorates from neglect. When Pope Gregory XI returns to Rome in 1377, he takes up residence in the Vatican area close to the fortifications around Hadrian's Tomb, which is near the old St. Peter's Basilica.

Since the Reconciliation (Lateran Treaty of 1929), the Lateran is officially not Italian but Vatican territory. The Lateran Palace is headquarters of the Roman Bishopric (in the person of the pope). The Lateran Basilica is held by the Roman Catholic Church as *Omnium urbis et orbis ecclesiarum mater et caput*, 'the mother and head of all churches in the City and the World.'

Miltiades is considered the 44th pope. The first pope was Peter (c. 64, in the time of Nero).

PART NINE

ESQUILINE DISTRICT

(Regio V. Esquiliae)

CHAPTER 29

ESQUILINE

One of the most spectacular places in outer Rome is the southeastern corner of the Esquiline district. Several major aqueducts and roads come together there. The Via Praenestina comes in from the east-southeast, enters the city, and bends a bit more northwest. At an ancient gate in the Servian Wall, the Porta Esquilina, this external highway becomes the *Clivus Suburanus* (Suburan or suburban sloping road). From there it descends into the giant stewpot that is central Rome. We will shortly visit that smoky, noisy valley in which as many as a million people live, work, and die. First, though, we must explore the surprises of the Esquiline.

This corner of the city is a very busy one. Here, as in every other part of the city, urban sprawl has overrun the crumbling, ancient city wall of Servius Tullius. We find here a collection of large buildings, none quite as spectacular as the largest in the city, but still quite impressive. Here we begin to see more of the many gardens that surround Rome.

If we stand looking away from the city, the Via Praenestina splits into two highways. The left fork continues east as the Praenestina, while the right fork becomes the Via Labicana heading southeast. We see many fine tombs here by the roadside, though none quite as distinguished as those on the Appian Way outside the Porta

There are splendid gardens throughout the city in every available temple, courtyard and all up and down the Janiculum across the Tiber. The northern edges of the city and the Esquiline to the east are framed in magnificent garden estates. We'll see the famous Gardens of Caesar as we prepare to leave Rome.

Capena where Marina and Lucius showed us around. Looming
over both roads is the Anio Vetus aqueduct. We also see the Aqua
Appia and the Aqua Marcia. The Aqua Appia is Rome's oldest major water conduit and runs mostly underground. It dates to 312 B.C.
In its trough flow over 75,000 cubic meters of water a day (75 million liters, or just under 20 million gallons). The Aqua Appia hooks
left and passes along the southern edge of the city, on or along the
Servian Wall, then into the valley between the Aventine Major and
the Aventine Minor. The Aqua Marcia, constructed in the 2nd Century B.C., comes in on high arches through Tivoli, and brings nearly
200,000 cubic meters of water per day (200 million liters, or about
53 million gallons).

The Roman engineers use gravity to move water. They design a
slight downhill slope in the direction of movement. Since cost is an
issue, they try to lay the channel underground whenever possible.
What they must take into account is a direct line from the source of
the water to its ultimate destination. This may be a distance of many
miles, sometimes over difficult terrain. If they cannot go into the
ground, then they must raise the entire aqueduct evenly upward by
enough height so a gradual incline of a few inches per mile is evenly
maintained. For health reasons the water cannot be allowed to
puddle or stagnate at any point. Finally, there must be just enough
water pressure at the terminus in the city to keep spigots flowing
without rupturing couplings, storage *castelli*, or outflow cisterns.

These considerations dictate how high the water must be carried.
In some cases, the water channel may be raised well over 100 ft

To get a handle on the water flow, let's imagine a modern back-
yard swimming pool that measures 15ft × 10ft × 6.6 ft deep, or
roughly 4.57m × 3.05m × 2.012m. This swimming pool holds
1,000 cubic feet or 28.32 cubic meters of water. The Aqua Marcia
would fill it 53,000 times in one day. The Aqua Appia would fill it
20,000 times in one day. By the way, assuming a standard modern
bathtub contains about 8 cubic feet of water (without you in it,
though your yellow rubber duck may float on top), the Aqua Marcia
would fill your tub over 6.6 million times each day.

(over 30m, the height of an eight to ten story building) atop two or three piggyback courses of arches. As a relevant example, the *Pont du Gard* (Bridge over the Gard) aqueduct near Nîmes, France rises on three tiers or galleries to 155 ft. (47m) spanning the river. The arches become successively smaller and more numerous from bottom to top.

A remarkable feature we see in the Aqua Claudia as it approaches the city is that it carries arches of another aqueduct, the Anio Novus, on top in a channel about equal to that of the Claudia. In ways like this, the Romans save resources by piggybacking one aqueduct atop another wherever possible. They'll also run arches over existing structures, as happens on the defunct and crumbling Servian Wall along the southern edge of the city.

The Roman love of water extends to a type of water temple called a *nymphaeum* (from nymph, female water spirits of rivers, lakes, and seas). We pass a large nymphaeum whose central feature is a fanciful fountain set inside a gleaming, ten-side, marble-walled hall. The inside glows with a mellow, deep light thrown back and forth among multicolored marble surfaces polished to mirror brightness. The hall echoes with the splashing of fountains adorned with mythological sculptures. The nymphaeum is set in a park complex filled with flowers. These include the Horti (gardens) of Licinianus, of Epaphroditianus, and Torquatianus. These prominent citizen have contributed great munificentia for the popular benefit. Visitors can wander in and out through several doors with the smell of blossoms following one everywhere.

For all its crowding, Rome encourages the cultivation of all sorts of flowery and green spots. Such spots make excellent locations for altars and shrines. This fits the Roman mentality that they are, at heart, still simple peasants living in the animistic world of the *numina*. Romans don't just enjoy the beauty of flowers and trees. They sense the sacred presence of genii and spirits among them. Rome has always been a holy city that exudes worship from every pore.

Speaking of water, there is a major *castellum* or reservoir at the corner where three major *viae* converge (the Praenestina, the Tusculana, and the Tiburtina; in other words the roads from Praenestium, Tusculanum, and Tibur).

Rome is a surprisingly small space. In 150 A.D, measuring east to west, the city proper is nowhere more than 2.5 miles (4 km) across. Including the Transtiberim adds on average about another kilometer. Measuring generously north to south it is just over 3 miles (5 km) on average counting the entire area out to the future Aurelian Wall. This covers approximately 7.75 square miles (20 square km). Compare this with greater modern Rome which covers 582 square miles (1,507 km sq). The area of the ancient city constitutes but one of twelve modern administrative districts.

Given these statistics, let's do some quick comparions of urban densities. If we accept the modern estimate of 1.2 million inhabitants of the ancient city, it means that there were 60,000 people per square kilometer, or 155,000 per square mile. The modern city of Mumbai, India (the former Bombay) has the highest urban population density with 20,000 people per square kilometer or 50,000 per square kilometer. That is only 83% of Rome's urban density. The urban density of the five boroughs of New York City is about 10,000 people/sqmi or 26,000/sqkm, or 44% as dense as ancient Rome's. London is 20% as dense as ancient Rome's population while Moscow is 16% and Jakarta is 25%.

High population density has many consequences. We've already seen that Rome installed one of the most abundant fresh water supplies of any city in history. Rome learned from her Etruscan teachers and has aggressively gone after fresh water. The Romans have created the infrastructure for efficient and plentiful throughflow, thus making theirs in many ways a healthier city than, say, the future London or New York in the 19th Century.

Two of the more fascinating consequences of population density is what to do with the dead and what to do with refuse. We learn about both here on the Esquiline. The answers will shock and astound 19th Century archeologists when they begin the first major, systematic excavations in the modern era. Until the 1870s, the Forum Romanum will be known as 'the cow pasture,' and its treasures will lie buried under meters of soil. Then, scientific archeologists like Rodolfo Lanciani (1848–1929) begin a systematic discovery of the past.

We have already seen the lavish sepulchers of the wealthy outside main gates, to display one's *munificentia* to the passing world.

Under Roman law, the dead must be buried outside the city Pomerium. When the Servian Wall was built, the Pomerium was not yet officially extended along with it, and the Esquiline was thus officially outside the city, though within its walls. On top of the Esquiline were a number of public cemeteries, essentially for the middle class or the poor working class. The middle class might afford a small monument, whereas the poor workers (free artisans) might make do with a *colombarium* niche in a wall for their cinerary urns. This will still be the practice for many Romans in the modern age. This brings us, then to the subject of *carnaria* (from *caro*, 'meat,' giving us 'charnel').

For centuries, it was the practice to throw not only refuse down into the available natural ditches and canyons at the eastern extent of the city, but also the bodies of pets, draft animals, slaves, and paupers. For the very first Romans, it probably meant a walk beyond the edge of their town, along country paths that would later become city streets but then led only to outlying towns and villages. One can well imagine the 'out of sight, out of mind' aspect. The practice continued through Republican times, and has only been discouraged in Imperial times, with considerable resistance. Under Augustus these open pits began to be covered over with fill, and then paved to make way for entire new neighborhoods whose occupants are ignorant of what lies beneath them. It will only be in modern times that the truth becomes clear.

Lanciani describes a common burial and refuse ditch 1,000 feet long and 300 feet deep, containing hundreds of crypts dug 30 feet deep into the walls, and 12×12 feet at the mouth. These had been sealed, and the ditch covered over, for at least 18 centuries. They were filled with "a uniform mass of black, viscid, pestilent, unctuous matter" in one could still identify a few bones. Apparently new crypts were excavated, while previous ones filled up and were sealed. Imagine the lot of the slaves who had to labor here with poor ventilation and primitive tools under unimaginable conditions. Lanciani has us picture how awful it must have been during times of pestilence, when the crypts were open at all times to receive a flow of corpses.

In addition to the charnel ditch just mentioned, Lanciani finds an even more revolting place. It is the Roman custom to keep an area free of structures and growth for some distance behind defensive walls. This is called the *Agger*. Initially, the line of the Agger followed the line of the Pomerium. Also, originally, the defensive works raised by Etruscan kings were long mounds of earth. The way they did this was to create a moat, and to pile the earth from the resulting ditch (100ft/30m wide, 30ft/9m deep) on the inside edge to create a defensive earthworks of similar dimensions; this would make an attacker first drop 30 feet into the ditch, cross it under fire, then climb 60ft/18m to reach the defenders at the top. Servius Tullius, one of the Etruscan kings, added the Servian Wall at the outside edge of the ditch, to make the attacker's job yet far more difficult. Behind this wall, was a bare, open, raised area constituting the agger. As we mentioned, much of this district was outside the sacred bounds of the Pomerium. For centuries, particularly in times of plague, Romans tossed the bodies of slaves, animals, criminals, and paupers in here. Then, under Augustus, this entire *carnarium* (meat-place) was paved over and forgotten. Lanciani mentions that during construction work in 1876, a huge section of earth collapsed into a hole 30 feet deep. Apparently, the minute the enormous mass of corpses was exposed to air after 20 or more centuries, they crumbled to dust and left a hollow into which the buildings under construction collapsed. By Lanciani's calculations, at least 24,000 corpses had been thrown into just that space, which he estimated to be 160ft/49m long, 100 feet wide, and 30 feet deep.

After many decrees and police notices, the emperors have managed to get people to dump their refuse outside the Servian Wall. The hauling business here is a major industry, and we follow a constant stream of activity out through the Porta Esquila. If you're a Roman, you either bring your dead dog or your dead slave or your broken amphora to the dump, or you pay someone to haul it away in the middle of the night on a wagon. Mind, most neighborhoods have drains and sluices, so you'd dump most of your garbage down the manhole in the middle of the street. If your clivus or vicus doesn't sit above a cloaca, there is usually a central gathering point from which slave crews haul away the trash. Even for the Romans, a corpse is a somewhat different matter. You are likely to see bodies wrapped up and carried away on a bier.

There is a scene yet more horrific than anything yet mentioned. Up here, within the stench and grotesquerie of the discard area, is a place of execution for slaves and common criminals. We don't want to go near, particularly not if we have to push our way through the mob of howling guttersnipes and drunken riffraff who stand in a line. They are kept back by two dozen of the urban finest. Behind them hang several tortured figures. Our eyes glaze over, and we cannot even count exactly how many poor souls suffer there. Several have been crucified, and stand writhing on the foot-blocks of their upright post while tied with reusable ropes to the cross-ties. At least two other souls have been impaled on nearby uprights, and are dying a monstrous death as the weight of their trembling bodies slowly forces them down. These men are simultaneously being tortured by being denied water, and the heat beats down on them. We wonder if one or more was falsely accused, hastily tried, and unable to bribe his way out. Even with laws protecting slaves from unduly harsh masters, the master is owner and can have his slave put to death. We wonder if one or more is suffering for being Christian. We turn away, roiling in our own thoughts. While the cruel games of the circus seem a uniquely Roman refinement of the genre of mass murder exemplified by many regimes throughout history, these methods of execution stain much of human history.

As we approach the Porta Esquilina in the Servian Wall, we see crews of men with wagons outside the gate. They wait all day, for any hauling job that may be brought to them. They then haul the refuse, corpses and all, another 400 feet from the wall, north of the Via Tiburtina. There sit a row of large, slimy, black stone blocks. That's the city's official limit, beyond which the offal can legally be thrown, as Lanciani puts it, "to putrify under the burning sun." First, we hear the shrill cries of carrion birds in the distance. We walk northwest along the Via Praenestina (past the businesslike, gray barracks of the Cohors II of urban vigiles on our left, and the Garden of Pallantianus across the street). We enter the Esquiline Field. We see on our left toward the Viminal Field a black cloud of birds roiling over the charnel field. We don't actually go all the way to the stones. We can smell the whole affair from a reasonable distance. It's enough to make us gag. We catch a glimpse of mounds of garbage and bits of rag waving in the wind. Birds fight over a human arm sticking from a mass of soil and pick the fingers clean of flesh. We see pinkish, blackish sinuous shapes that may be the entwined remains of dozens of paupers and slaves. We also glimpse the black enormity of a dead and gas-bloated ox lying on his back with all four legs leaning away from each other and his horned skull pointing to one side at the end of a massive neck. If there is a way of picturing hell, perhaps this is one of its chambers. Lanciani in 1884 reports of this spot that ". . . I was obliged to relieve my gang of workmen from time to time, because the smell from that polluted ground was absolutely unbearable even for men so hardened . . . as my excavators."

Ironically, one of the larger meat markets, that of Livia, sits outside the Esquiline Gate, not far beyond the Cohort II headquarters. The Via Praenestina curves west to join the Via Tiburtina which then enters the Esquiline Gate and drops down along the famous clivus into Subura.

PART TEN

ISIS & SERAPIS DISTRICT

(Regio III. Isis et Serapis)

CHAPTER 30

TEMPLES OF ISIS & SERAPIS

The district is bounded on the south by Regio II (Caelian Hill), on the north by the Clivus Suburanus from the Porta Esquilina west, on the east by Regio V (Esquiline) at the Servian Wall, and on the west by Regio IV (Temple of Peace). Regio III includes the Colosseum Valley and the Oppius. Its greatest feature is the Flavian Amphitheater, known to later ages as the Colosseum.

Temples of two major Egyptian deities have given this district its name in the *Notitiae* and *Curiosum*. The temples are located in the southeast part of the district. There is also, on the Via Labicana, an arch dedicated to Isis. Isis, a major Egyptian divinity whose cult has been brought to Rome, is the wife of Osiris (god of the lower world and judge of the dead) and mother of Horus (sun god, represented by a hawk). Her worship came to Rome around the end of

It is always worth mentioning the megalomania and special evils of Nero. He had a colossal bronze statue of himself built. It overlooked his city within a city from a height of 120 feet (almost 30 meters). After Nero's death, Vespasian removed its head and replaced it with a representation of the sun god, with rays emanating from a halo. Commodus (180–192) replaced the head with a likeness of himself as Hercules, but subsequent emperors restored it as a sun god. A 7 meter square (21×21ft) pedestal built under it by Hadrian will exist into modern times, but otherwise the colossal statue of Nero, the Colossus, vanishes into the mists of history. Only its name survives, in that of the Flavian Amphitheater: the Colosseum.

the Republic, during the time when Rome first conquered the empire of Cleopatra Ptolemy.

Serapis is a Mediterranean hybrid deity whose story is typical. Centuries before Caesar conquered Egypt for Rome, Alexander the Great conquered Egypt for Macedon (or Greece). Alexander died 323 B.C., and his empire was split among three of his generals. Ptolemy got Egypt and became its first Ptolemaic or Greek pharaoh. The Greeks were fascinated by the cultures they had conquered, and the predictable exchange of genes, gold, and gods took place. Under Ptolemy I Soter, the Egyptian Apis (or Eg. *Hapi*, 'hidden;' worshiped in the image of a bull; known as Osorapis when deceased and entering the underworld) was reintroduced as a new deity with many Greek features.

During the next century, the Romans conquered Greece proper, absorbing the peninsula into their empire. The fanatically ultra-conservative Roman leadership (in men like Cato) resisted tooth and nail, but Greek mythology, philosophy, medicine, and arts flowed into Rome. Zeus became congruent with Jupiter, Hera with Juno, and so forth.

Nearly three centuries after the Greeks were smitten by ancient and exotic Egypt, the Romans fell under her spell. Once again, the fascinated conquerors joined in an exchange of genes, gold, and gods. The worship of Isis, Osiris, and Horus is a cult of death and rebirth. Serapis is a conflation of Osiris and Osoapis, and belongs

About the origin of the word *pyramid*, there is a famous story that, when Alexander's soldiers were camping out along the Nile, they looked into the distance and saw some strange, pointy mounds protruding from the sand. Those were the long-buried and forgotten tombs of pharaohs from the earliest dynasties (some 24 centuries earlier!). The troops were in the habit of making quick-bread or pancakes (fire cakes) by dropping damp dough on a hot rock. The troops noticed that the shapes of the distant monuments roughly resembled those of their pancakes. These firecakes were named *pyramidoi* (from *pyr-*, fire, the fire they were cooked on), so the soldiers called the monuments out on the horizon 'firecakes,' or pyramids, and the name forever stuck.

to the same general cultus. Serapis morphs into a sun god, congruent with Zeus Serapis, and also with healing and fertility.

As we walk down the Clivus Suburanus, where it descends from the Esquiline, the road is wet and slippery. It is a dreary stretch of road—at night, one sees an endless chain of wagons, pulled by straining beasts of burden, and wheels skidding on the slippery paving stones. A good deal of it is traffic heading to the dump of horrors we visited outside town. Some of the wagons have a death-smell about them.

On our right, as we descend toward the Colosseum Valley, we see the dark chasm of Subura with its million flickering lights. Our road curves away from there, toward our left. There, we see the gleaming walls of the twin Egyptian temples across the small valley-cleft. The clivus descends along the northern of two tongues of elevated land that stick out from the Esquiline, the Cespius. The other a short distance to the south is the Oppius. As the road descends, we see the magnificent Porticus of Livia (wife of Augustus), over 300 ft long and 225 ft wide, containing all sorts of shops and shrines. Here we really start seeing the crowds that will throng around us through the next parts of our journey. The Porticus Liviae is very popular, and extremely beautiful in its marbles and fountains. It strikes us again and again that Rome is a city of temples, but many of the temples are unabashedly as much of the people as of the gods. The *munificentia* required of the wealthy are perhaps the last echo of the relative democracy that archaic Rome possessed.

The major feature of the district, however, are the *Thermae* or Baths of Trajan, which lie just below the portico. Until later times, when Caracalla and Diocletian build their enormous thermae, this one will remain Rome's largest and most magnificent. They sit upon the buried structures of Nero's monstrous Golden House. Trajan's Baths measure 340m (one fifth mile) by 330m at the outside walls.

Walking through this vast building, we feel dwarfed and intimidated. This is nothing like Publicolus' neighborhood balneum up in the Horse Head. This is like going to a swim meet in Grand Central Station. The main building has a frigidarium, central hall, tepidarium, and caldarium running north to south, plus dressing rooms and colonnaded courts. The outer rectangle includes libraries, gymnasia, and a huge rounded theater. The floors are beautifully tiled as we walk, revealing mythological scenes. In the caldarium our feet get toasty on the tiles, heated from underneath. That's the hypocaust (under-fire) that's operated by platoons of slaves feeding wood and coal into great stone ovens. If we listen carefully, we hear the sound of water rushing—from the nearby aqueduct, through the walls, under the ground, and away through the latrines and kitchens of the city, ultimately into the Tiber.

Just beyond these thermae, between it and the Colosseum, stand the much smaller Baths of Titus, which were hastily built to coincide with the opening of the Colosseum (Flavian Amphitheater). Vespasian, founder of the Flavian Dynasty (Vespasian, Titus, Domitian), died in 79 A.D. before the Colosseum could be fully dedicated (79 was also the year of disaster in Pompeii, as Vesuvius exploded). Titus, who reigned two years, dedicated the Colosseum and his baths in 80. Titus seems to have rushed to complete his baths to coincide with the celebrations surrounding his father's amphitheater. He also have had a sense of foreboding about not being able to accomplish his munificentia duties. He died in 81 A.D. at age 42. Many suspected his brother Domitian to be complicit.

Tucked into the Oppian slope inside this district are some minor buildings. We are temporarily back in the more public and ceremonial regions of Rome. We are heading toward the Colosseum and the Roman Forum before completing our tour around the northern part of the city. The rest of our visit in this region brings us to the valley that used to contain a stagnum or pool of Nero's Golden House. That place now is the locus of the Colosseum, and the area around it is focused on the games.

As we walk down into the valley where the Colosseum sits, we are struck by the many buildings around it, all supporting its function. We pass a large basin called the *Lacus Pastorum* (from *pastor,* shepherd). We can readily imagine that in much earlier times, there may have been a watering hole in a meadow here to which shepherds brought their flocks of sheep. On that spot now stands a nice stone basin with a fountain in the middle, in which pigeons bathe, and ducks quack. Families come by here to sneak glances at the gladiators, and let their children throw bread to the birds.

In the north slope of the Caelian Hill (Regio II) stands the restored Temple of Divine Claudius looking north to the Flavian

Amphitheater. On the east side of the Colosseum Valley in Regio III stand three great gladiator schools or *ludi* (from *ludus*, 'game'): Ludus Magnus (great), Ludus *Dacica* (Dacian), and Ludus *Matutinus* ('early morning,' connected with Janus). The Morning School is so-called because it specializes in training the hunters who fight in the venationes (hunts), which generally are held in the Colosseum in the mornings. From holding pens in that complex come rank odors of foreign big game. We hear the clangor of swords and shields, the shouting of coaches, and the yells of fighters, combined with the shrieking and roaring of birds and animals being held for their final hour.

If we look east along the Via Labicana, just outside the old Porta Caelimontana of the Servian Wall, we see the austere columns of the Imperial mint. It is simultaneously a temple dedicated to Apollo and Victory. In one of those many echoes of the animist past, this temple which is also a bank and a mint is dedicated to the *genius familiaris monetalis* (vague animist guardian spirit or local genius associated with the place and its functions; remember that *genius* shares a root with *gens*, 'tribe,' and *geno* or *gigno*, 'bring forth').

There is a neighborhood or vicus over there, where the *monetarii*, bank clerks, if you will, and other temple servants live. Lowly slaves (the ones who keep the fires banked, pour the molten gold and silver, and carry the heavy coins and ingots) are housed in barracks nearby, while corporate officials and chief priests (same thing) most likely live in nice spreads on the Palatine or the better areas of the Caelian. Also living with their masters in nice digs are the accountant slaves, often educated Greeks. Being creatures of habit, the Romans always keep an Etruscan or two around for those extra bits of supernatural data. Those Etruscans live in reasonable comfort with their Roman wives while also maintaining ancestral spreads up in Etruria.

About a mile and a quarter east of here, near the Praetorian Guard fortress, is a complex of buildings for holding wild beasts. Venatores ('hunters' or game wardens) bring these unfortunate animals down the winding road we just traveled, to a building called the *Claudium*, where they begin their last hours. When the time approaches, the venatores lead them through an underground tunnel directly into the pens under the arena (sand) of the Colosseum,

▤ Counterpoint. At no moment in our walk through ancient
▥ Rome are we more likely, than now, to revile the Romans, much
▤ less comprehend their sanction of these blood sports. And yet, it
seems significant that the imperial palaces on the Palatine had tunnels leading directly to the Circus Maximus to one side, but not to
the Colosseum to the other side.

It seems undeniable that most Romans thought the circus or the
arena was a just end to a criminal life. The games originated in religious practice of ancient funerary tradition. Nevertheless, it is unthinkable that most Romans spent their entire lives daily watching
these mind-numbing horrors—on practical grounds alone, because
most people had to work hard to get by.

and then into the lifting elevators that bring them up for their last
glimpse of daylight before they meet the nets and tridents of their
tormentors.

Several great streets cross the city and end near the Colosseum.
From the east, the Via Labicana ends on the north side of the Ludus
Magnus, between the school and the Shepherds' Fountain. The Via
Tusculana ends between the south side of the Ludus Magnus and
the northernmost corner of the Ludus Dacicus, or school for Dacian fighters. Nearby is the *Samiarium*, which serves both as a first
aid station for wounded gladiators, and a repair place for broken
weapons and armor. Also nearby is a dark, stinking hall called the
Spoliarium, or morgue. It receives the bodies and body parts of both
humans and animals who perish on the sand. Most of these cadav-
ers are then carried by wagon, in the dark of night, with an escort of
torch bearers, to the dumping pits beyond the Esquiline. It doesn't
surprise us, however, to see cooks and their helpers from the imperial kitchens, and from the houses of the very wealthy, paying the
venatores for choice cuts of rare animal meat. The wealthy love to
surprise their guests with a mysterious cutlet, or a chop, or a soup,
that turns out to be giraffe, or hippo, or some rare African hawk.

Behind the Ludus Magnus is a large building (the *Summum
Choragium*) in which the moveable stage machinery and general
equipment for the Colosseum are stored. All day long, hundreds of

freemen-specialists in the imperial service, as well as slaves, convey canvas-covered machines of wood or metal to and from the Colosseum. We see piles of pine cones, which are burned in the arenas to mask the stench of blood and body parts churned into the sand and rotting in the sun. There is also a washing station to clean the gore away before machinery is put back in storage. The freemen have their own vicus here, in which they live with their families. It is somehow comforting to see their small houses with their compital shrine and children running around it at play. It's homey touch amid such a horrifying landscape dedicated to games of death. It is a touch of apparent normalcy amid a section of the city that seems alien to the modern mind.

As much as we abhor what goes on in the Colosseum, much less understand it, we do have enough fascination to at least peek. The torments of this place, which many ancients condemn, are well belabored in other books. A glimpse will suffice for our purposes today.

CHAPTER 31

COLOSSEUM: SANDS OF DEATH

On an oppressive, humid summer afternoon, we stand overlooking the arena. The sun has gone for the day, hiding behind steamy gray clouds. Surprisingly, we are not overwhelmed by the awesome size of the place. The stands all around are packed with over 50,000 spectators of all classes. They seem to be a drunken, rowdy lot. We spot a few reserved men in spotless togas around the emperor's empty box. The air is close and dense, filled with laughter and bellows for blood and death. We see the hierarchy of seats, from those of the patricians near the bottom, then the middle class, and high up in the worst seats are women and slaves.

This is a magic and dreadful moment, a dark experience. What impresses us immediately about the Colosseum is not its size, but its intimacy. By modern standards, it would be a modestly large city ballpark. We are not conscious at that moment of size, but of how tight and close is this entire landscape of observers and actors in this holocaust. Over about five centuries, well over a million human beings, and countless magnificent animals, die for the amusement of Rome's most sadistic citizens. This is the cork in the bottle, the finger in the dike. It is what keeps the lid on the city mob, and keeps rulers in power; this, and free food and wine.

Most Romans have spent some time here. Most of them think little of the fact that the Fates elevate some, while dashing many others. More than one emperor has had his severed head carried about the city streets by a mob. Judging by the capacity of the Colosseum, it can hold about one half of one percent of the city's population at any one time. By contrast, the Circus Maximus alone can hold somewhere around one third of the city's population at any one time. If we include the other circuses in the city, about half the population can be entertained at one time. There are other venues of cruelty, like the *naumachia* (for sea battles). Cruelties do take place in the circus, and their extent and nature depend on what sort of man is emperor (Nero vs. Antoninus). We may assume that the majority of Roman families, when they have a holiday, are more likely to visit a park or attend the races. Very few have much leisure time, despite the many holidays officially declared for state purposes. Most people live by their wits, and the hard-working shop keepers and artisans can hardly afford a day off. The two real leisure classes of Rome are the very highest and the very lowest—bad emperors on top, and the city mob at the bottom. The smattering of polished looking men and their consorts, in the box seats at the bottom here in the Colosseum, give themselves away as being of a particularly cruel and voyeuristic nature.

Professor Amanda Claridge tells us: "The Colosseum is by a considerable margin the largest amphitheater in the Roman empire." It is not round but actually ovoid, like a Gaelic football, which is rounder than an American football. She gives its length as 189m (620 ft., just over half as long as *RMS Queen Mary*, or the aircraft carrier *USS Constellation*, 323.8m/1062.5ft). The maximum width is 156m (512 ft), while it is 48m high (158ft., about like a 12-or-15-story building.

The fundamental design of the Colosseum is relatively simple. Vespasian's builders stacked huge blocks of stone in three concentric concrete drums, each larger than the other, starting with the smallest on the inside. The outer side of the outer ring or drum was faced with many fine niches containing sculptures and other artwork. The drums are connected on the inside by poured concrete ribs and arches that radiate outward. Seating is vaulted over these supports in an upward slope; the lower sections of seating being of the common travertine marble of which modern Roman curbstones are made; while the upper sections are wood. A fire in 217 destroys the wooden seating up top and renders the Colosseum unusable until its repair by 240 (reminiscent of similar disasters at the Circus Maximus). Gladiatorial contests continue into the Christian era, about 443; and *venationes*, or hunts, continue until at least 523. After this, a church and cemetery appear in the decaying structure. Nineteenth Century botanists found hundreds of different species of flowers and plants, many presumably from seeds brought with the special foods of exotic animals from Africa and Asia. These were eradicated to slow the erosion of the building.

The crowds exit and enter, as they do in all Roman arenas, through passages and stairways above ground called *vomitoria*. Under the ground are at least three sizeable tunnels for bringing fighters, animals, and machinery to the complex of underground holding pens beneath the sandy fighting ground. One such tunnel connects the Colosseum with the Ludus Magnus. Stories that naumachia were held here don't seem credible, since the building would be difficult to make water-tight. The Romans had special public *naumachia* elsewhere, including one near the Vatican Hill. There are four parallel walls under the sandy oval of the arena, and these structural walls both hold up the fighting surface, but contain as many as 80 lifts exist to lift fresh fighters or game into the arena, using trap doors. Major hydraulic lifts at either end of the arena serve to bring heavy machinery or the occasional elephant or hippo up. The sandy oval itself is an ellipse 83m long by 48m wide (160ft × 272ft).

We walk through the main portal, and seems like a dark hand closes around us. The noise inside the drum is deafening. We are assaulted by many foul odors. Vendors hawk snacks and drinks. At least once every ten minutes, a huge bloodthirsty shout arises as some victim pours its lifeblood into the sand. We hear again the clangor of metal on metal, and the thud of lead-weighted net upon iron-studded wooden shield. The whack of sword on helmet, the ripping sound of bare feet making swift maneuvers through sand also contribute to the din.

We spot the occasional male or female lupa here or there, soliciting business under a cloak while standing in the shadows, while an obliging throng of customers form a shield around the pair going at it. We see several wealthy men and women in their box, frozen in attitudes of rapt attention, with wide greedy eyes lapping up the carnal overload.

We too find ourselves drawn to the metal railing that separates the free from the doomed. How amazing! Just ten feet away, a handsome young *retiarius* or *tridentarius*, wearing only a loincloth, is split open from chest to abdomen. Even as he keels over forward, we see the plum-dark colors and shapes of his organs, and the white sausage material of his intestines as they pop out in a tangle like rope. We catch for just a second the bemused, dazed look while his eyes close and something like a smile replaces the grimace around his mouth. The giant in padded clothing, wearing the fish-fin helmet of a Myrmillo, swaggers over to put a heavily armored leg on his victim's back while the sand pours full of blood. The retiarius is supposed to be the fisherman, with his trident and net, only this fish has won today's fight. The Myrmillo waves his sword and shield, showing brawny arms with wrist-greaves. He tilts his filigreed-masked helmet back so that we see his scarred, sweaty face. We glimpse his small teeth and tongue in a mouth contorted with exertion and triumph. The crowd roars deafeningly.

Meet Whale.

They don't call this guy *Orca* for nothing. He is said to have over a hundred kills to his credit, not all of them in the arena. Originally a slave from Germany, captured in a frontier battle near Moguntum, he was taken to Egypt to labor on the grain ships. When he began killing people, his owners became interested in the possibilities of the arena. After a few bouts in local arenas from Alexandria to Carthage, he was shipped in a cage to Rome. That's how he arrived for his first fight: a wild-man in a lion's cage. He was promised the possibility of freedom if he performed well. Orca won his first dozen fights, killing some of the best fighters sent against him. He earned millions of sesterces for his owners and gained his freedom. He doesn't drink but he has a weakness for the ladies. He seems to enjoy killing. Consequently, he has come back to the ring on his own. He continues his run as Rome's greatest popular hero. People who have never seen him sing about him in taverns, bet on him from Spain to Judaea, and fight among each other over his stats in the arena. He owns a lavish villa on the Esquiline, and enjoys the company of a dozen women every night. Many of the women are the beautiful young wives of great patrician families. They burn incense to the gods and act demure by day, then run in

the streets of Subura at night like the commonest *lupae*. At least two
or three such women, and one male admirer, have opened their
veins in unfulfilled hysteria over their passion for Whale.

Orca steps aside, and a grotesque, eerie procession appears
from a side door. In the background, other fighters continue with
their killing, for the program must never rest. A slender, unearthly
figure in black appears. He represents Pluto, god of death and the
underworld. He approaches slowly at the head of a procession, and
trumpets wail like an elephant's screaming. We grit our teeth and
want to hold our ears. Slowly, the procession reaches the body.
Pluto leans forward with a silver mallet and strikes the dead man's
head. This gesture is meant to signify ownership. It will also either
wake him if he still lives, or finish him off. The other attendants include slaves carrying a steel bucket filled with red-glowing coals. A
figure dressed as Mercury (transporter of the dead to the underworld) pulls a red-hot iron from the coals and singes the body.
Then the procession turns and walks away in silent, grotesque dig-
nity. Meanwhile, two near-naked common slaves come running.
One picks up the dead man's armor. The other carries a hook on a
pole, with which to run the man's neck through so that they can
haul the body away. All this happens in minutes. Finally, slaves arrive to rake the sand free of body parts. They will also carry off the
wettest clumps that will soon rot in the sunlight.

We stagger back while other victims fall before us—one decap-
itated, the other getting an arm sliced off. We happen to look up
and see the tiny shapes of sailors crawling in the rigging above to
pull a giant canvas awning over the eastern side of the stands. This
keeps the late sun from beating down on the crowd from the south
and west as the day progresses.

For a moment, it seems as if the sun would burst forth orange
or red, the color of blood in the sky. We feel a sick yet somehow ex-
hilarating feeling in the gut that few moderns know about. It is the
fever of the arena, which awakens in us a pure animal lust for murder, a song of our carnivorous ancestors. It only lasts a moment, before we tear ourselves away with a shout of protest and stagger from
that furnace of death. It is a feeling we will never forget, though we
hope never to experience it again. For just a instant, we unsuspect-
ingly became drenched in sheer bloodlust. The tragedy of this

moment is that now we understand the particular savor of the arena. It is a taste we never realized we possess.

No wonder that many individuals commit suicide quietly in their dark subterranean cells rather than face a painful, humiliating death under the laughter and jeering of a vast throng of gawkers. For just a moment, we were in touch with a part of our soul that we'd never known existed. No wonder some of the Romans came back day after day, year after year, for more than half a millennium.

How did this all start? It grew out of the funeral games of the Etruscans. The Romans picked up this custom, and lost the original religious aspects while adding their own particular spin. The games are a show of merciless power, an ostentation of ruthlessness by which Rome shows the world a thing or two.

PART ELEVEN

TEMPLE OF PEACE DISTRICT

(Regio IV. Templum Pacis)

CHAPTER 32

IMPERIAL FORA

Happy to leave the Colosseum, we pass the Meta Sudans. That means Sweating Fountain, or more literally a *meta* or marker like those in the circus, which it resembles. It has stood here since time immemorial and will still exist in modern times, though lost in hedges near the Arch of Trajan. Meta Sudans is a cone-shaped pile of earth two meters (6 feet) high, from which water spurts.

Regio IV, Temple of Peace, is bounded on the west by Regio VIII (Forum Romanum), on its lower eastern side by Regio III (Isis and Serapis) and above that Regio V (Esquiline), and to the north by Regio VI (High Lane).

Our walk takes us northwest a kilometer or so, through the Roman Forum. Just as the Meta Sudans is a convergence point, so the *Milliarum Aureum* (Golden Milestone, actually a decorous bronze pillar) at the other end of the Forum marks the terminus of all of Rome's major roads to the world. The distances to remote cities aren't actually measured from this *milliarum*. They are measured from the city gate in the Servian Wall from where each road leaves Rome.

We pass once again by the magnificent Basilica Paulli on our right and Basilica Julia on the left. We feel dwarfed, hypnotized, by the rows of columns on their porticoes. As we approach the northern end of the Forum Romanum, we note that the portion on our left is actually in Regio IX, while that on our right lies in Regio IV. We will now head into Regio IV.

If we kept straight ahead, we would pass the *Carcer* (the Tullianum, or Mamertine Prison) on our left and the Curia on the right. We would be assaulted by the odor of a huge public latrine on our right, before we'd pass under the shadow of the Arx and follow the *Clivus Argentarius* (incline of silversmiths). That would bring us out into the old Campus Martius, now Regio IX where the Flaminian Way and the Flaminian Raceway are among the dominant features. We'll come back that way at the end of our walk in the city, before crossing the river to Transtiberim.

Instead, for now, we turn right to walk between the Curia of the Senate and the northeastern end of the Basilica Paulli. This leg of our journey will take us through the Subura in Regio VI, and we'll hook around going westward through the northern end of the city (Regiones VI, VII, and IX). In other words, we'll make a counter-clockwise sweep through the northern areas before coming back in a southerly direction, and crossing the Tiber at the Tiber Island to enter Regio XIV (Transtiberim).

Immediately, as we walk along this Clivus Argiletus, we begin to hear the distant noise of Subura. First, we pass through the Imperial Fora. These were added during the First Century B.C. to the early Second Century A.D. First, Julius Caesar added the Forum of Caesar, primarily to extend the ancient Forum Romanum. There followed the Forum of Augustus, the Temple of Peace (after which the Regio gets its name in the Notitiae and the Curiosum), and the Forum of Trajan. The last major construction was the Temple of Deified Trajan, erected by Hadrian in 120 A.D. We could spend an entire day in the Roman Forum alone. At least one or two more could be spent in this huge complex of statues, porticoes, libraries, shrines, temples, and other buildings of administrative or religious purpose. Though we won't linger here, we are struck by at least two feelings. One, we are dwarfed by the huge and symmetrically tasteful buildings like the Temple of Mars Ultor (Avenger). We admire its porticoes, columns, and great rises of steps. Second, we are struck by the absence of truly public buildings for the people (markets, insulae, baths). This is truly a rarified, imperial place where the law courts and administration of the empire are centered.

CHAPTER 33

ARGILETUM

Passing through on the Clivus Argiletus, we enter the rim of Subura. Down we go, into a smoky, noisy, thronged valley that is home to hundreds of thousands of souls. The origin of the name Argiletum isn't certain. It may refer to a type of clay *(argilla)* mined here for making bricks. On our right is a small clivus (of coppersmiths) filled with smoke and the clicking of little hammers, steel on silver. Below that, the next street is that of sandal-makers. We hear the tapping of somewhat larger hammers, steel on hobnails and leather.

The Argiletum leads east from the marble and ceremonial world of the forums into the living, breathing world of humans and commerce. It is the great book market of the city. Here one can step into shop after little shop. Some of the shops are dark, dusty nooks. Others are bright, sunny corner stores open on two sides. The bookstores offer both scrolls and bound volumes. The scrolls sit rolled up in wooden dovecotes that cover a shop's entire back wall. From each scroll dangles a little tag with its title or subject. The bound volumes, many in beautifully embossed green or red leather with silvered or gilded titles, sit in stacks. Some stand on edge with the back out, like in a modern library.

Not surprisingly, there are ancillary businesses all around. Some shops sell writing equipment. Most stationers cater to both the traditional trade in wax tablets and styli, and the paper or papyrus technology, using reed quills and black or colored inks. Many Romans still prefer the wax tablet, considering that it can be endlessly reused. 'Tablet' is something of a misnomer. It is actually a sort of shallow box, usually with a wooden lid, with a flat surface of wax underneath, hemmed in by the wooden or tin sides. To reuse it, one simply warms it so the wax melts. One can also drip candle wax into it to cover the old. When the wax gets dirty and grimy, the user can pry it out and pour in new wax. The wax comes in various colors. A writer may experiment with such things as a black layer over clear wax. The contrast allows the sharp-tipped stylus to gouge out more visible letters or doodles. The shops have an agreeable mix of smells. There's the aroma of fresh paper. Some of it is actually papyrus from Egypt. Some of it is made of shredded rag and tree fibers. There are the scents of ink and wax. Many of these substances are perfumed to varying tastes ranging from the florid to the musky to the briskly masculine. There is an underlying smell of smoke and burning wax, since sealing wax is for sale. People like to try before they buy, using a guttering candle set before a small shrine of the Muses or of Apollo.

Whatever the shops sell, they are filled with weights and measures. Business is conducted in coin, so there is a constant rattle and jingle amid the hubbub and laughter of conversation. Where there are people, there are shops for food and wine. Everywhere in Subura, one walks through a mix of wood and charcoal smoke, layered with burning cooking oil, roasting meat, boiling cabbage, and frying fish. Here and there, walking by a restaurant, one catches a whiff of sour-sweet red wine or a delightful fruit compote sweetened with honey, and poured over fresh bread. One walks past a grill on which pork sausages pop amid sizzling onions, or a shop specializing in poultry, where several savory stuffed geese marinated to a dark brownish-red dangle over a coal fire, shooting out sizzling points of glowing fat.

CHAPTER 34

SUBURA

Subura is the valley between the southern end of the Viminal Hill and the western end of the Esquiline (or Oppius). We won't go that far west, but remember that we came from that horrible charnel field on the Esquiline, and as we entered the Porta Esquilina, the Via Tiburtina.

What Babylon was to the Bronze Age, Subura is to the Marble Age. Everything under the sun—and just as likely the moon—is possible in this teeming valley. It sprawls across the center of Rome, under her eastern hills. As in all cities in all ages, the fundamental laws of real estate apply here: Supply and demand; location, location, location. If you are wealthy enough to own a palace, you'll want a ritzy address on the Palatine. If you have been pushed out of that neighborhood by emperors, you'll settle for something on the Aventine. Naturally, if you're that rich, you also have a few hideaways in other parts of the city. You would also want a nice estate in the Alban Hills to escape the fevers of August and maybe a seaside cabana down around Neapolis where Pompeii used to be.

If, on the other hand, you're a middle-class citizen, a working stiff, or just plain on the dole, somewhere in Subura there's a place for you. In overcrowded Rome, the seas of five and six story buildings lap at the western part of the city. As sacred as the Arx and the Temple of Jupiter Best and Greatest are on the Capitoline, just look down the cliff and see a tide of humanity living in vast apartment blocks (*insulae*, 'islands'). We already saw one on our way from Ostia, in the Casa Balbi where we spent the night. That was a clean, cheerful way station compared to some of the crime-infested tenements of the city. It's not that all apartment blocks are run-down and dangerous. The laws of the marketplace operate freely in Rome beneath the veneer of the dole that keeps the mob in check. Someone running a better sort of place, closer to sources of good food and water, can charge a bit more and thus keep out the riffraff.

CHAPTER 35

PEOPLE OF SUBURA

Subura is people. Hundreds of thousands of them. They run the spectrum of Rome's population. They are mostly the everyday free-born and freedmen, but there is a fair smattering of slaves. Subura is smoke, Subura is fire, Subura is noise. Subura is cooking smells and manure and garbage and flowers in a garden. Subura is insulae piled like crashed ships, one behind the other, teeming. It is a row of shabby homes in which the future millionaire, the New Man, gets his start. It is the small villa gleaming among its garden flowers behind a high wall. It is the cobblestone alleys where drunks and prostitutes prowl and the destitute lie down to die at night. Subura is home for some, and far from home for others. In winter, the two or more square miles of clay roof tiles glisten with sleet and flour-dusted with frost. In summer, the Mediterranean sun beats down relentlessly. In autumn, leaves swirl up in the wood-smoke air, along with the sad light of an amber lantern and the wistful notes of a flute. In spring, green ivy crawls into the sunshine from shady nooks, and flowers explode in colorful and fragrant profusion. Death is always a step away, but life goes on. It is Subura.

Coming down into the teeming warren, we find ourselves surrounded by so many people, so much life, that the very atmosphere seems to take on a different texture and smell.

We come down into the Fauces (Throat) of Subura where the shops become less intellectual and more utilitarian. Shoemakers, ironmongers, merchants in woolen goods, and every other imaginable little handicraft are represented here. Rome doesn't have much of what we would call mass production, unless it is bread making, for example. The term 'manufacturing' is ironic, however, since it

We can piece together some of ancient Rome's past from various sources, including great monuments left on the hills. The everyday Roman world is often harder to reach. Entire neighborhoods grew up and vanished over thousands of years. We find shreds of Republican ruins here and there—under the imperial ruins of the Palatine, or, on the Aventine, under Caracalla's baths—but the fragile and organic life-breath of Subura winked out as people emigrated in the decades after the Sack of 410 A.D. Poorly built insulae that could barely stand up during their builders' lifetimes crumbled to dust, or have made way for new structures like the modern Termini rail complex on the Esquiline. Subura, in modern times, is truly a lost world.

means 'hand-making' and that is precisely how things are made in Rome. A skilled tradesman opens a shop and makes gloves, or toys, or tunics, or whatever. Generally, the members of a craft work near one another. This gives them advantages, like buying raw materials in bulk and attracting more customers who need to buy a certain thing to one place. We have already seen how the carriage trade clusters near the Porta Capena (Regio I), as do the *vitrarii* (glaziers), olive oil workers, and carpet makers. They both complement each other, and compete at the same time. A large, older, corner shop, or one that occupies a large middle section of a street with an attractive store front may tend to get more traffic. The back shops may have more specialists. They may get less trade but they can charge more. Somehow, it all works out. A manufacturer will hire apprentices and journeymen, who work hard and get less pay. Many a manufacturer will buy slaves to do the hard work (like pumping bellows in a smithy, or sawing wood in a carpenter shop). Now though slaves are increasingly protected by gentler laws, and they require a lot of upkeep. Sometimes it is just cheaper to hire more apprentice boys. There is little difference, anyway, in the surface appearance of how one or the other is treated. The human side of the system is complex.

The underlying modus operandi can best be summarized by the treatment of a little donkey mentioned in Petronius' *Satyricon*. The poor beast lives its life walking in circles pulling a mill wheel until it drops dead. If it stops for anything longer than a quick drink of water, a slave whips it. The mere sound of the whip tapping a warning crack on the sidewalk is enough to make the exhausted animal lurch forward for another half hour or so, until the next crisis of fatigue. That is the pace of life in the city or the farm, in just about any place or time. It is certainly no different here.

There are other aspects of the ugly side. We see a blind little emaciated boy with a stunted arm, begging and crying piteously by the wall. A drunk is keeled over in his own vomit. An elderly woman in rags, obviously mentally ill, wanders out thrusting her begging bowl under people's chins. All the while she spits out accusations and curses, prophecies and portents. A middle-aged master whips his child slave, who has dropped a flat of apples. A wealthy teenage girl pulls her tearful slave girl's curls. These, and a thousand more, are all glimpses of life whirling through the Argiletum as we head downhill. Mostly, it is life on the hard side, with people doing what they can to support one another, comrades in adversity.

There is a great deal of conviviality. Even the numerous pick-pockets gather in dark alleys toward the close of day. They want to fence their stolen goods, which may wind up in a buyer's stall not far away, by dawn. With that money, they can then eat and buy cheap wine. Then they may gamble the night away in smoky, shuttered dens. The flutist and the tambourine man keep the atmosphere lively. The belly dancer earns her pittance standing among a crowd of drunken gawkers. She may secretly pull a quick trick in a corner when the owner isn't looking. She doesn't want to share with him, and most tavern keepers discourage whoredom from their shops. It always brings more trouble than it's worth. There is an entire street of *lupanaria* up on the Caelian for that. Every tavern employs two or three bouncers. These men are usually would-be wrestlers who lost their way between the wine shop and the gymnasium of life. Their job is to keep order among men no better or worse than they are. There are plenty of gangsters *(latrones)* and knifemen *(sicarii)* in Subura particularly, and gangs of toughs and drunks make dates to rumble in deserted streets or compital squares by moonlight.

We come down into the section known as Subura Maior, which complements a Subura Minor to the north of here, toward the foothills of the Viminal Hill. Even in broad daylight, there are some streets on which the sun never shines. They wind like black, cold ribbons among the six-story high-rises looming all around. As ever, the Romans make best use of space by keeping shop on the ground floor, and renting out apartments or flats above. The higher ground along the Esquiline and Caelian foothills has plenty of shining villas with splendid gardens behind high walls, guarded by armed slaves. What you find here in the heart of Subura are the working class and the poor. Ironically, there are fewer slaves here than anywhere else in Rome, since only a few shop keepers can afford to own one. Conversely, half the people here are either freed slaves themselves, or descendants of freedmen. This is the first place an escaped slave will run if he can demonstrate he has been hideously abused. People here are sympathetic, and will hide him until he can slip out of town. Those bold enough seek help before a kindly magistrate.

The *insulae* ('islands,' on the cheaper side tenements of the unemployable, on the somewhat better and pricier side, the apartments of poor workers) teem with life. Their heavy wooden portals

This is little different from Victorian London or New York, or many Third World corners of the modern age. The scenes involving slaves, described earlier in the Argiletum, could just as easily have happened in 1850s Charleston or Savannah. Most of the people we see here, as in the rest of Rome, are Mediterranean. They could pass for modern Arabs or Italians, Greeks or Frenchmen. There are small but significant minorities of both black-skinned, kinky-haired Africans and blond or red-haired descendants of Nordic slaves. They all live side by side in the same hardscrabble life. There is plenty of friction among them, and it may be racial at times, but more likely it will be religious or ethnic. All the Oriental and polytheist cults are represented here, along with Christians and Jews. The archaic religion (more in Appendix B) is state-supported and respected by most, but avidly practiced by few, and mostly by the elderly and the uppermost classes. The average man or woman on the street is more likely to be a disciple of a foreign deity like Horus or Kybele.

are open from dawn to dusk. They are guarded by a couple of husky latchkey porters after dark. The hallways at ground floor echo with the cries of very small children playing. There is no childhood per se for any but the wealthy. It is common for children as young as seven or eight to start toiling at their parents' trade.

In the 1st Century, Augustus ordered a shrine built near the crest where Clivus Suburanus (Subura hill-street) climbs up the Esquiline, and intersects the Vicus Sobrius. The name of this street and neighborhood invokes the austere and self-denying traditional Republican virtues. The nickname quickly acquired by the compital shrine of Mercury Sobrius is 'Mercury Nondrinker'. This is quite ironic, judging by the singing and carousing one hears at night. We turn north from the Clivus Suburanus to continue through Subura, but rising gradually as we pass through the balance of Regio IV and into Regio VI. We walk among hundreds of noisy high-rises, whose somber and stained walls overlook myriad tiny streets and alleys.

We walk through a fairly typical insula that borders between the occasionally employed and the working poor. It is neither the worst nor the best of such places. Passing by the outer shops facing the street on the first floor, we find ourselves in a dank and stinking corridor. The smell of urine here is overpowering. Only indirect light filters in through austere vaults facing skyward into the building's central courtyard. The wall surfaces throughout this building were whitewashed long ago, but that has worn away to reveal brick. The mortar holding the bricks together is riddled with white efflorescence from dampness. Indeed a kind of soggy, mournful air breathes through this place. We step out into the courtyard for a breath of fresh air.

We find a timeless sort of tenement scene that is as homey as it is depressing. Elderly women in threadbare stolas sit about, sipping cheap wine from clay cups. They supervise tiny squalling children in a sandbox. In the dark corners of this irregular square sit old men, also drinking wine. They lean on their canes as they argue about the green and blue horse teams, or the deeds of Orca in the arena. We listen to a debate over which conquered province had the loosest women when they were legionaries under Hadrian.

Having regained our breath, we venture up a stained and dirty stairwell. One hears the echo of a workman's loud and cheerful whistling as he stands on a ladder, repairing an oil lamp that some child smashed with his ball. A husband and wife argue. A father yells at his son, who drinks all day and doesn't work. The son yells back that he is only virtuously walking in the steps of his sire. Then we hear the crash of a wine jar against a wall, and nimble feet slapping the ground as the son seeks shelter elsewhere. Two teenage sisters are arguing over a boy named Cornelius, who has been two-timing them both while running with at least one other girl in the next neighborhood.

These Romans live communally. In some cases a family inhabits a corner of a single room. All four such families share a central stove. Never mind that these rat-trap buildings are notorious for suddenly collapsing and killing their occupants. Building codes are often honored in the breach. Shoddy mortar, hasty construction, and poorly cured lumber are but some of the many reasons. The insulae are frequently set ablaze, either by lightning or by careless cooking. For all of that, this is better than living on the street. Most families manage to inhabit a space of their own. The best rooms are in the middle stories. They are far enough above the street noise, but far enough below the rain and wind blowing in through leaky roofs and shutters. If the building is on fire, it is easier to jump from a third story balcony than a sixth story one. As we stroll along the upper story corridor that makes a trapezoidal run around the central courtyard, we still have that impression of melancholy. We sense it in the damp and unfinished brick walls, the stale cooking and urine smells, the cries of children. Yet, in that inevitable Roman fashion, every section of the building has at least some small shrine. Most of them are to Neptune, the water god, who protects from fire. The water nymphs likewise have little niches that one can touch, walking by, for good luck or as a prayer.

We emerge from the building into a small cobblestone street, where we glimpse a homey scene. A row of shops opposite us are already half-boarded and locked for the day. The street is crammed between two high-rise buildings and overhung with balconies. This results in its being perpetually dusk in here. The air has a tang of sausage casings and bread, wine and fresh onions, and is filled with echoes. We hear laughter, a man singing, a shoemaker tapping continually with his mallet, cooks rattling pots in a kitchen, and chil-

dren crying out in play. Two women walk by, in long gilded brown
stolas, with scarves modestly thrown over their rich black hair. True
Roman women, they carry their shopping bundles and whisper to
each other about some private matter. One leans her ear close to
the other, who holds a hand over her mouth as she smiles and
speaks furtively. A butcher looks up from the gloom inside his
shop, just as he is about to lower his cleaver on some pork loin. The
metal glints reddish like an evening sun in his oven light. Just as we
are about to step out into this time warp, there is a loud outcry. The
two women glance back, scream and run onto the narrow little
sidewalk. We too jump back just in time as a cascade of foaming,
dirty water swirls by. A man shouts, and three street urchins run for
their lives, laughing. They have opened the petcock on a small water closet up the street. Many of the Roman streets have these,
tucked into a corner here or there at the top of a vicus or clivus.
They have spigots halfway up for people to draw water. Down near
street level a gate or petcock can be temporarily opened to sluice
the entire street clean—after a warning to pedestrians. This street
will be flooded ankle-deep for some time with white-foaming water and floating trash. It will be awhile before someone trudges to
the castellum and gets the gate shut. We step back into the insula
to exit the other side.

As we leave this building, and the teeming Subura thins out
gradually into quieter neighborhoods, we start going up the Quirinal Hill into a financially better heeled part of the city. The next
part of our walk will begin at the Castra Praetoria just beyond the
Servian Wall.

Ostia is a coastal town facing the Tyrrhenian Sea. This is a typical 2nd century A.D. Ostia apartment building. During the 2nd century, approximately 40,000 people were living in Ostia.

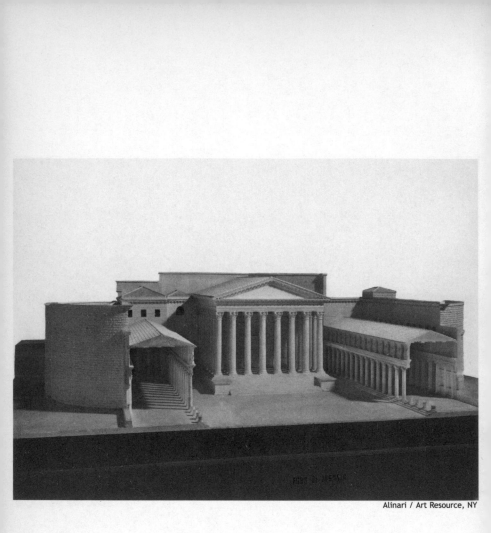

A reconstruction of the Forum of Augustus and the Temple of Mars Ultor.

Aerial view of a reconstruction model of Ancient Rome. The Circus Maximus (left of center) is located between the Palatine and Aventine Hills. Under Julius Caesar (around 50 B.C.), the arena was expanded to accommodate approximately 150,000 spectators.

A reconstruction model of Ancient Rome. The Colosseum was originally known as the *Amphitheatrum Flavium* (The Flavian Amphitheater). Construction on the Colosseum began around 72 A.D. and was completed around 80 A.D.

A reconstruction model of Ancient Rome shows how sophisticated and dense the city was. Rome is one of the world's oldest cities and has a history that stretches over 3,000 years.

Aerial view of a reconstruction of Ancient Rome.

Werner Forman / Art Resource, NY

The Appian Way was the most important of the Roman roads. Construction on the Appian Way began in 312 B.C. The original road connected Rome with Ariccia, Forum Appii, Terracina, Fondi, Formia, Minturnae, Sinuessa and Capua.

The Arch of Titus is located on the Summa Sacra Via, west of the Forum. The triumphal arch commemorates the sack of Jerusalem in 70 A.D. which ended the Jewish War.

Interior of the Colosseum. Detail from the reconstruction model of Ancient Rome.

Hypothetical reconstruction of the Roman Forum in Imperial times. Depicts the southern part of the city.

Hypothetical reconstruction of the Roman Forum in Imperial times. Depicts the northern part of the city.

The interior of the Pantheon. The Pantheon was erected in 17 B.C. by Roman general Marcus Agrippa (64-12 AD). It was originally built as a temple to the Roman gods.

Roman bridge across the Tiber at the Isola Tibernia. The Tiber was an important river for Roman trade and commerce. It is sometimes referred to as the Blond River because of heavy sediment deposits which give the river a yellowish cast.

The Castel Sant'Angelo as seen from across the Tiber River. Originally built as a funerary monument to Hadrian in the second century, the Castel Sant'Angelo has also served as a fortification and a prison throughout its history.

PART TWELVE

HIGH LANE DISTRICT

(Regio VI. Alta Semita)

CHAPTER 36

HIGH LANE

Regio VI takes the name *Alta Semita* (High Lane) from a street that follows the ridge of the Quirinal Hill (modern *Via Venti Settembre*). It is bounded on the south and southwest by Regiones IV and V, on the southeast by Regio VIII, and on the east by Regio VII.

The Alta Semita itself passes eastward through the Porta Collina in the Servian Wall. It becomes the Via Nomentana, eventually heading to Nomentum 14 miles from Rome. Then it passes along the northern border of the Praetorian Guard camp and barracks. As it comes out of the Porta Collina, it crosses at right angles the Via Salaria Nova (New Salt Road), which heads northward into the Tiber Delta.

We stand on the parade field between the Porta Collina and the Praetorian Guard barracks. Nearby is a large castellum to store water brought in on the Aqua Marcia. The barracks of Cohort III of the urban vigiles is across the Via Tiburtina from this castellum. South

In about 400 years, the Vivarium will become one of the many melancholy notes surrounding the silent and overgrown wilderness into which Rome declines in the European Dark Ages. While much of the inner city reverts back to a marshy graveyard as in archaic times, isolated places on the edges of the city become incubators of the future. The Vivarium becomes an important monastery where some shadow of Classical learning may be preserved into medieval times. It will be remembered for many centuries as the Vivariolum.

of the Praetorian Guard barracks on the other side of the main road is a rectangular, quasi-military camp with cages along one wall, called the *Vivarium*. It is a sort of a zoo for keeping the larger wild animals destined to die in the arenas. Nearby is the *Amphitheatrum Castrense*. Before the Colosseum was built, spectators could pay to enter this amphitheater and watch *venationes* ('hunts').

We head through the decaying Porta Collina and back in the religious city limits. Walking westward along the slope of the Quirinal Hill, on our right we overlook a valley dominated by the Gardens of Sallust. Beyond that, in the direction we will eventually go, Regio VII begins, rising along the Hill of Small Gardens. Above the myriad small family garden plots on the slopes, we see wealthy estates in the distance, hidden among great sweeping willows and other trees.

In the spirit of munificence, some wealthy patricians permit common folks to amble through their gardens. Those who are less generous do not. Sallust (86 B.C.–34 B.C.) was possibly a *novus homo* (new man) of the late Republican aristocracy. His political career was unusual, for he began by being elected Tribune whereas most ambitious Romans began their careers with the Quastorship. He rose from humbler stock (local aristocracy) and became the only member of his family to serve in the Senate. He eventually found success as a supporter of Julius Caesar. As tribune (53 B.C.), he was vocal in attacking Cicero. Sallust served without particular distinction as a general, and became the first governor of the newly formed province of Africa Nova (New Africa: modern Algeria). He remained in office until the year of Caesar's assassination. Retiring to Rome, under fire for alleged improprieties, he resigned himself to writing history books and political critiques that have come down to the modern era. He writes of the Catiline conspiracy that threatened the late Republic. He writes about party strife during the war against Jugurtha. New men like Sallust, Cicero, and the dictator Marius rocked the boat for the

In Renaissance times, the hills in the northern part of the city will see the splendid mansions and huge garden estates of fabulously wealthy families like the Borgia and the Medici. So, the parkland tradition of these districts will long survive.

traditional aristocrats from old families, who generally had the system sewed up tight for themselves. Sallust's writings suggest the Republic was undone by power struggles between the old aristocrats who controlled the Senate, and the Novus Homo senators who whipped up public support for their own schemes. Sallust died at about age 53, and his gardens were bought or seized from his family by Tiberius. Luckily, the current emperor has opened them to the public and we can walk through their park-like setting. The gardens include a sepulchral vault, equestrian facilities, and an Egyptian-style obelisk. Several temples predate the estate of Sallust. Among them are three ancient temples of Fortuna, and at least one of Venus. As we walk along the high road, we admire these marvelous and refreshing gardens. We see fabulous homes and estates below us. Meanwhile, our own road is lined by poplars and cypresses on either side. It too has its share of remarkable buildings.

On our right along the Alta Semita as we head southwest stands an ancient shrine of the Capitoline Triad (Jupiter, Juno, and Minerva). This shrine (rebuilt many times) has origins older than those of the temple of Iuppiter D.O.M. on the Capitoline Hill.

Next, to our left, is a magnificent round temple. This is the mausoleum of the Flavian Dynasty (69–96), erected by the hated Domitian. Hoping to start a dynastic tomb, he brought the ashes of his father Vespasian and brother Titus here from the Mausoleum of Augustus. Domitian was born in a rather plain street near here, Ad Malum Punicum (At the Red Apple)—sounds almost like there must have to been a tavern, with a name so picturesque. His father Vespasian skyrocketed to prominence during the Year of Three Emperors (68–69). Vespasian ruled ten years, and Titus two. Domitian seems to have started well, but become violently paranoid in the final period of his 15 year reign. He killed or exiled many senators, knights, and imperial officers. He even held his wife and closest family members in a regime of terror. Ultimately, Domitian was hacked to death by members of the Imperial household. His corpse was rescued before the mobs could get hold of it, and secretly taken to an ancient nurse named Phyllis, who had cared for him as a boy. Phyllis arranged for his cremation and then smuggled the ashes to this temple, where she mingled them with those of his niece Julia. At some point Domitian had left his wife Domitia, daughter of

Nero's famous general Corbulo, and had cohabited with his niece (daughter of Titus). Popular pressure forced him to remarry his wife who seems to have had a hand in guiding the assassins to her husband. Domitian's memory lives in the diabolical company of Nero and Caligula. Ironically, Domitian's resplendant marble temple, which sits gleaming here among the trees, is regarded as one of the finest in Rome, and synonymous with Rome's eternity.

Set back some distance from the Alta Semita, on our left, is a large shrine and altar called the Ara *Incendii Neronis*, Altar of Nero's Fire. Domitian built one of these in each region, where priests and people can make propitiations for divine protection from fires. The altars are memorials to the great fire of 64 A.D.—an early form of advertising propaganda, one might say, which reminds people about the dangers of fire in a crowded city with much flammable building material (timber roofs, wall supports, etc.). All these altars are dedicated to Neptune. Among the four elements (earth, wind, water, and fire) attributed to Classical Greek philosopher Empedocles, fire and water are opposites.

We come to a crossroads of the Alta Semita and the *Clivus Salutis* (inclined street dedicated to the goddess Health, who has a temple nearby). From here, we can look across to the Arx, not far away to the southwest. We are able to gaze down on the Imperial Fora. We ask directions from a florid, pleasant-faced old priest in a frayed white toga and wide-brimmed straw hat, who is picking flowers in a garden. The priest jokes that we'd better pray at his temple, because one's health might go uphill or downhill at the whim of Salus.

Salus is not the only ancient deity here. This hill was originally settled by Sabine people, and retains some of their names. The genius and name Quirinus itself may derive from an archaic Sabine town called Cures that stood on this hill. The nearby Porta Sanqualis in the Servian Wall derives its name from the somewhat exotic deity Semo Sancus, also of Sabine origin during or before the Etruscan monarchy. We pass by a small, Etruscan-style temple of age-dark stone encrusted with moss and ivy. Inside is a statue of Tanaquil, the wife of low-born Lucumo of Tarquinii. Tanaquil was a prophetess of some power, and she predicted if they settled in Rome their fortunes would soar. They changed their names, he to

Priscus Tarquinius (Priscus of Tarquinia), she to Gaia Caecilia. Tarquinius ruled Rome from 616 to 578. When he was murdered, Gaia instigated to have her son-in-law Servius Tullius assume the crown. Her symbols are the distaff and spindle, representing her skills at spinning and weaving (reminiscent of Penelope in *The Odyssey*). A bronze statue of this Tanaquil sits in the temple of Semo Sancus. Her distaff and spindle are preserved as relics in a large metal box, and guarded by a small priestly cult sacred to the state. Northeast of here stands a temple of the Sabine goddess Flora.

We pass the gray fortress-like barracks of Cohors I of the urban vigiles on our left, overlooking an insignificant-seeming *amnis* (stream). This Amnis Petronia is an important supernatural boundary. In the early republic, when the city fathers headed to the Campus Martius to meet in the Comitia Centuriata (the original assembly predating the Senate), they had to pause here in the true spirit of their animistic religion. With great solemnity, they would take spe-

In this part of Rome the Emperor Diocletian will build the largest Roman baths ever. Between 298 and 306 A.D., just in time for the reign of Constantine, Diocletian will order the construction of these baths on the Viminal Hill—just south of the Alta Semita, south of the Gardens of Sallust, and southwest from the Castra Praetoria fortress. Built on the model of the large thermae of Trajan and even larger thermae of Caracalla, this complex will cover 28.5 acres (nearly 1.2 million square feet). The central hall alone will measure 280 m × 160 m (918 ft × 525 ft) and be several stories high. With its many Roman innovations, like intersecting barrel vaults in the central axis, Diocletian's Thermae will soon enough serve as the model for the Basilica of Constantine and for many great buildings into modern times. The ruins of the complex will be incorporated into, among other structures, the Church of Santa Maria of the Angels (central hall of the baths, converted by Michelangelo) and the Church of San Bernardo at the Baths (another hall). The Roman National Museum occupies a large number of rooms. Perhaps most interesting is the fact that a corrupted version of the name *(thermae)* survives in the form of modern Rome's huge central railroad station, the Termini.

cial augurial readings (the *auspicia peremnia,* from *per,* 'across' + *amnis,*
'river,' taken when crossing bodies of water).

We now walk through the Porta Salutaris in the Servian Wall
(built or begun by that same sixth king, Servius Tullius). We head
downhill toward the Field of Agrippa in Regio VII.

CHAPTER 37

PRIVATE DOMUS

Modern text books give the impression that the average Roman lives in a standard home with an atrium, a peristyle, an inner courtyard, and so forth. The truth is, most Romans live amidst squalor in giant tenements. A very small number live in those luxurious palaces on the Aventine.

However, the backbone of the Roman upper middle class—the well-off, the successful businessmen, a lawyer from a minor but old family—may in fact own the Roman dream. That's the house moderns read about in history texts. One only has to ask oneself: Looking at the picture, could I afford this home in my own modern city?

We visit Caius Julius Ralla, a middle-aged lawyer who spends most of his days in the law courts of the Forum Romanum. His specialty is business law, and he tends to accept cases involving private maritime trade. Frequently, for example, this involves investor suits of negligence. When a poorly loaded or outfitted cargo vessel sinks, the losses can be quite significant. Ralla frequently travels to either Ostia or to the New Port on the northern side of the Tiber mouth to investigate evidence first hand, interview witnesses, and build a case.

Ralla starts his day at dawn, complaining of the rumbling carts outside that kept him tossing and turning all night. He sits on a low wall in his peristyle garden, quietly eating a small breakfast of juice, bread, cheese, olives. He listens to his wife and her two female slaves getting their sons ready for school. He has two sons and two daughters. The girls, who are still very young, will play in the park today under the watchful eye of one of the slave women. The boys are older, and attend school. Ralla does not own a pedagogue (slave escort for the specific purpose of tutoring a boy, accompanying him to and from school, making sure he gets there on time, and so forth). However, he pays his neighbor Pomponius to have their pedagogue pick up young Claudius on the way to school in the Campus Martius. It's a big day for the younger son, nine year old Marcus. He will attend his boys' group at the local shrine of Diana today. The boys are dressed in special uniforms suggesting themes sacred to the Huntress. They will carry candles, sing hymns, and walk in a solemn procession through the Gardens of Sallust. Some will play flutes, while others will carry poles to whose tops are attached small busts of Diana. Ralla is quite proud and fond of his boys. He is pleased at their piety and civic dutifulness. They will grow up to be like their father—solemn, devoted civic servants who are the backbone of the state.

Ralla's home life is good. His wife is attractive and pleasant. He himself is an easy-going lord and master of his domain. The Roman household is the state in miniature. Ralla is the family priest on holy days, and he leads the daily prayers at dinner. Marcus and Claudius generally alternate at who gets to throw the crust of bread or meat offering to the penates, who hover about the sacred hearth fire. Ralla himself tosses a few drops of wine. His wife, Marcia, is the chief priestess in the kitchen. She, and all of the children, tend the lararium (shrine of family ancestors) that stands in a closet in the atrium. The two slave women, as well as an elderly man slave who tends the garden and does odd jobs, live at the far end of the garden in a row of small cellae. The slaves are part of the family, though they eat and sleep separately. Dinner is usually a bit more formal, especially when Ralla and Marcia entertain friends. The dining nook (triclinium) is cozy and comfortable. The wine flows freely along with good food and conversation. Sometimes they hire a halfway decent musician and singer to regale them with sentimental favorites.

In the morning, all that is history in the gray dawn light as Ralla hurries from his garden picking his teeth. He has hugged and kissed his wife and children. Now worry lines rim his forehead and his eyes are filled with plans and calculations about a big case he must argue before the magistrates at the Basilica Iulia.

First, however, he must preside at a uniquely Roman custom, the patronage. He enters the atrium without ceremony. A dozen men of various ages and conditions of dress come more or less to attention and cease their whispering. "Good morning," Ralla says crisply as he takes his seat in a chair. He will be the only one sitting, in true magisterial fashion. His clients take turns pleading for money, help, intervention in a court case, advice about a divorce problem, or just plain come to fawn over him and praise his patronage. Some of these are his former soldiers when he was a quaestor in the Praetorian Guard. Others are ex-slaves he or his father or grandfather manumitted (freed) in their time. Two are impoverished business acquaintances with whom he has developed contracts. In all, he has about twenty clients, but they don't all show up each morning. This is how Rome works, from the emperor on down. The emperor himself goes through this ceremony most mornings. Like the rumbling traffic at night, it's part of the Roman condition. The pyramid of patronage is one of the major glues that holds the empire together, as it did the Republic.

For a few minutes of patient, pleasant banter, the clients laugh politely at Ralla's jokes and entertain Ralla with a few small anec-

You saw the movie: The Godfather, starring Al Pacino, released 1972. The title *Il Padrone* in Italian comes from the Latin *patronus* (from *pater*, father) meaning protector, guardian. Like Michael Corleone in the modern movie, Ralla is a patron to these men and their families. He is a provider, fixer, facilitator. They come to him when they need help, and when he holds court, they must attend out of courtesy, unless they are very sick or otherwise unable to show their respect. No, Ralla has never made an offer the other person can't refuse for fear of his life. Ralla does, however, give orders (legal ones) and they get followed—or else. A good patron presents himself as sober, fair, and a leader—the embodiment of *virtus* that is the Roman ideal. The very word comes from the root *vir* (man) and suggests a whole range of manly qualities that a good Roman patron must project so that the world will continue functioning.

dotes about their families. Ralla doesn't tell jokes well, but he is so sincere in his fumbling that most of them enjoy his attention for its own sake. A few among them are not the most honest or worthy of men, Ralla knows, and he keeps an eye on them. What they don't know is that they come to him separately to complain about each other, and Ralla mends 'situations' while keeping secrets very well. It isn't easy for these men to spill their hearts in public, particularly to beg for money to get through a rough spot. It's all done on the up and up, though, in the form of a contractual loan. Ralla has a wooden chest of documents and money by his side, with a huge lock on it. The key is kept hidden in his house. He keeps records with a stylus and wax tablet, and hands each man a small bag of coins that must be repaid—sometimes with interest, sometimes not. Within an hour the business is done, and the clients thank him and leave. The elderly slave man appears and locks the door.

Now Ralla goes back to the garden, where the sun is starting to shine warmly. He has a few fond moments alone with Marcia. She has been reading a small book of charms and spells a woman friend has given her. The woman had gone on a journey to Tuscany, and brought back gifts for all of her friends. Ralla is a practical man. He does not have much use for Etruscan mumbo-jumbo, unless it is a true ritual sanctioned by one of Rome's state temples. "Why do you spend your time on that silly business," he teases her gently while nuzzling a kiss behind her ear. She smiles enigmatically and says in her most coy manner: "I read these spells because I want to set snares of honey to trap you, my dear sweet fly of a husband."

"And I will gladly buzz into your beehive if that's where you keep the honey."

They laugh together, and the children, hearing their parents being happy, come running to share in the laughter. The slave women chase them, waving aprons and cups of milk and bowls of porridge that the children left behind in their enthusiasm. On either side of the peristyle (colonnaded) garden are the small, simple sleeping quarters of the family.

Marcia and the slave Felicia help Ralla drape the cumbersome toga around his frame. Soon enough he steps outside the garden gate with his briefcase in hand and starts the long, but interesting and refreshing hike down into the center of the city. As he strides down narrow streets, up and down inclines, he keeps one eye on the swarm of humanity. Inwardly, he is already in the solemn and marble halls of the basilica, preparing his pleadings in the case of a ship of 150 amphorae of Faliscan wine that went down off Capri. It sank because of the negligence of her master. The scoundrel then left his ship as it sank. All hands drowned, while he managed to save himself and tried to hide in the hills above the island. He was caught trying to slip back into Rome to retrieve a fortune he'd buried in his yard. Unfortunately for him, the investors had spies waiting to capture him and bring him to court. The investors will pay Ralla handsomely to prove that the company that hired the captain was negligent. They should have known that the captain had lost at least one other cargo under suspicious circumstances. It is a case Ralla knows he can win, and he whistles to himself as he disappears around a corner in Subura.

PART THIRTEEN

BROAD STREET DISTRICT

(Regio VII. Via Lata)

CHAPTER 38

BROAD STREET

V*ia Lata* (Broad Street, Broad Way, or Broadway) is the name slowly being given the portion of the Via Flaminia as it approaches the city. The Via Lata district (Regio VII) is bounded on the south by Regio VIII, on the east by Regio VI, and on the west by Regio IX. This is a narrow district on its east-west axis, but the longest district of them all on its north-south axis. This district has plenty of magnificent parks, statues, and villas. Like much of the northern edge of the city, it is sparsely populated compared to the parts south of here (all of which we have already visited).

In this district is the ancient shrine of the Capitoline Triad (Jupiter, Juno, whose origins are older than those of the corresponding temple of Iuppiter D.O.M. on the Capitoline Hill. We already saw it as we came west along the Alta Semita through the adjoining district.

Via Flaminia remains officially that until the Aurelian Wall goes up c. 270. After that, the portion of the Via Flaminia inside the Aurelian Wall will be called Via Lata. We assume, for our purposes, that the name started adhering to the street earlier. In reality, most people heading north to tend their little garden plots on the Collis, and enjoying the parks and gardens of the wealthy along the way, might have referred to this district by some obvious, handy name like Suarium or Hortulorum, but this is pure speculation.

CHAPTER 39

PORTICUS EUROPA

On our left, as we enter Regio VII, is the Hadrianeum, a Temple of Deified Hadrian. The temple is actually in Regio IX, but don't be confused; remember, Regio VII is a long, narrow district—narrow east-west, long north-south.

We head across the Field of Agrippa to the Portico of Vipsania or Portico of Europa. This is a beautiful portico lying on the south side of an extension of the Old Salt Road (Via Salaria Vetus, entering the city diagonally from the northeast) that connects with the Via Flaminia (where Regio IX begins, right near the end of this important portico). The Europa contains a huge map of the world ordered by Agrippa in the time of Augustus. The map shows the Roman empire in splendid detail. We see stacks of bricks and other workmen's supplies off to one side. The portico will soon be partially walled in to protect the fine floors. The pillars have beautiful Corinthian capitals. Although the official name refers to the daughter of Marcus Vipsanius Agrippa by his first wife, Pomponia, all of Rome knows this portico by the name Europa because of this map. Vipsania was given in marriage by Augustus to his step-son Tiberius, who loved her very much. After the birth of their son Drusus, Augustus made Tiberius divorce Vipsania and marry Julia, daughter of Augustus, for dynastic reasons. Vipsania died soon after. Agrippa had another daughter named Vipsania by his second wife, and that daughter is remembered by the name Agrippina. The gardens around the Porticus Europa are sunny and airy, filled with flowers, and framed in laurels. We walk through the porticus, cross the Salaria Vetus extension.

BORDERS
BOOKS MUSIC AND CAFE
1937 MacArthur Road
Whitehall, PA 18052
610-432-5520

STORE: 0345   REG: 02/96   TRAN#: 0536
SALE   05/07/2005   EMP: 00224

WALK IN ANCIENT ROME
    7752463   QP T   16.00
LINDOR BALL
    0000324   EB N   .40
LINDOR BALL
    0000324   EB N   .40

       Subtotal   16.80
       PA 6% TAX   .96
3 Items   Total   17.76
       CASH   20.00
       Cash Change Due   2.24

05/07/2005 10:48AM

Check our store inventory online
at www.bordersstores.com

Shop online at www.borders.com

We amble north on gravel paths through open fields, toward the *Suarium* (Swine Market). From a distance, we can smell smoke from curing pork. Up here is an almost rustic area of large estates, parks, hunting preserves, and vegetable farms. It is not surprising to find a special market for pork. The Romans love ham and pork.

It is obviously going to be difficult to carry freshly slaughtered pork down into the Subura on a hot day, given that it would spoil. We are pleasantly surprised, therefore, to find that the farmers, who have brought their pigs here to market, have opened rough concession stands. There, one can safely buy fresh bread, pork, wine, and the best *garum* around. We can also find all sorts of spices, knick-knacks, and anything else an idle shopper might impulsively pick up. There are fruit and vegetable stands, and the usual cooked dormice can be had on every corner.

Not far away, to the north, is a large castellum of the Aqua Virgo, an aqueduct that enters the city from the same direction.

CHAPTER 40

HILL OF
SMALL GARDENS

One of the leading features we find at the very northern edge of the city is the Small Gardens Hill.

Having eaten and revived ourselves at the Suarium, we wander northeast for a short while on the Salaria Vetus. We pass an old temple of Venus Erycinae, representing a cult of the mother goddess brought in from Greek Sicily around the time of the Punic Wars. Her cult has been quite popular for a long time, and represents one of the earliest incursions of an Oriental mystery cult into Rome under the guise of Aphrodite and Venus. A bit farther up the road is the Vicus Minervii, where nowadays many of the freeborn

In the future, after the 4th Century, this hill will be called the *Pincio* (Pincian Hill), after a wealthy family that owns much of its land. Until then, it is known as the Collis Hortulorum (Hill of Little Gardens), which lies across the north and northeast edge of the city. It curves clockwise into the Quirinal (Regio VI), with the Gardens of Sallust in the valley in between. Like Europeans into modern times, Romans like to garden a little plot of land to supplement their table. No wonder Domitian's vicus is named By The Red Apple. Likewise, the poor poet Martial lived in a vicus on the Quirinal called *Ad Pirum*, By The Pear. In later times, the Pincii family will one day build a fine house here. The Pinciana's beautiful marble will be carried off after the end of the Western Empire. Rome's Gothic ruler, King Theodoric, will install many fineries, plundered from here, into his palace in Ravenna, in northern Italy.

artisans live who are associated with the parks and palaces of the wealthy.

We turn west now, following well-trod and wide paths of the urban farmers. We pass many a family out for a stroll. They walk hand in hand, mother, father, and children. A little boy stops to buy a honey cake with a coin his father gave him. At the same time, a little girl purchases flowers to put in her hair (giving one flower as a gift at a little shrine to Juno Sororia (protectress of girls at puberty). It is quieter up here in the north, away from the city crowds. It is relaxing, and the air smells sweet. Even with so many families and elderly, priests and the farmers with the occasional pig on a leash, it seems peaceful.

The great archeologist Rodolfo Lanciani tells the story (paraphrased here) of an excavation in this part of the city during the late 1800s, in which workmen came across a statue of a boxer. The boxer was sitting upright some meters under the soil. He sat for nearly 2000 years, buried under layers of constructions covering the centuries of the Classical, Medieval, Renaissance, and Modern periods. He was found looking up as if surprised to see the sun again, and about to ask who it was that dared to disturb him.

We soon cross the relatively narrow Regio VII (Broadway, or Via Lata) to enter Regio IX (Circus Flaminius).

PART FOURTEEN

FLAMINIAN RACEWAY DISTRICT

(Regio IX. Circus Flaminius)

CHAPTER 41

UPPER CAMPUS MARTIUS

Regio IX occupies the ancient Campus Martius and is bounded on the south by the Servian Wall at Regiones XI and VIII, on the east by Regio VII at the Via Flaminia, and to the west and north by the curving Tiber. The Regio is named after a circus in the southern part of the Campus Martius, which shares its name with the Via Flaminia that enters from the north. The Via Flaminia itself, however, becomes the Via Lata, heading southeast into Regio VII (Via Lata) from which we have just come.

Walking on the Via Flaminia in the northernmost part of the city, by the Gardens of Domitian, we turn south toward the *Campus Martius* (Martial or Military Field). Not far away, to our right, is the Tiber. Just about a kilometer ahead we see the Servian Wall. Above it, on the Capitoline Hill, we see the Arx on the left, and the Temple of Iuppiter D.O.M. on the right corner of the cliffs. Coming from the fresh air and open spaces of the Little Gardens Hill, the city looks vast and smoky. A thousand little twirls of smoke rise in a general grayish-yellow haze. The sun is directly south, it being around noon, and its glowing orb looks as if its edges are swimming in liquid bronze. Numerous military couriers of the Frumentarii ride by in either direction on horseback. They usually travel in threes and fours for mutual protection, though only the senior man carries the diplomatic pouch. Those communications may be heading only as far north as Tuscanum, or they might be heading to some outpost in Helvetia, Austria, Belgium, or Germania.

There are a few noteworthy sepulchers from the old Republic as we walk along, but nothing like the Appian Way on the southern edge of the city. The road forks, with a branch running straight past the river bank and intersecting with the road coming from Hadrian's Tomb. We take the main branch, the Flaminia (Via Lata).

After walking by a small forest on our right, we come to the Mausoleum of Augustus, which looks almost Art-Deco. It is a huge, impressive, round structure sitting on a slight mound. We recall that burial within the city Pomerium is prohibited, even to emperors. At the same time, burial in the Campus Martius is a great honor because this is where Romulus died. It is restricted to the most deserving persons, and must be sanctioned by the Senate. Augustus built a dynastic tomb here to house the ashes of his successors for generations to come. The travertine drum, which forms the lower level at street level, has a diameter of 87m (285 ft.) and rises about 10m (28.5 ft.) straight up. There is a ridge around the upper edge of the drum. A sacred garden or grove surrounds the top. One sees thick bushes of various powerful plants, and a ring of thin, tall cypress trees all around. (see also, without columns, Scarre 22) Cypresses are sacred to Venus. Inside the park-ring atop the drum rises a *tholos periptera* (round temple of Greek origin, with a dome or *tholos* surrounded by peripheral stairs and sometimes columns) upon several rounds of stairs. The round building is surrounded by columns. Over this rises a small ring of sacred plants, and within that a dome with a gilded statue of Augustus on top. What gives the building a startlingly modern flavor, reminiscent in part of the monumental excess to which Mussolini and the fascisti will take the straight, clean lines of Art Deco, are the two obelisks standing by the sides of a small, plain entrance. Each obelisk is 14m (46 ft.) high, with a slight taper topped by a pyramidal point. The door reminds one a bit of the entrance to the Sybil's cave at Cumae, but is entirely manmade rather than carved into rock. The heavy wood and metal doors are sealed shut and guarded, but we understand there are multiple *cellae* or rooms inside. The ashes of various important persons are in there, starting with Augustus and his wife Livia. It is also possible that his predeceasing heirs Gaius and Marcellus, and various emperors and select members of their families have been included. The last to have his ashes entered here was Nerva, 98 A.D., on the day of an eclipse of the sun. The very next emperor after Nerva, Trajan, had his ashes buried in a golden urn at the foot of his great triumphal column, which stands at the end of the Imperial Fora.

Near Augustus' tomb, and at the edge of the road, is a large square crematory altar, the *ustrinum*. Here the bodies of Augustus, Tiberius, Germanicus and his daughter, Tiberius the son of Drusus (brother of Nero), and other royalty were burned at high temperature. Each person's ashes were rendered down through a grate into a fine alabaster jar to be sealed within the tomb itself.

Across the street is the Porticus Vipsania (Europa, with the map of the world in it), where we were earlier. Now heading south on the Flaminia, we pass several connecting streets on our right, running straight toward the river. On our left is the Suarium or pork market in Regio VII. Not far away in the opposite direction is a landing dock, named *Ciconiae Nixae*. It is named after a stone tablet showing two storks leaning beak to beak against each other. This dock on the banks of the Tiber is a landing place for smaller boats bringing wine and other produce to the Suarium from farms upriver. Many of the pigs sold at the Suarium are raised there, but a farmer bringing a prize breeder is always welcome. In recent years, with the shift to large corporate farms, the business has become more efficient, and now much of the traffic comes from slaves on larger estate vessels. Feeling sorry for several sweaty slaves wrestling a heavy wooden barrel ashore, we walk on.

Across the river from us is a busy navy shipyard that supports the enormous industry of the *naumachia* (naval battles staged in artificial lakes), which we'll visit later. In the early republic, Rome's tiny navy was sheltered on the city-side, under the protective Servian Wall. Now the only real mission of the navy in the city is in support of the games in the circus and the arena. There is a naval detachment who is responsible for bringing delicate and exotic animals directly to the city rather than risking the rumble of wagon transport on stone roads. Downriver from the shipyard, just north of the Tiber Island bridges and at the northern edge of Transtiberim, are a series of Tuscan wine warehouses.

As we continue our walk along the Via Flaminia, we see on our right two very famous monuments built during the reign of Augustus. The first is near the street, the *Ara Pacis* (Altar of Peace). The Senate erected the Altar of Peace in 13 B.C. to commemorate victories of Augustus in Spain and Gaul. Every year, the magistrates, priests, and Vestals offer sacrifices here. The altar is richly decorated with the finest Augustan reliefs, showing a religious procession and sacrificial rites. We notice that the emperor and the priests all have their toga draped over their heads. This is every Roman's instinct (male or female) in reaction to any matter that is grave, shocking, religious, or even happy.

The other monument is set back a bit. It is the *Horologium Augusti* (Great Sundial of Augustus). This magnificent device represents a forward-looking aspect of the Augustan age. Rome got its first sundial around 263 B.C. It had been seized in Sicily during the war with Hannibal, and was erected in the Forum. What nobody in Rome realized was that the sundial was calibrated by the far more technically adept Greeks for its latitude in Sicily. The sundial sat in the Forum for a century before anyone realized it was off by the amount of time corresponding to the difference of four degrees latitude. Augustus, the greatest innovator of all Roman history, laid out a large ground-plane of white marble. On the south edge of this field, in line with the solar movement, he erected an obelisk as *gnomon* (Gr. 'indicator') whose shadow sweeps over the marble field below and indicates the hours dependent on the season of the year on the carefully calibrated lines cut and inlaid with bronze quadrilles and markings.

The sundial, or solarium, not only points to the hours of the day, but also points at certain moments to the Augustan monuments all around. It's clear that Augustan architects had a very comprehensive, elegant, and cohesive plan for the northern Campus Martius. In that spirit, this part of the Via Flaminia clearly has started looking like a Grand Avenue or Broad Way (Via Lata). On Augustus' birthday, September 23, the sundial points its shadow directly to the *Ara Pacis*. It is almost as if Augustus had harnessed even the power of the sun to do his bidding, and to serve the Roman Empire.

The obelisk or gnomon of the horologium augusti in modern times stands before the Italian Parliament building and is about 30m or 100ft. tall.

From our position here, we see that the architects have carefully kept open a direct line of sight between the Mausoleum of Augustus and the Pantheon of Agrippa, south of here. We start walking south again on the Via Flaminia.

CHAPTER 42

LOWER CAMPUS MARTIUS

After the Great Fire of Nero (64 A.D.) the emperors have each added many new buildings, particularly on the Campus Martius. There is always a sense of urgency, no matter how well liked or disliked the emperor to continue the essential *munificentia* for the benefit of the city and the people. Knowing the great works of Augustus, there has been a strong feeling to restore the city somehow since so many public buildings perished along with the humbler homes of the poor. The area we are walking in now, on the southern Campus Martius, contains a nearly interconnected complex of both old and new public structures. We only have time to point out a few of the more important structures in this area.

A great street runs west-east, from Hadrian's Tomb across the Aelian Bridge, and dead-ends in a T-intersection with the Via Flaminia (or Via Lata). We might call this the Via Aelia, after the bridge, or better, Via Triumphalis. After the Etruscan kings were expelled, and the Republic was set up, the Romans enacted laws to safeguard their liberties. Among these was a law forbidding military processions or exercises within city limits. The Campus Martius, which lies outside city limits, became the official parade ground and place to celebrate triumphs. This street has been the scene of many magnificent processions.

In a row along the southern edge this street we see the Trigarium. Running west to east, this is a huge complex of stables and training areas for horses and charioteers. It takes its name from *trigarium*, a chariot of three horses. All sorts of horseback athletes train here. We hear the snap of a whip, and shout from several men, as two men on horseback race from one end of a long strip to the other on white mounts, under a cloud of yellowish dust. East of this is the Stadium of Domitian (replacing temporary stadia of Caesar and Augustus), which is the second-largest structure in this area. Domitian erected this long rectangular stadium for athletic contests in the far less bloody Greek mode. This indicates that many Romans sought entertainments other than blood sports. Like the Circus Maximus, its arcades are filled with shops of all kinds, including brothels.

To its east are *thermae* of Nero. Between these baths and a small temple dedicated to Hadrian's mother-in-law, Matidia (said to be the only house of worship ever erected by a man to his mother-in-law) an old building has been demolished for the line of sight between the Pantheon and the Mausoleum of Augustus. The Theater of Hadrian sits near the corner where Via Aelia dead-ends at Via Flaminia.

Continuing south on the Flaminia, we pass a great rectangular park with grass, trees, and drinking fountain surrounded by high walls of travertine marble. This is the largest structure in this area. It is an ancient place, dating to the early Republic, called the *saepta*. The walls probably recall the need for safety while the leaders of all the important *gentes* (tribes) came down from their hills and valleys to debate and vote on important issues. We pass temples of Isis and Minerva Chalcidea, tucked against the *saepta*, dating to Domitian.

We cross a humped stone bridge over the little Amnis Petronia. The stream we crossed earlier today on the Alta Semita. Suddenly, we find ourselves in a densely populated area that stretches all the way under the northern edge of the Capitoline Hill. Part of this population explosion lies in Regio IX, and part of it in Regio VIII (Forum Romanum), before running around the Imperial Fora and the Argiletum, and down into Subura. We avoid going back that way, and continue past a temple known simply as *divorum*, of the gods. It was built by Domitian for the emperors of his deified dynasty (he was the only one not deified). We pass the *Diribitorium*. It is a large, ancient hall in which *diribitores*, election officials, counted the ballots cast in the saepta. Although the hall is locked and quiet today, we can imagine the echoing clatter of ballots in dim light under high roof as dozens of serious fathers of the Republic watched one another with hawk-eyes to make sure no electoral miscounting went on.

We have nearly come full circle now in our walk around Rome proper. To our left rises the Capitolium, and beside that we see the huge, rounded northern end of the Basilica Ulpia that forms the end of Trajan's Forum (in the Imperial Fora). The Via Flaminia ends here, splitting into two smaller roads. One leads left into the Clivus Argentarius, or incline of the bankers (money lenders; from *argentum*, silver), of which we spoke earlier as we passed through the Forum Romanum. It is no surprise that these private bankers conduct their trade here, under the shadow of the Capitoline with its treasury, and the nearby temple-mints like Juno Moneta. A wealthy broker can borrow a sum of money from the temple at a low interest rate, lend it out and charge a higher interest rate, then pocket the difference, just as they do in modern times. This clivus is the street that passes between the *carcer* (Tullianum or Mamertine Prison) and the Senate Curia. We'll walk to the right, on a street called Vicus Pallacinae.

This district before us is named after the Circus Flaminius whose name derives from the famous main road of the Campus Martius. At 260 m (853 ft.) long and 100 m (328 ft.) wide, the circus is enormous, yet it is still dwarfed by the Circus Maximus which is three

The modern town symbol of Orange, a lovely Provence town in Southern France, is an image of a crocodile chained to a palm tree. That's because Julius Caesar's legions, when they first arrived in Egypt during the mid-first century B.C., were astonished to see a crocodile chained to a palm tree near the Nile, and some cruel entrepreneur charging admission for gawkers to have a closer look. When the soldiers of Caesar's Legio II retired, they received homesteads in the Gaulish town of Arausio, which became Orange. The Romans razed much of Arausio, laid out a typical quadrate Roman city with two main streets perpendicular to one another (cardo and decumanus), and built great monuments. The modern town proudly remembers its Roman makeover with the sense of wonder the legionaries felt when they saw their first crocodile.

times as long and half again as wide. The Circus Flaminius dates to 221 B.C. It was built by the censor Caius Flaminius Nepos. Many games and ceremonies of state importance have occurred here. In particular, triumphs could be held here in full military splendor, since it lies outside the Pomerium. During the dedication of the the the Forum of Augustus in 2 B.C. the floor of the Circus Flaminius was filled with water, and 36 crocodiles were killed in a spectacular *venatio* (so-called 'hunt').

Leaving the Flaminian Circus, we pass the porticos of Octavian, Philippus, and Octavia. We pass the Theater of Marcellus, a semicircular structure whose seats face toward the Tiber. Between 10,000 and 14,000 spectators can attend this theater. Marcellus, adopted heir of Augustus, died in his youth, forcing the succession to Tiberius.

We pass by *Ad Porta Flumentana* (By the River Gate), a neighborhood of very wealthy houses under the Capitoline Hill, in the Campus Martius. This area is associated with an ancient river gate in the Servian Wall. We have now indeed come full circle, because we are back at the ancient Tiber port with the cattle and vegetable markets.

We will now turn north along the Tiber docks. We walk along the sharp curve that contains the Tiber Island, on our left, with its Temple of Aesclepius, god of Healing. The island will always be the site of hospitals, right through the Middle Ages and into modern times. We pass the Pons Fabricius that would take us to the island. From there the Pons Cestius leads into the heart of Transtiberim with its Jewish and other quarters.

For the next little while, the Tiber will flow on our left. To our right is the Theater of Balbus. Balbus was a wealthy Roman, who dedicated the theater in 13 B.C., during the reign of Augustus. It could hold about 7,700 spectators in its semicircular slope of stone seats. We pass a splendid Temple of Neptune and the Porticus of Argonauts associated with it. There are many people happily, busily milling about, and great shopping to be had. This truly is a Broadway, as the lower end of the Flaminia is often referred to. It has theaters, shopping, and many taverns and restaurants. We pass the Porticus of Pompey near the Agrippa Bridge. There on our right is the Theater of Pompey, Rome's first permanent theater was completed in 55 B.C. Pompey, one of the first Triumvirate along with Crassus and Caesar built his theater in the face of the last Republican conservatism. Since theaters were still frowned on by the puritanical Romans, he placed a small temple to Venus Victrix (Venus Victorious) atop the seats, to suggest the seats are steps leading up to the temple. He was able to dedicate the whole structure as a temple rather than a theater.

We'll turn right and walk on beautiful footpaths surrounded by flowers, around the western rounded end of Pompey's Theater. This brings us to the central portion of this area, which we have so far skirted. We pass the Odeum of Domitian (from Greek *odeon*, a place where poems are recited or sung with music) which seats 5,000 and is one of the wonders of Rome. The area is roughly triangular and full of structures—all of which we have thus far seen—except for the greatest and most famous of all. There it is, in the line of sight from the Mausoleum of Augustus.

Here is an interesting and ironic footnote. Julius Caesar of course did away with both Crassus and Pompey to make himself dictator in 46 B.C. Two years into his life dictatorship, Caesar was stabbed to death by conservative senators (Cassius, Brutus, et al) who wanted to restore the Republic. The spot in the Roman Forum, outside the Curia of the Senate, where they knifed him was in front of a statue of Pompey.

After the civil war that the followed the death of Julius Caesar, Gaius Octavius (Gaius the Eighth) assumed power. After the late Caesar was deified in 38 B.C., Octavian gained in stature and styled himself as Caesar. He had the Senate proclaim him Augustus in 27 B.C. This was an archaic term with some amount of implied sanctification. This title vanishes over time, but It becomes customary for the adoptive heir of the Augustus to be called Caesar.

The title Caesar survives until 1917 in the Russian Czar and until 1919 in the German Kaiser. In fact the system of ancient Roman ranks, adopted by the Holy Roman Empire, reinforced in the Feudal ages, still governs the aristocracy of Europe with kings, princes, dukes, and so on.

CHAPTER 43

PANTHEON

This building is, in a sense, the keynote of our entire walk in ancient Rome. Our entire journey has built up to this point. We chose the year 150 because it is part of that relatively small bright window in the long dark corridor of history. It is a time when everything seems to be going perfectly well for the empire. We've seen the constant preoccupation of the Romans with religion. They consider the

Where the Americans in 2003 send an army to Iraq with over 100 lawyers, the Romans send their army with 100 priests. The Roman priests are not just chaplains (sent to take auspices and preside over religious ceremonies) of a handful of state-recognized churches sent to minister to individual soldiers. They are official government functionaries on whom, it is believed, the entire success of a military campaign depends. A militray commander ignores their advice at his peril.

A good example involved Admiral Publius Claudius Pulcher (Handsome). In 249 B.C., during the First Punic War, he sailed against the Carthaginians with a fleet of 123 ships. On board were all manner of priests and augurs, plus a number of chickens used in the auguries. The chickens refused to eat. This was taken as a very bad sign. A wise Roman would have turned the ships around and gone home. Not Claudius. He threw the chickens overboard, saying "Since they won't eat, let them drink." Everyone blanched with horror at this sacrilege. He rushed off to battle, lost 93 of his ships, and was soundly trashed. When he got home, he was accused of treason (for sacrilege, more than poor judgment), and heavily fined.

state and its religion, its army, its leader, its priests, and every other aspect to be part of one total package.

To understand more about the Pantheon, we should understand its history. While Augustus built a spectacular complex of buildings (his mausoleum, giant sundial, and altar of peace) in the northern Campus Martius, his great friend and ally, Marcus Agrippa, got to redevelop the southern portion. Agrippa built a complex of important structures in the lower Campus Martius. He routed water the Aqua Virgo via a channel, *Euripus* (happy or nice river bank) so that it filled a large stagnum, or artificial lake. This serviced his thermae, which loomed out of the corner between the Diribitorium and the Saepta.

Most importantly, he built a temple in 25 B.C. This was not the Pantheon visible in modern times, but a temple of Mars and Venus dedicated to the Julian gens. Julius Caesar and Augustus belonged to this gens, and Agrippa had married into it when he married Augustus' daughter Julia. The temple had seven cellae, dedicated to the planetary deities. The Venus statue wore earrings made from Cleopatra's pearls. Agrippa brought the best sculptors of the Mediterranean world to create statues of himself and Augustus for the

The Romans have long memories, and they remember the most terrible defeat of the otherwise spectacular reign of Augustus. In 9 A.D., Quintilius Varus, supreme general of the Rhine Legions, was moving his forces from summer quarters on the Weser River (near today's Hannover in the north) to their winter quarters on the Rhine. Germainc tribesmen fell on the men of the lost legions and Rome suffered one of the worst defeats in her history. Legions XVI, XVII, and XIX with 20,000 soldiers were massacred, ritually killed, or sold into slavery. Varus is said to have committed suicide. The site of this disaster was not found by archeologists until 1987. The disaster cost 10% of the entire Imperial army. Augustus is said to have wandered around his palace in mourning; he was more than once seen banging his forehead on a door, saying "Quintilius Varus, give me back my legions." It is also said Augustus left Tiberius a note in his will, recommending he not expand the empire beyond its current frontiers.

The Barberini Pope Urban VIII removed the bronze nails and other details of the portal around 1600 to make the *baldacchino* (canopy) above the main altar of St. Peter's. For this act of vandalism, Renaissance Roman society spread the epigram: *Quod non fecerunt Barbari, fecerunt Barberini.* "What the barbarians did not do, the Barberini did."

temple. This temple burned in 80 A.D. and Domitian restored it. Lightning struck and burned it again, and Vespasian restored it. Finally, Hadrian had most of it razed from the ground up and rebuilt it around 125 A.D. as the home of all gods. The front of the building retains the *pronaos* (Gr porch) of Agrippa, with its eight heavy columns and triangular attic (the part that sits atop the columns, as in many Greek and Roman temples, and is covered with relief sculptures). The enormous doors, on their original hinges into modern times, date from Classical times and still swing with perfect balance.

The major building consists of a huge rotunda or drum of brick-faced concrete 6.2m (20 ft.) thick. Atop the drum sits a perfect hemispheric dome of concrete with a 9m (30 ft.) round hole or impluvium (lit., 'lets rain in'). Under the impluvium in modern times will still be the original brass-edged drains. The floor is of granite, porphyry, and colored marble. The inner diameter of the drum, and the height from floor to impluvium, are exactly equal (43.89m, or 144 ft).

In the 16th Century, when Michelangelo designs the dome of St. Peter's, he purposely makes it several feet lower than the dome of the Pantheon. This is a gesture of respect and admiration from a Renaissance genius to his counterparts of the ancient imperial past.

The inside of the concrete dome contains the multitude of staggered niches in which all the cults of Rome (but two: the Jews, and their subcultus, the Christians) were allowed to display images of their divinities. It's a far cry from just 200 years earlier, when foreign cults (except the cognate Greek gods, Zeus-Juppiter, Hera-Juno, etc.) were not permitted within the sacred

Pomerium of the city. In the Pantheon, we see a Rome confident in her origins and nature, and open to all the cross-currents of her empire. More than any other building, the Pantheon is emblematic of the *Pax Romana*.

The inscription above the pronaos of Agrippa in modern times still proclaims: *M. Agrippa L. f. cos. Tertium fecit.* "Marcus Agrippa, son of Lucius, created this in his third Consulship."

We now leave for Transtiberim. It is a short walk to the Pons Aelius and the Tomb of Hadrian across the river.

PART FIFTEEN

ACROSS THE TIBER DISTRICT

(Regio XIV. Trans Tiberim)

CHAPTER 44

MAUSOLEUM OF HADRIAN

Regio XIV includes everything across the Tiber, plus Tiber Island. It consists of much more than the portion inside the Aurelian Wall (the Servian Wall did not cross the Tiber). It also includes the Janiculum, the Vatican Hills, and great outlying parks and gardens.

Crossing the Pons Aelius, we come upon Hadrian's Tomb, which sits by the opposite shore, overlooking a large meander of the Tiber. Across the river from it we see the Horologium of Augustus, whose metal topping ball shines in the sunlight.

Hadrian's Tomb is similar to that of Augustus in many respects. It is undoubtedly modeled on it. Coming across the bridge, we enter a ritual and decorative space of four travertine pillars on which stand bronze peacocks. It sits in a travertine space enclosed by a low wall. The main element is a drum, which sits on a square podium whose dimensions are almost identical (84m diameter, 10m high) with those of Augustus' main drum (87m by 10m). Atop the podium or base is a drum 64m in diameter and 21m high. Hadrian's Tomb does not have the two obelisks flanking its entrance. It does have the ring of bushes and cypresses at the top. In the center there is a tholos or domed temple in the Greek style, topped by a resplendent statue of Hadrian. Hadrian loved all things Greek, so the tholos

Just as the Mausoleum of Augustus served as resting place for subsequent emperors, Hadrian's Tomb will also become the dynastic resting place of the Antonines. In all, about 20 urns of ashes of the Antonine and Severan emperors, and various family members, will go into the tomb before it is sealed forever.

is not surprising. Inside the drum are vaults radiating outward as supports for the heavy temple and earth on top. The entrance faces across the Aelian Bridge along a short extension north from the Via Triumphalis. This road runs east-west, and crosses the Tiber via Nero's Bridge. Hadrian's ashes, and those of his wife Sabina, were laid to rest in a stone chamber in the middle of the monument which can be reached by a circular ramp inside the drum.

This general style of building is not entirely unique. The mega-wealthy widow of Crassus, Caecilia Metella, had a tomb erected that will stand into modern times on the Via Appia. That tomb has a drum measuring 30m in diameter and 11m high, and will also see use as a fortification in the Middle Ages. Like Hadrian's Tomb, it has an inner drum surrounding the burial chamber.

A little of the future history of Hadrian's Mausoleum is irresistible. In 270, when Aurelius builds a great defensive wall around Rome. Hadrian's Tomb becomes a fortress included in these works. It remains a fortress until modern times. It also serves at various times as a prison and even a papal torture chamber. During the 1400s it becomes papal property once and for all, and is called *Castel Sant' Angelo* (Castle of the Holy Angel). Pons Aelius becomes Ponte *Sant' Angelo*. From St. Peter's Square to the Castel runs a street called, in the 20th Century, the Via Della Consiliazione (Avenue of Conciliation, after the Lateran Treaty of 1929 whereby the modern Vatican state is created). Alongside this street runs a high, fortified wall with a path between its ramparts, known as the Passeto. It is on this Passeto that the Medici Pope Clement VII flees for his life in 1527, during the Sack of Rome by a predominantly Protestant army of German Lutheran mercenaries. Guarding his retreat are the corps of Swiss Guards. These were formerly Swiss mercenaries, reputed to be the best in Europe, and hired in 1506 as a corps of 200 by the warrior Pope Julius II for direct duty in the Vatican. Unlike most other mercenaries, these soldiers demand not only top pay, but all the beef they can eat each day (same deal as the Beefeaters at the Tower of London), a custom maintained into modern times.

CHAPTER 45

VATICAN HILL

In 150 A.D., during the Pax Romana and the brilliant, calm reign of His Majesty Imperator Titus Aelius Caesar Hadrianus Antoninus Pius Augustus Pontifex Maximus, the area around the Vatican Hill consists mostly of villages and farms. The area is neither well-reputed for the fertility of its soil nor the quality of its wines. To the north of here, and well into modern times, are meadows with sheep.

The Vatican Hill itself is a raised ridge of at least two prominences. Below it extending north-south is the Janiculum, a long ridge. The two ridges (Vatican and Janiculum) are joined by an east-west ridge at the middle of the western side of the Janiculum. Beyond the Vatican ridges is a small valley with gardens, including the Horti of Caesar farther south. Around the Vatican are some suburbs. Generally though, it is a marshy area whose low spots are prone to flooding, like many of the other low areas in the region. Roads run to the city from the coast and the north, and these roads are lined with impressive sepulchers—mamy from Republican times.

The most prominent feature of the Vatican is the Circus of Nero and Gaius, among a Garden of Agrippina and a Garden of Domitian. A large necropolis runs along the northern edge of the circus. Also known as the *Circus Vaticanus,* it was started by Gaius (Caligula) and finished by Nero, so it carries the praenomen of two of history's best-known tyrants. It served as a private course for chariot racing, with an Egyptian obelisk on the spina. Claudius and Nero both used it for their entertainments and orgies. Clustered around the circus are massive imperial structures. Most impressive is a palace the size of a large basilica, three stories high, with many colonnades and balconies on all levels. It has a central courtyard and a round tower at the southeastern end with a dome on top. There are many outlying temples and a stagnum. The palace has all the stables, equipment houses, and training schools needed by such a great entertainment center.

The Circus of Gaius and Nero is of special interest to Christians. It is believed that Saint Peter was crucified upside down here. As Rome fell into ruins, among the Christian sepulchers in this circus is one located on the *spina* about halfway between the midpoint and the east-northeasterly end. According to tradition, this is the spot on which St. Peter died and was buried. It is also the location of the modern main altar of St. Peter's Basilica. Visitors to the modern St. Peter's can walk around the back of the main altar, where the Pope celebrates Mass, and walk down a flight of steps into the ancient catacomb to see the burial spot said to be the apostle's.

CHAPTER 46

BURIAL PLACES

In all directions around the city, particularly along the large roads, are burial places. You may recall that by the dictates of their earliest, animist religion, the Romans cannot bury their dead within the sacred and supernatural city limits. Even emperors, from Augustus to Hadrian, built their *mausolea* outside the Pomerium. The humblest of Romans, slaves, often did not receive any sort of burial. Their owners discarded their corpses, either by throwing them along with the trash on the giant dump outside the Esquiline, or leaving them for others to remove.

From earliest times, the Latins cremated their dead, whereas the Etruscans and many other Italians buried them. Augustus, for example, built an elaborate cinerary oven before his mausoleum for his own cremation and the remains members of his dynasty. We saw the fabulous tombs of the very wealthy—for example, the pyramid of Cestius and the cylindrical mausoleum of Cecilia Metella south of the city. The less well-heeled could pay to have smaller marble tombs erected farther out along the highways like the Appian Way. The middle and working classes and the poor had to content themselves with having an urn of their ashes inserted into wall-tombs *(colombaria)*, very much like those of modern Romans.

Christians expected to be resurrected bodily at the final coming of Christ, and felt it was more appropriate to opt for burial rather than cremation. Most were urban, many were poor, and generally the only place to go was underground. Over the centuries, they dug long tunnels underground and sealed their dead into wall niches. Polytheists also had their catacombs, though they buried their pots of ashes in them.

The catacombs figure in the preposterous misperceptions polytheists and Christians had of each other. Christians acquired a negative image, largely due to a combination of imperial propaganda (like that of the self-serving Nero), rival religious agitators, and the dangerously anarchistic-seeming and aggressive proselytizing of some of their more zealous members. Many Romans believed the Christians were insane, godless atheists who wanted to destroy the world to speed up the return of their dead leader. They were considered unpatriotic traitors who hated the emperor and everything Rome stood for. Romans felt their way of life slipping away in the massive influx of foreign languages and cultures. During times of persecution, the Christians were forced to perform their religious rites away from the public eye. They had to worship in catacombs and private homes. This secrecy added to the growing rumors that they ate babies and had wild sexual orgies. Later, Christians will tell equally wild stories about their vanished polytheistic neighbors and oft-time oppressors. For more information on religious history, see Appendix B.

CHAPTER 47

SEA BATTLES

We leave the Vatican and walk south, southeast, along the Janiculum Hill toward Transtiberim proper. Along the way, we come across one of those remarkable centers for sea battles that are unlike anything the world has ever seen. There are several of these around the outskirts of Rome, and we must see at least this one, the Naumachia of Augustus (Gk *naus*, ship + *mach*ē battle).

There have been at least half a dozen of these special stadia, which are essentially holes filled with water. In them live wars are staged for the benefit of myriad spectators watching from surrounding stands.

One of the first naumachia was built by Julius Caesar to celebrate his triumph in 46 B.C. when he officially declared himself dictator. It was possibly built in the Codeta (a field of myrtle trees in the northern Campus Martius). The structure increased the marshiness of the area and bred disease. It is likely that it was filled in without a trace. Another theory is that is was obliterated by the extensive works of Augustus and Agrippa. Most of the subsequent naumachia have been dug across the river in the Transtiberim where we now walk. One is the Vatican naumachia, in the area we are just now leaving. Another is the naumachia of Domitian. We are in luck—the naumachia of Augustus is in full swing as we approach.

Of all the strange sights, nothing is quite as jarring as seeing three huge navy warships crawling through a meadow under full sail. We happen upon this scene as we descend from the Janiculum Hill toward the Tiber shore. We are roughly opposite the Suarium. Due to the thousands of spectators lining the way of the ships, we don't realize at first that they have entered along a canal dug into the earth from the naval shipyards. Now we understand that the easiest way to get a bireme from point a to point b is to float it. Lightened of all ballast, with their oars stowed upright (like a row of toothpicks from this distance), and devoid of crew, the ships are being towed by slaves and sailors pulling ropes from paths along the canal side. A helpful passer-by explains that this is an effective way for the navy to get rid of an obsolete ship and simultaneously raise cash to build several replacements.

Roman warships come in several sizes and configurations. From the Latin word for 'oar,' *remus,* we get monoreme (a ship with one bank of oars on each side), bireme (two banks), trireme (three banks), quadrireme (four banks), and quinquereme (three banks with two men to an oar on two, and one on the third, making five in total). The main use of oars has to do with maneuvering in battle. The ships have sails for moving over distances, and it's unlikely the rowers had much to do on a windy day. One imagines that these rowers are the most motivated sailors in history. When two ships ram each other, the one that hits hardest and first tends to sink the other.

Originated during the Bronze Age by the Phoenicians and Minoans, the Greek bireme is about 24m (80 ft) long, 3m (10 ft.) wide at the beam. The Athenian trireme, with which the Greeks won the great Battle of Salamis in 480 B.C. and stopped Persia, was about 35m (115 ft) long, 5m (16 ft) wide, and had a draft of about 1m (3 ft). The trireme has staggered banks of oars, so that the rowers sit on different levels relative to each other. Part of their challenge is to keep the oars moving in tandem to avoid having them strike each other. The typical trireme has a captain, 30 officers and seamen, 170 rowers, and a small staff of heavily armed *epibatai* (marines, or sea soldiers). The Romans, who are farmers at heart, have learned what they know of naval arts from their former enemies the Greeks and the Carthaginians.

The trireme is the ideal war galley. With its shallow draft, it is supremely maneuverable, and fast whether under sail or being rowed. The typical warship has in its center a castellum, sort of a castle, from which archers can shoot down into enemy vessels. The marines' primary use is for boarding and fighting. The desired out-

▤▥ A modern rostrum is any platform or stage used for public speak-
▤▥ ing. This term has an interesting history. In ancient times, a *ros-*
▤▥ *trum* (pl. *rostra*) was a metal beak on the front of a warship, used
for ramming. The word comes from the same root (rod-, gnaw) as
'rodent.' In fact, 'rat' comes from the same root. In 338 B.C., Rome
won her first big naval battle at Antium (Anzio) against the Volscians.
The Romans took the bronze ramming beaks from their enemies'
ships and installed them before the speaker's platform at the south
end of the Forum Romanum (at the foot of the Capitoline Hill). Consequently, public speakers were said to be speaking from the rostra.

come is a quick ramming, to either sink the enemy or incapacitate
them, so that the foundering vessel can be towed as a war prize and
refitted (with new rowers). The *corvus* was another important, Roman tactical invention. The *corvus* was a bridge that attached to a
grappling iron and allowed a warship to hold an opposing ship
alongside and board it.

Given the shallow draft, a canal no more than 2m deep (6 ft.)
and 5m (15 ft) wide is needed to tow the ships from the Tiber to
the naumachia. This is the same canal used to fill the artificial lake.
It is a simple, expedient way to create a huge entertainment venue.
Interestingly, the naumachia, which is about a kilometer inland,
does not have permanent seating. Perhaps this is because, away
from the center of the city, it doesn't demand the same ostentation
in marble and precious stone. Because it is relatively inexpensive
and impermanent, it provides the best creative minds of the Roman
entertainment industry a lot of leeway to develop new surprises
and twists for each major festival. When the wind is right, one can
sail across the channel into the stagnum. We find a rather primitive
oval edged with travertine blocks, and wooden bleachers capable
of seating 250,000 or more. The three triremes coming in now, and
six others anchored awaiting their entrance at some dramatic moment in the fray, each need a circle of about 33m (100 ft.) to operate. The stagnum in the middle of the naumachia before us is an
irregularly shaped depression filled with water to an average depth

of 3m (10 ft.) and a width from 100m (330 ft.) to 200m (650 ft., one eighth mile). The depth makes drowning a real danger, but not such that a sunken ship totally disappears from the crowd's view. At the same time, there is an area near the middle of the lake that is about twice that deep. The ships must have enough room to maneuver, yet not be too far so that the spectators can't see the action. There are four separate *portulae*, little harbors—one for each fleet, and one in reserve for surprises. The ships' square sails, and smaller, square sprit-sails on the bow, billow with wind and look ready to race out for combat.

There is a good wind today, and the air is filled with the smells of roasting dormice and pork, plus fresh bread and incense. Musicians and jugglers perform everywhere. Police are out in force, as muggers and pickpockets try to work the crowd. The idea is to make families feel safe in coming here. The stands groan with the weight of spectators munching snacks, drinking wine or juice, and commenting eagerly. They point to the waiting ships.

Today's main battle will be between a blue fleet (the Satyrs, with blue sails), a red fleet (the Centaurs, with red sails), and a yellow fleet (the Harpies, with yellow sails).

The emperor and his family arrive from across the river via the Nero Bridge from the Via Triumphalis. They come in a great train of white-armored Praetorians guarding the purple wagons in which his Majesty and family along with the Vestals sit. All the city's main priesthoods, from the Arvales to the Flamens, are represented today. To keep the impatient crowd under control, plenty of action goes on. It's important to get the royals past that quarter million (in case they're having a bad day and decide to trample the parade—nothing could stop this large of a crowd if they panic or riot). Once the VIPs are safely inside a fortified palisade, high up on the best seats with the best views, the main action can begin.

Several speakers on a high wooden tower address the spectators, much like modern sports commentators. They use megaphones similar to actors' masks, and their amplified voices carry across the water. It's a constant running commentary: "Who bets on Yellow? Who bets on Blue? Who bets on Red? Whom will Mars favor today? Whom will Diana fill with arrows? Whom will Vulcan smash with his hammer? Oh! There are the first hunters!"

The first spectacular event begins. Actually, it's a big surprise. It's something of a mystery, and a quarter million voices fall silent. What's going on?

The wind rattles through our ears, and one can hear a pin drop. An odd-looking little boat sails out from the shore near the emperor's box. It has a flat deck on which several clown-actors and dwarves caper about, chasing a couple of near-nude young nymphs. The little craft is rowed by a dozen Nubian slaves in Egyptian headdress and loincloths. The sun gleams on their sweaty backs.

From the opposite side, in the reserve harbor, come two smallish biremes under full sail. In today's excellent wind, the biremes just pop out suddenly and start racing in a big arc toward the center. They leave a pair of long, lazy wakes on the otherwise placidly lapping greenish water. We can't see who or what is on the biremes because they have colorful canvas raised on either side to shield the decks from view. By the minotaurs and other mythological images painted on the canvases, we immediately know that something from *The Odyssey* is about to be reenacted (liberally, by Roman stage masters intent on pleasing a largely illiterate crowd).

As the biremes threateningly circle the little rowed craft, the crowd starts getting excited. Will the biremes fight each other? Slaughter the clowns? Under Antoninus, the viciousness of Nero's games is more subdued (though still awful by modern theatrical standards). It is a great venue for professional fighters and actors to make a lot of money.

"I think something is in the water," the announcer says. We see something vague, a large shadow maybe, in the middle of the lake, totally under water and out of sight.

The little boat rows in a wide circle, and one by one, the clowns and nymphs dive off. As the skiff circles around, one by one the divers come to the surface holding colored glass balls. Each ball gleams with rainbows of captured sunlight. The announcer excitedly rattles on, describing and analyzing everything we see, and adding little hints of this and that for the crowd's benefit. Their voices rise to a hushed, murmur as the tension builds.

The divers have done something under the water. They have released something by removing the glass balls, which have ropes trailing down.

A trumpet signals that something major is about to occur. The divers go down again showing their feet before they disappear. What's going on? The skiff circles around, picking up the divers as they surface, and heads back toward the edge of the lake.

Now the two biremes are at opposite ends of the lake. They turn and face each other. Up go the full sails, out go the oars, and they race toward each other as if to ram head-first. As they pick up speed, the canvas sides fall away. One bireme is full of men on horseback, wearing Bronze Age armor. The other bireme has wild men on board, clad in fur and waving clubs—the Laestrygones, a race of giant cannibals from *The Odyssey*.

Now we hear a strange, wailing sound from a choir of women with strange but lovely voices. They can only be the fabled Sirens, who lure sailors to their deaths by shipwreck. Odysseus has his men lash him to a mast, and fill their ears with wax, to survive this charming but deadly singing. The two ships appear headed for a collision.

Suddenly, the water starts to bubble and foam. The crowd raises a deafening ocean of shouts, trumpets roar, drums rattle. The planners could not have provided better sound effects. It's almost painful to hear, and we consider covering our ears. Steam appears, drifting around like fog. Something huge is slowly rising from the water. At first, we see only blinding sheets of glass catching sunlight at various angles and mirroring it into our eyes.

Mihercle! My Mercury, what is this? The whole crowd is on their feet, on their toes, holding each other's shoulders, straining to see over the heads of those standing on the bleachers before them.

The island of the sirens rises from the lake, where it was anchored by various devices. It is round, made of timbers, and covered with artificial rocks whose surfaces are inlaid like mirrors. Hypnotically, the dancing sprites of reflected light bounce around. They even reflect the emperor's handsome, bearded face and small even teeth as he claps and laughs delightedly.

The island is 18m (60 ft) in diameter. It is flat around the edges and covered with half a foot of sand, except for a few boulders here and there. In the center is a cone-shaped mountain 6m (20 ft) wide at the base, with several wide ledges for actors to stand on, to a height of 6m. Even as the last gouts of water pour off the mountain and run off the edges and grating under the sands, a giant puff of smoke erupts from the mountain top. Its lid flies off, and a ball of flame erupts like that of Vesuvius (well remembered from its catastrophic explosion only 71 years ago).

The two ships ram into the opposite shores of the island. The wild men disgorge onto the island and disappear into the mountain. There they will find costumes and stage props for their next act. All eyes are on the horsemen. As their ship sinks, they begin to have a sword fight. Their horses are specially trained to swim, and make for each other. It's a stretch of true mythology, staged for the joy of the moment. Already, the water is roiling purple with blood and gore. Even the foam around the struggling combatants starts looking wine-red.

For another two hours, an endless series of acts overlap one another, first here, then there, so that there is never a lull in the action. There are over 2,450 criminals to be executed today, brought in from as far away as Germany and Egypt for the occasion. In one event, a shipload of criminals float past while the siren sings. They stand tied to posts on their boat, with wax in their ears. Their terrified screams and wide eyes are drowned out by the crowd's hoarse yelling. As their ship runs aground on the island, they are set upon by four lions released from the hold of the ship and the result is, well, a *carnarium*. Hordes of clowns and nymphs abound to haul away the wreckage from each act. Puffs of smoke and dazzling mirrors signal it's time to look elsewhere for the next attraction. Female gladiators cut down terrified, overweight, middle-aged men sent to fight for their lives in comic armor with little bent swords. Some of the female fighters have their right breast removed in the fashion of amazons (Gr *a* without + *mazos* breast) to facilitate drawing a bowstring like a man. The Laestrygones come out with their clubs and beat to death a group of younger male convicts who have been given slender fighting staves to protect themselves. One or two of the fur-clad gladiators do go into the water, not to resurface, but it's a quick ten minute slaughter. The convicts were condemned anyway, most for murder and other capital crimes (perhaps including sacrilege or atheism). The crowd roars its approval. Good riddance, they yell, nicely done.

Finally, as the crowd begins to weary, the island sinks beneath the water, and the lake is clear for more action. Here and there floats a body part, but the clowns in their little boats rush about to clean up. The climactic sea battle begins. First, the red and yellow ships fly at each other. They are manned by a combination of specially trained gladiators, and some convicts who have been promised to have the death penalty lifted if they do well and are on the surviving ship. The red ship catches the yellow ship amidships. The yellow ship goes down quickly with all hands. Archers on the red ship finish off those swimming in the water. At the same time, the blue ship bursts from her *portula* and drives on the red ship. The prow rises and falls, and the ram glitters wetly. The defenders on the red ship stand ready with poles. They manage to deflect the blue ship just a bit, and the two triremes end up alongside each other. This is what the crowd loves. As the hulls grind together, nets drop, and men slide onto opposing decks with knives and swords ready. Showers of arrows cut many down. We catch the glint of swords, the clang of metal, the shouts of the scared and injured. We feel a shudder, and see the red ship take a hit. A rammer has unexpectedly run out from the reserve harbor. We hear the wailing of galley slaves, and then their sudden silence as the red ship lists to one side and settles. Now another reserve ship races out, and throws burning pitch. Torches twirl through the air, slowly, arcing gracefully, and then splatter against blue's castellum. Burning men jump down to the water. Well, this livens things up a bit, doesn't it?

"Now here comes a special treat," says the announcer. "Remember the games at the Colosseum? Bets went heavily on the fights between the great hero, Orca, and two newer Thracians named Meat Hook and Glory Boy. The Whale held them both off and the referee declared a tie to save all three for today's great event."

The crowd roars wildly as a pair of skiffs row out to the island. The volcano continues its reddish flashing and dull roars in the background. On one shore emerges the mighty Orca in his Myrmillo outfit. It consists of heavy armor, shield, sword, and the characteristic wide-brimmed helmet with a huge fish-fin on top. From the other side come Meat Hook and Glory Boy, two *tridentarii* who work together against their massive opponent. For a while it's a standoff. The two Thracians, wearing only loincloths, wield their nets and tridents with great speed and skill. Orca has advantages in both strength and speed. There! Glory Boy's arm comes off at the shoulder, ripping off part of his chest. He staggers about with his ribs gleaming white against purple flesh and yellowish muscles. Blood spurts out in a single great fountain that dies out, even as Glory Boy pitches forward on his face. A few minutes later, Meat Hook has Orca backed off to the edge of the island, but Orca gets in one wide wheeling slash of his sword which takes Meat Hook in the middle. As he doubles over, Orca slashes his head off. Again, that brief spray of blood. As Orca reaches down to pick up the severed head, something bumps the island. An elephant bursts in panic from a secret cell where it was being kept for a later act. Orca flails his arms while the crowd stands on its toes screaming for more. Orca's face begins to flood with sheer panic as he slowly topples over backwards into the water. For a minute or two, he flails about, screaming in a high pitched voice that cuts through the crowd's laughter and yelling. "Help me!" he screams. "I can't swim!" With the crowd laughing, he sinks beneath the water and drowns.

We've had about all we can take, and leave with the earliest citizens to head back before the traffic jam. Leaving the naumachia, we have a half hour walk through sparsely settled, brushy marshland until we reach the outskirts of the true Regio XIV, Transtiberim (across the Tiber, the modern Trastevere from the ancient name).

CHAPTER 48

TRANSTIBERIM

We follow a new road past the villa of Clodius. Near the river is a large wine storage house, the Cellae Vinariae Novae et Arruntianae Caesaris Nostris. This name may translate roughly as "Wine Merchants' New Warehouse Dedicated To Our Younger Caesar." There is an Etruscan name in there, *Aruns* or *Arr ns*, usually given to a younger son, while the elder is called *Lar* or *Lars* in their language. If this reading is correct, it seems to have an unmistakable hint of affection in the ancient Etruscan manner (the mysterious smile, the unbridled life of which the Romans are both mortally disapproving and envious). The suggestion is that a good deal of the wine this far up river, on the northward side, comes from Etruria, from Etruscan vineyards in Tuscanum (Tuscany). From here, small boats ferry the wine either to the Suarium (via the Twin Storks dock across the water) or down to the old river port with its cattle and vegetable markets. The wine merchants' complex is rectangular, like a horrea or granary.

It has vaulted store rooms on the first floor and long porticoes enclosing complex courts on the second floor. In the courts, merchants haggle, accountants keep their books, and corporate investors plan trade expansion. In the courtyards outside the storage halls below, artisans and slaves follow their trades (barrel makers, hoop smiths, siphon makers, caulkers, boat makers, *et al*). We continue on this Vinariae road or vicus, quickly coming to the walls and structures around the Pons Agrippae. That's the bridge that Augustus' friend Agrippa built, leading toward the Theater of Pompey.

As we approach the Transtiberim, looking far off to our right, toward the sea which is 20 miles (33km) west, we see the arches of

two large aqueducts coming toward the city. The Aqua Alsietina terminates at a naumachia of Augustus west of Transtiberim, and supplies water to the district. The Aqua Trajani terminates in the giant
grain processing center at the far western edge of Transtiberim.
Some of its water is stored in a huge castellum, but a lot is increasingly used to drive the water wheels of the *molinae*, or flour mills.
Although the Romans don't expand into an industrial society, it appears that water power is cheaper than human or animal power in
this instance. The large bath complex Balneum Ampelidis receives
its water from the aqueducts, and services that area. A little closer
in is the complex of support structures for the naumachia of Augustus, which receives water from the aqueducts as well as the river.

Transtiberim is a settlement, a spill-over, within a tongue of
land that sits in the large lower bend in the Tiber. Across the river
from the northern shore of this land is Tiber Island. The rounded
tip of this tongue points directly across at the old river port, toward
the Temple of Portunus. The southern edge of this tongue is across
the river (via the Sublician Bridge of pontifex fame at the heart of
Roman history and religion) to the marble docks and the huge
shopping center of the Porticus Aemilia. Three important bridges
cross into Transtiberim from the city: The Cestius, from the island;
the Aemilius, from the Portus; and the Sublicius, from the docks.
Most important is the Pons Aemilius, which enters the nose of
Transtiberim and then splits into two main streets. The upper street
(at some point to be called Aureliana) heads west to the Tyrrhenian Sea coast (33 km, or 20 mi). The lower street from that fork becomes the Via Portuense (Port Road) heading southwest along the
Tiber to the New Port opposite Ostia, where we started our walk.

Within the busy, brawling, raucus mini-Subura that is Transtiberim, three or four other large streets form a careless grid dead-
ending at will. The biggest of these is the street coming northwest
across the Sublician Bridge, crossing the Port Road, and dead-end-
ing at an auxiliary barracks of the VII Cohort of the urban vigiles.
The police and fire service headquarters is a large one, and set almost dead center in the Transtiberim, equidistant from the three
important bridges.

Near the Pons Sublicius is a vicus of tanners and leather workers. Cattle and pigs go to the Forum Boarium or the great *macella*

(markets) of the Caelian and Esquiline, or to the Suarium (pork market) in northern Via Lata. In those places, and in neighborhood butcher shops, the animals have to be slaughtered and sold fresh before the meat starts spoiling. The hides find their way across into Transtiberim. We can well imagine the size of this industry, given that 1.2 million souls eat meat, which produces a lot of hides. Those in turn wind up in everything from sandals and boots, to saddles, book bindings, gaskets, purses, buckets and belts. We must not forget expensive, stylish women's *strophia* and *subligacula* of softest leather (breast strap and undies) resembling the modern bikini.

CHAPTER 49

POIGNANT GARDENS

The outlying, southerly structures of Transtiberim, along the River Road heading out along the Tiber, include a temple of the Dea Suria, or Dea Syria. Also in that area is a large statue of Hercules Cubans (reclining, as if at a feast). This statue is the centerpiece of a popular shrine within the Horti Caesaris, or Gardens of Caesar.

It is night time as we wander along the dim, torch-lit paths with their marble statues and fragrant flower beds. These gardens are where Caesar entertained Cleopatra in 44 B.C., the year of his murder. Her presence in Rome probably was what made the ultra-conservative senators snap, and seize their opportunity to stab him on the *Ides* (middle day) of March. We can almost feel the presence of the Egyptian temptress, with her exotic servants and her music wafting among the staid Roman columns. Cleopatra was no ravishing beauty, but she had personal magnetism and sexual charisma, that drew Caesar and Antony to their doom, and herself with them. She was the last of the Ptolemy line to rule Egypt. Julius Caesar was the death rattle of the old Republic.

In a rather desolate area north of these gardens, at the foot of the Janiculum, is another poignant spot. It is the Lucus Furrinae (Sacred Grove of Furrina, or Furina). Little is known about this ancient deity, whose festival, the Furrinalia, were held every July 25 in antiquity, but which has largely died out by now along with many of the ancient ways and beliefs. This grove is where, in some sense, the future of Rome was sealed in 121 B.C. Here, Gaius Gracchus ordered his servant to kill him after trying unsuccessfully to extend freedoms and liberties to the common people (plebs) of Rome. The same faction of wealthy families killed his brother Tiberius a few

years earlier. This was the beginning of the end of the Republic. The
final turbulent 75 years of the Republic were beset with civil and
social wars, dictatorships, and disruptions. Three hundred wealthy
families came to own all the wealth of Rome, and among those, 20
or 30 controlled the government. There was, to begin with, the struggle between the old, traditional families who sought to maintain
traditions, versus the so-called Homines Novi (New Men) like Marius, Cicero, and many of their contemporaries. They were rising
through the ranks, but most never quite broke through the glass
ceiling of old money and old prestige at the very top. Julius Caesar

In time, the grove of Furrina becomes the site of a series of Oriental gods including the synthesis Iovis Heliopolitanus (Heliopo-
lis being also the site of ancient Baalbek in Lebanon).

One can imagine the *Götterdämmerung*, the Twilight of the Gods,
that went on here in the final generations before the Sack of 410.
Rome is abandoned by her emperors, who rule by proxy from capitals in Germany (Trier), Northern Italy (Ravenna), Serbia, and Constantinople. The aqueducts continue to function, and the ships come
and go with grain, and life seems normal on the surface, but something essential is gone: the numina have been banished, and the religion that will dominate the coming Middle Ages rules. The City of
Rome has lost her emperor, but has gained her Pope. Where the civic
and religious power were one, they are now separate

In a final irony, the last polytheist temple erected here is by Julian the Apostate is dedicated to Chronos, Father Time. Some historians interpret startling evidence as suggesting human sacrifice in
Julian's temple during the twilight years of the Roman empire. If
true, this would starkly remind us of the demon-filled decline of the
Etruscan state a millennium earlier. Archeologists cite the finding of
a human cranium under a statue of Jupiter Heliopolitanus, and the
presence of statues with the tops of their heads cut off, and tombs of
possible victims in the sanctuary of Julian's temple. One can only
imagine the dark and grisly rituals that might have occurred here in
the last generations of the Roman Empire, right under the noses of
the Christian bishops who effectively ran the show.

himself came from one of the oldest *gentes* (Julii). This may explain the Senate's acquiescence when Augustus asked for total power on the premise that he was going to restore the Republic. Augustus proceeded to do the opposite, and their old world slipped ever farther out of the Senate's grasp. Some of the cruelty of emperors starting with Tiberius reflects this underlying and undying war between the conservative old and the radical new, between the old Republic and the new Empire.

CHAPTER 50

THE NEW PORT

The Port Road takes us west at times in a straight line, ignoring the meandering of the Tiber. At times it dodges among swamps and hills. In many ways, our walk here is a mirror image of our walk eastward on the opposite side of the Tiber, on the Ostia Road. We pass the same sorts of small tabernae and hostels, and the same sorts of slave children peddling water and sweets.

The Emperor Claudius (41–54 A.D.) built a new, sheltered harbor (*portus*, port) a few kilometers north along the coast. Because the Tiber makes a huge meander, the new Portus shortens the cargo trip to Rome considerably. The artificial port is hexagonal rather than round, so it's easier for ocean-going ships to tie up at straight-edged docks.

A drawback was that goods had to be carried overland, either to the nearest Tiber shore a kilometer or two away, or directly to Rome on the Via Portuensis. To make this trip easier, the Emperor Trajan (98–117) in the 2nd Century added a huge new outer harbor sheltered by a huge surrounding groin and a tall lighthouse. Trajan also built a ship channel (Trajan's Canal) to the Tiber.

For modern travelers flying in and out of Leonardo da Vinci International Airport at Fiumicino, the harbor of Trajan is still there. It is a mystifying hexagon of jade-colored, opaque but lustrous water, having lost its purpose and its way, as the Roman Empire finally did. It still sits there in the middle of nowhere, as enigmatic now as the far more ancient Egyptian Sphinx.

At the outer entrance to the great harbor complex, where the stars shine on the glittering waters of the Tyrrhenian Sea, stands a great pharus or lighthouse. It was built by filling a huge barge with concrete. On this base rises a lighthouse whose fire signals night and day to ships coming from all over the empire. Ships leaving Latium are filled with travelers of all ages, nationalities, and descriptions. They stand on deck warmly dressed and looking backwards with a mix of emotions. The blazing lighthouse lens is the last they see of Rome.

HISTORICAL BACKGROUND

Neolithic to Bronze Ages (10,000 B.C. – 2,500 B.C.)

Humans have inhabited the Italian Peninsula since the Ice Ages. Paleontologists have found Neanderthal fossils dating to 50,000 B.C. near Rome. The Neanderthal race died out during the Ice Ages.

We live during a time of warming called the Holocene Period. After the glacial time ended, by around 8,000 B.C., Homo Sapiens spread evenly but sparsely across the newly thawing European sub-continent. Our kind clustered earliest in Mesopotamia (today's Iraq), where large areas were then much more lush and wet than they are today. Today's deserts were then dense forests, meadows, or marshes filled with game. Tribes of modern humans roamed as Mesolithic hunter-gatherers. When they settled down to farm and herd, they adopted a more sophisticated Neolithic way of life in the first real towns and cities. The term 'civilization,' often used as a value judgment, simply denotes 'living in cities' (L *civis*, city). The term 'stone age' as in Neolithic (*neo-*, new + *lithos*, stone) can be misleading, since such people did quite sophisticated things with wool, cloth, clay, and wood, to name just a few materials. Around 6,500 B.C., people started using soft metals like copper.

Civilized people claimed ownership of land and chattels. With that ownership, they needed laws to protect their rights. They required priesthoods to sanctify it all, and ensure their good standing with supernatural powers. In short, as more people lived close together, the complexity of their society grew exponentially.

Civilization radiated outward from the Middle East—eastward into the Indus Valley (Harappa, Mohenjo-Daro), westward into Asia

Minor (today's Turkey) and into what is today Greece. Some religious cults, which spread to Rome many centuries later, seem to have roots as far east as Persia and even India. Civilizations advanced in the more populated Middle East and Egypt, while Europe lagged for many centuries. The western Mediterranean would lag in development for millennia, as a kind of 'wild west' of the archaic world.

Bronze Age (2,500 B.C. – 1,200 B.C.)

Around 2,500 B.C. came the remarkable discovery that if you added a little tin to your copper, it became hardened enough to make swords, arrow heads, armor, chariot hardware, and even ploughs. Out went stone, in came metal—hence the Bronze Age revolution that ruled the known world between 2,500 and 1,200 B.C.

During the Bronze Age, Middle Eastern civilization slowly spread across Asia Minor (today's Turkey) into what would one day be called Greece. The first great civilizations began to flourish in Egypt and Mesopotamia. A people called the Achaeans settled Asia Minor and Greece during the Bronze Age. Their civilization, with its epic wars and travels, would be reprised in the much later Greek epics *The Iliad* and *The Odyssey*.

The Minoans (centered on today's island of Crete) were a great Bronze Age trading nation. Their ships plied the Mediterranean. In Mesopotamia, great civilizations including Sumer, Chaldea, Akkad, and Babylon developed at various points. The Sumerians invented writing about 3,000 B.C., using wedge-shaped cuneiform impressions on clay, and a great multitude of symbols.

In Egypt, over 30 dynasties would rule during a period of nearly 3,000 years. It lasted from the Old Kingdom pharaos who built the great pyramids, until the last pharao was to succumb to Roman power in 30 B.C.

The same general developments took place in other regions of the world, like in the Americas and in East Asia. By 'known' world we speak here broadly in the viewpoint of people in the Mediterranean and the Middle East.

The Bronze Age was a splendid time of thriving commerce and civilization until it all ended with, one could say, a bang.

Dark Age (1,200 B.C. – 800 B.C.)

Not long after 1500 B.C., the most violent volcanic explosion in historical times blew the island of Thera sky-high, and signaled the beginning of a long, lingering decline lasting several centuries. The eruption sent tidal waves across the Med and caused earthquakes across vast distances. There is some discussion that Plato's philosophical treatise *Atlantis* may be a dim recollection of the horrors of that time. Over the next 300 years (and all these dates are fuzzy), the Mediterranean world drifted out of the sunlight of the Bronze Age. In approximately 1,200 B.C., it sank into a dark time of which we have few written records.

As the First Millennium B.C. opened, Egypt was battered by the invasions of an amalgam of sea raiders. The Assyrians conquered Anatolia and eventually much of the Middle East. Around 1,000 B.C., David became the first king of Israel. His son Solomon succeeded him in 961, dedicated the First Temple at Jerusalem in 953, and ruled until 922. This was the high point of what might be called the Empire of Solomon. His realm split in two kingdoms whose subjects would wind up lost in the Babylonian and Ninevean Captivities.

The great sea power was Phoenicia. By 500 B.C., the Persian dynasties of Cyrus and Cambyses ruled an empire that included the

The end of the Mediterranean Bronze Age seems to coincide with the presumed era of the Trojan War. Most likely, the early Greeks may have been marauding the older, wealthier cities of Asia Minor. One can imagine raiding parties, in the off-season, venturing along the lush hills behind the shores of places like Troy, looking for easy prey—a few sheep, a small town, any target of opportunity. There probably was not a sustained ten-year siege of Troy, but rather a lengthy period of probing raids and occasional assaults. Then, on a pretext (perhaps Helen, the 'face that launched a thousand ships'), it's just possible that a war took place like the one described in *The Iliad*. The chaos and disorder of the age remind one of how the Norsemen or Viking raiders would one day terrorize Britain and much of Europe during the dark centuries after the Roman legions had departed.

entire Middle East from the Mediterranean to the Indian Ocean, from Egypt to Anatolia. They had swallowed up all of the fragmented kingdoms including Israel and empires including the Assyrians.

The upheavals at the end of the Bronze Age, and the subsequent Dark Age, caused mass migrations of people away from the population centers of the Middle East. Some of the immigrants wandered west from the Balkan Peninsula, around the northern Adriatic, to a still sparsely populated Italy and down into the Po Valley. The westward migration of tribes typically caused one tribe to either push the previous arrivals out of the way, or to bypass them, and penetrate deeper into the boot of Italy. Aboriginal people of Indo-European stock had lived in the Tiber delta since time immemorial. The *Latini* (probably from *latus*, referring to the flatness of the land) came during the Bronze Age and settled in the Alban Mountains south of the Tiber. Here they built defensible strongholds with access to copious fresh water.

Early Iron Age

The Bronze Age world slipped into a sleep of centuries, like the sun disappearing over the horizon for the long night, and in the morning about five centuries later, around 750 B.C., the Mediterranean awakened as an Iron Age world.

The early Iron Age saw a very different mosaic of civilizations. The Egyptians were still there, for example, but the Minoans of Crete and the Achaeans of Asia Minor had vanished. The Assyrians who ruled Asia Minor and the Middle East were replaced by the Medes and then the Persians.

In place of the Minoans, the Phoenicians rule the sea lanes. Where the Cretans traded on the inner rim of the Med, the Phoenicians push out into the Atlantic as far north as Britain, to trade with the Beaker Tin folk. They went as far south as the islands along the African shores of the Atlantic.

This is where the splendid purple dyes originate that eventually wind up on the edges of Roman senators' togas. The word 'phoenician' comes from the Latin *puniceus*, 'red' or 'purple.'

We call the Iron Age culture of Italy (10th to 9th Centuries B.C.) the Villanovan, from the name of a village near Bologna where in

These Phoenicians actually call themselves *Kena'ani,* 'of the purple land,' after the murex shellfish found off their shores. Their influence adds the word *kena'ani* to the Hebrew lexicon with the secondary meaning 'merchant.' You may know them as Canaanites, the folks whose lands the Chaldean Avram invaded when fleeing his native Ur during a famine early in the Bronze Age. The long-vanished Philistines, left their name in the eventual Roman province of Palestine. Avram and his *Habiru* ('wanderers', or Hebrews) brought a supreme gift with them from Chaldea, writing. Their alphabet, unlike the Sumerian, uses a short phonetic alphabet of 22 sounds, like that of the later Greeks. The way the strokes of the Hebrew letters are formed reflects how cuneiform wedges were incised in clay. When Avram, or Abraham as he later called himself, came to Canaan, he also brought along some of Mesopotamian culture including the *Epic of Gilgamesh.* This informed *Genesis,* which, along with Greek and Latin flood stories like that of *Pyramus and Thisbe,* in turn would influence Virgil's *Aeneid.*

1853 archeologists identified the first artifacts of the period. The Villanovan people brought with them, from the so-called Urnfield Culture of eastern Europe, the practice of cremating their dead and burying the ashes in urns. The urns were often shaped like military helmets, or else like huts (one wonders if the helmet urns were for men, and the home or hearth urns for women).

Classical Mediterranean World (c. 750 B.C. to c. 600 A.D.)

The dark age gave rise to Classical Mediterranean civilization, much as the European Middle Ages of our Common Era gave rise to Renaissance and Modern times. Just as Medieval and Renaissance people looked back to the long-ago Classical era with admiration and wonder, so the emerging Iron Age civilization of the Classical Age (which birthed Rome) would look back on the wonders of the Bronze Age.

Greeks from Mycenae took over the rule of Crete. The Minoans vanished from history, leaving their legends including that of the

Cretan bull, or Minotaur, which helps inform the cult of Mithra that we find in later Rome.

The Phoenicians, whose great period is from 1200 to 800 B.C, leave many coastal settlements, of which the most famous is Carthage near modern Tunis. This North African city will become one of the early Roman Republic's two greatest enemies (the other being the collective southern Italian colonies of various Greek city-states).

Around 750 B.C., a new civilization with strong Anatolian or Middle Eastern overtones started to dominate metal-rich Tuscany, north of the Tiber—the Etruscans. Herodotus suggests that the *Tyrrhenoi*, as the Greeks to the south were to call these people, may have come from Lydia in Asia Minor. There is no conclusive consensus among historians about the sudden, mysterious appearance of these unique people. One shred of evidence points to a tribe among the Sea Peoples who ravaged the Mediterranean during the Dark Ages. Egyptian hieroglyphics refer to the invasion of these dreaded marauders. They included Achaeans, Lycians, Philistines, Sardinians, and an unknown group called the Teresh, whose name may be another variant on Tyrsoi (a Greek variant for the Etruscans). The Latins would refer to them as the *Etrusci* (possibly *e-*, *ex*-Tusci or Trusci; though the adjective *turskum* has survived from the Umbrian dialect of Latin, describing them). The Etruscans called themselves *rasna* in their alien and indecipherable language that seems unrelated to any other known language in the ancient world. The Etruscans, for all their enormous advances in areas like metal working and civil engineering, had a relatively primitive alphabet. The Etruscan alphabet reminds one of the alphabet which the Bronze Age people of *The Iliad* and *The Odyssey* borrowed from the Phoenicians much earlier. The Greeks, on the other hand, developed a stellar civilization using a virtually modern alphabet. The modern word 'alphabet' comes from the first two letters of the Greek alphabet (*alpha*, a + *beta*, b, which in turn are related to the earlier wedge-shaped, cuneiform-derived Hebrew *aleph* and *beth*).

By 750 B.C., the Greek city-states start coming into their own. Somewhere in Greece, or possibly across the Hellespont in Ionia, a court poet of great sophistication, whom the world knows as Homer, weaves stories of Bronze Age war and wandering. His stories are so brilliant and captivating that moderns still study and admire *The Iliad* and *The Odyssey*.

The Assyrians, then the Medes, and finally the Persians loom on Greece's eastern side, preventing expansion; so the Greek city-states expand westward. It's just a short cruise across the Adriatic to the eastern coast of Italy. The Greek colonies, independent of each other, and answering only to the parent city in Greece, conquer Sicily and the southern half of Italy. They call this *megale Hellas* (Great Greece), while the Latins will refer to it as *Magna Graecia*.

Meanwhile, a human wave is stealthily building across Europe north of the Alps, a world away and not to be encountered for another three and a half centuries: the Gauls. But that is a long way off, and we are more interested in the little pinprick on a bend of the Tiber that will in time become what moderns call The Eternal City.

Rome first appeared as a tiny settlement in a bend of the Tiber around 750 B.C. In the world that gave birth to Rome, there was not an abrupt switch from using bronze to using iron. As with the concept of 'stone ages,' there is a bit of a misnomer in this 'metal ages,' since people didn't stop using bronze. Instead, they added the use of iron to their repertoire. Iron attracted lightning, for reasons the archaic Romans didn't understand. They long considered iron to be evil and unclean, and banned it from sacred structures all through ancient Roman history.

APPENDIX B

ROMAN RELIGION: NUMINA MEET SHINTO

Modern Questions, Ancient Answers

Moderns ask: Why did the Romans so violently persecute the Christians? Did God smite the Romans? Were they immoral? Many moderns seek to answer such questions, which require truthful inquiry into the ancient Roman soul. The necessary information about Roman religion lies buried under the propaganda of medieval churchmen, and yet earlier under layers of imported religions that mask the real Roman religious identity. Medieval people inherited the scattered mosaic of Roman civilization with many pieces missing. They knew that the Classical world had been incomparably greater than their own world, even if they did not quite understand how and why. Early Medieval bishops not only had axes to grind, but real-life problems to solve. They had a world to hold together. We won't be judgmental about them here. We do, however, want to peel away layers of naive disinformation (e.g., 'the Romans vanished because they were immoral,' or 'God smote the Romans because they had too much sex'). We want to plumb the true nature of the Roman soul with an open mind, and perhaps learn more about ourselves.

We are visiting ancient Rome at the height of the Roman Peace. It is the sublime moment when the most things were working in Rome's favor and the least number of factors were working against her. A major milestone was the completion, around 125 A.D., of the Pantheon—a house of worship for all religions in the Empire (except the Jews and the Christians). The Romans 200 years earlier, during the late Republic, would not permit a foreign house of worship anywhere near their city. (A notable exception was the early acceptance of the cult of the Magna Mater, related to the worship of Cybele, and the sibylline practices at Cumae.) In 125, the emperor Hadrian welcomed the world's religions as a matter of state policy. His Pantheon, however, sat outside the *Pomerium* or sacred boundary of the spiritual city of Rome.

The Romans were an extremely conservative, religious people. Their state, religion, culture, and world were all the same thing. Temple and state were one and the same. Augustus had the Senate give him the *imperium* (absolute civil power), but he also had them grant him the titles of *Pontifex Maximus* (highest priest) and *Augustus* (revered). Ultimately, they also titled him Pater Patriae (Father of the Nation).

To understand the Roman soul is to begin to understand just about everything about them—their greatness, their humanity, and their failings. Rome has left a mark on human history that affects most of us daily, in our languages, our customs, our laws, even in our democracies.The Founding Fathers were deeply mindful of the Roman Republic as they crafted the underpinnings of the U.S. Republic in the late 1700s.

Christianity

To understand ancient Rome, and the world that gave birth to ours, we must work backwards and peel away layers of change that came as Rome expanded far beyond her city limits. First, we'll look at Christianity going back to 313 A.D. In that year, Constantine and his co-regent Licinius issued the Edict of Milan, a document that pulled the safety net of religious tolerance once and for all over the Christians. They joined the many other faiths of the Romans during the Imperial centuries. Christianity ultimately became the official (and only tolerated) state religion.

Oriental Mystery Religions

Working backwards once more, the next layer of religion we want to cut through are the Oriental mystery cults that attracted such enormous multitudes of Romans during the Imperial centuries.

Pagans, Heathens. Moderns casually refer to the Romans as 'pagans,' which is a unfortunate misnomer. It is not only meaningless, but derives from an ancient social slur. The archaic Roman religion (animism), after having been overlaid with various polytheistic layers and finally by Christian monotheism, was banished. It would long continue to flourish in the countryside where it first began. That's where the term pagan cones from: countryside is *pagus* from Gr *pagos*. In fact as we walk around Rome in 150, the city areas outside the *Pomerium* or sacred city limits, as defined by the Servian Wall, are still called country, *pagus*. This would include the wharves south of the Aventine and the Campus Martius. "Pagan" didn't mean some diabolical follower of evil. It just meant "country boy" or "homie". It would have been used in a way similar to when two modern Italian men meet, slap each other on the back, and call one another *paisan!* (fellow countryman!).

In late Roman times, the more sophisticated urban ruling class, now Christian, referred to those still secretly practicing the old, forbidden ways as "pagans". They meant it in the sense of 'rube' or 'yokel.'

Similarly, the word 'heathen' in English comes from the Middle and Old English (Anglo-Saxon) 'heath' for 'wilderness.' The modern German word for 'pagan' is Heide, from 'heide,' meadow.

In the late Classical age, violent confrontations, sometimes even gang warfare led by religious officials, was common among various urban factions, including polytheists, Christians, and Jews. Several famous incidents of destruction are noteworthy. In the late 400s, a Christian mob burned down the great Serapeum library at Alexandria on the grounds that any book other than the Bible is diabolical and must be destroyed. Only some books in an adjacent church library were spared, and the collection began being built again. In the 600s, the Moslem Caliph Omar ordered the library fed to the fires of the public baths, on the ground that any book other than the Koran is diabolical and must be destroyed. There were 4,000 baths, and the sum total of ancient Classical learning and culture took six months to vanish in their fires. Another incident was the murder of the last great Classical philosopher, Hypatia, who was tortured to death in 415 by a mob of Christians. They had been incited by their leaders by false rumors from adherents of rival religions. This mob gouged her eyes out, then scraped off her skin and her flesh with seashells in an orgy of hatred.

During the late Republic, it was still possible for traditionalists to legally keep cults like that of Mithras outside the city. Roman reactionaries like Cato—and much of the hard-nosed, corporate leadership of the 300 old families who owned most of the wealth hated music, theater, foreigners (particularly Greeks), and most of all hated strange religions. Nevertheless, as the Romans conquered Greece, Greece culture conquered the Romans. Roman leaders saw the Greeks as immoral deviants. If the Roman conservatives didn't care for the Olympian gods brought in from their new Greek province, they went absolutely bonkers about keeping out the Oriental mystery religions. What pried the door open in Rome was the fascination with anything Greek. Even though contemporary Greeks were viewed by the Romans as corrupt and untrustworthy, the Romans still greatly admired their culture—from Homer to Plato, from Pindar to Sophocles—they copied and absorbed it. In his comedy *Mostellaria* (The Haunted House, c. 200 B.C.), Plautus, the comic playwright, has two slaves taunting each other repeatedly about the woeful ways into which their absent master's young son has fallen, ". . . drink day and night, and Greek-it-up like mad." Yet Plautus gives his characters Greek names and they wander anachronistically from the Athenian harbor (Piraeus) through the Roman Forum without lifting an eyebrow. Oriental religion, caught on in Imperial Rome in large part because the Greeks themselves had already succumbed, and spawned their own Greek equivalents like the cult of Dionysius (celebrated in wall murals of the House of the Mysteries in Pompeii). Much of what we see as Roman had its roots in the Hellenic world—even the nearly 1,000 large and small baths that filled every corner of Rome. In a word, Greek was chic.

Many of these various cults[7] tended to fall into two or three universal traditions, with roots dating back into the stone ages. From at least 75,000 B.C. there is evidence of deliberate and ceremonial burial, which suggests some interest in an afterlife and a considerable social consciousness. During the Mesolithic (middle stone age) in Europe, modern humans were fairly sophisticated hunter-gatherers, perhaps even nomadic herders, but the point is they weren't settled down yet and farming. By 15,000 B.C. (e.g., Lascaux, France) Aurignacian people were painting sophisticated murals on cave walls. These murals, echoed by later cave art elsewhere, seem to revolve around the life-giving process of hunting. They seem to have a strong mythic element, probably shamanistic. Shamanism is a religious phenomenon in which the practicioner is able to enter a trance-like or ecstatic state and 'see' supernatural phenomena or visions, which the shaman then relates or interprets to the general population. This is precisely what occurred in Oriental imports to Rome, like the Kybele (Cybele) cultus. This religion (which probably has its archaic roots in the Mesopotamian Kubaba associated with Gilgamesh and his mythology) echoed throughout the Classical world, in the Sibyls. The Sibyls (the word comes from 'Kybele') were seers (shamans) who sat in a subterranean cave and let volcanic gases transport them into ecstasy. They would then either speak or write cryptic sayings whose prophetic content priests or priestesses then interpreted for the worshiper. The two most famous Sibyls were the Oracle at Delphi in Greece, and the Sibyl at Cumae (just north of Naples, not very far south of Rome). The cultus of the Sibyls played a significant role throughout Roman history, from the time of the ancient Etruscan monarchy.

The cultus of *Mithra*, which was particularly popular among soldiers, was imported from archaic (pre-Zoroastrian) Persia and Babylonia. *Mithra* had been a god of the sun as well as of justice, law, and war. The faith may have spread as far east as China. Mithras was generally represented as a handsome youth sitting astride a bull, whose throat he is cutting. The cultus was secretive, and no scriptures survive directly describing its beliefs or practices, but we know it called for loyalty to the emperor. This no doubt fed into the worship of deified emperors. Rituals included baptism in holy water, and eating a sacred meal of bread and wine. Worshipers gathered in a *mithraeum*, which was often underground or in a cave, but could be in any sort of enclosure symbolically taking the place of a cave. Modern researchers have used reliefs found in such places of worship to construct a cosmology. They suggest that since Mithra was a sun god, the rest of the symbology was astrological and refers to ancient Mesopotamian mythology. Whatever the details, it is clear that the bull's blood falls on the earth and begets life. The theme of death and rebirth recurs in just about all of these Oriental mystery cults. Other faiths of this type included the Egyptian-derived cults of Isis, Serapis, Anubis, Osiris, et al.

The theme of death and rebirth figures not only in hunting and gathering cultures, and in animal cults, but also in later farming cultures. Both types probably have their earliest roots in the late Stone Ages. About 7,500 B.C. Mesolithic (middle stone age) hunter-gatherers settled down in communities to become Neolithic (new stone age) farmers. This is when our ancestors discovered an amazing secret of death and rebirth involving the seed. This discovery influenced many of the world's religions for ages to come.

The farmers learned harvest wheat and learn to make bread, which tastes wonderful, and helps you stay alive. It smells great, and seems to have medicinal properties. The greater miracle, however, is this. You save some of the wheat seeds and throw them in the ground. Then you go away and come back a few months later. Miraculously, the dead seeds have come back to life as new wheat. This can only be a divine miracle. It is a sign and a gift from the earth deities which invariably seem to be female, reflecting human motherhood.

It's not all as clean as that, of course. Some people became herders, and of those some led their sheep, goats, cattle, horses, or other animals short distances to better feed and water. Others may have ranged afar; but they had to return periodically for the times of year that they learned were appropriate for planting and harvesting. This became bound up with the mysterious cycles of things moving in the sky. Things that moved as they were supposed to were good, and unusual things (*prodigia*, like comets) must signal disaster (*dis*, bad + *astrum*, star). Understanding these signs required a complex temple priesthood, with lots of secret handshakes and symbols, and that kept everyone in business.

Some of the cults that came into Rome, therefore, like that of Demeter or Ceres, were linked to the life, death, and rebirth cycle of wheat. Not only did all things Greek appeal to the Romans, but the Greeks under Alexander had conquered the eastern Mediterranean world and brought home to Greece a strong wave of Middle Eastern and Egyptian cults. Moreover, they adapted these, Hellenizing them. For example, in Egypt the Greeks picked up the cult of Serapis. Under Ptolemy I Soter, the Egyptian Apis was reintroduced as a new deity with many Greek features (Eg. *Hapi*, 'hidden;' worshiped in the image of a bull; known as Osorapis when deceased and entering the underworld). The Hellenized Serapis was a plum ready for plucking when Rome conquered Greece in the 2nd Century B.C.

Judaism

One outsider group, which fits into no layer, were the Jews. There was a solid and important Jewish subculture in both Rome (particularly Regio XIV, Transtiberim) and in her major cities in North Africa and other points around the Mediterranean. The Jews were a sizeable minority in the Empire. On the one hand, historically they were a thorn in the side, requiring at least two massive military operations to suppress Zealot movements. On the other hand, the large majority of Jews lived cooperative and productive lives within the Roman state. The Jews tended to be urban, and they had sizeable minorities in most major Roman cities. The pragmatic Romans frowned upon the refusal of the monotheistic Jews to pay token worship to the state and the emperor. However, the Jews created for the Romans important trade connections within the Empire and thus became indispensible. The Jews had been around for a long time. In fact, their diaspora around the Mediterranean was did not occur when the Romans were in power, but much earlier, during Alexander the Great's time. The wealthier Jews were not only formidable traders and bankers (which may have come into their culture from the indomitable Phoenicians), but they did something else that fit perfectly into the Roman model of ultimate respectability.

The Roman system of patronage, described here and in other books, involved a concept called *munificentia*, loosely translatable as 'doing good.' This concept involved the notion that wealthy men could show off their good fortune by providing benefits (*munificentia*) to the state and the people. As many as 15% of urban populations in Roman cities around the Mediterranean were Jewish. There were plenty of poor and working class Jews, particularly in Rome in the Transtiberim district (across the Tiber, today's Trastevere). There were, however, also plenty of commercially successful Jews. What the Romans no doubt liked about the Jews was that the Jews were great givers of munificia.

Between them, the Romans and the Jews practically invented the concept of *caritas* (charity). There were really two separate threads here, but they were so compatible that they easily overlapped. On the one hand, the Romans felt that it was a matter of religious necessity for the rich to share with the poor. Thus the wealthy Romans did splendid stuff that everyone liked, like opening soup kitchens for the poor, building theaters and baths and other public venues for entertaining the masses, and maintaining shrines. The Jews originally took care of their own, given the urgent conditions of the Diaspora. Nevertheless, when people were hungry, the Jews didn't have the heart to turn Gentiles away from their soup kitchens and shelters. This no doubt won them some number of converts (though they were not known to proselytize).

Christianity sprang up under the wing of the Jewish communities, since many of the early Christians were simply sectarian Jews.

For the purposes of this book, we define the following terms as follows. Monotheism is the belief in a single, omnipotent god. Dualism and trinitarianism are subjects we don't need to treat here.

Polytheism is the belief in many named gods with complex mythological histories. Polytheistic deities may be anthropomorphic (human-like, as in Zeus, Jupiter, Athena, et al). Polytheistic deities may be zöomorphic (totemic; possessing animal qualities, as in the Egyptian Horus, falcon; Anubis, jackal, et al). Polytheistic deities may be both, as in the case of Serapis, a Roman god of healing, brought across the Mediterranean by Greek and Macedonian conquerors of Egypt—a combination of Osiris (a deity of the annual fertility cycle, with ties to solar movements) and Apis, the bull representing strength and fertility.

Animism is the belief that we live in dual, parallel worlds, one of living people and objects, the other of spirits. In Japanese animism, these generally nameless spirits are kami. In archaic Latin animism, they are *genii*, plural of *genius*. Genii inhabit all things. They are all around us in things as ordinary as a door hinge or a cupboard. We'll learn more about this shortly, comparing early Japanese and Roman religion.

As the Christians diverged from Judaism, and formed their own religious communities (*ecclesiae*, from Gr word for assembly), they saw how successful the Jews were with their charities, and how the Romans looked favorably on those who lavished upon the people. This encouraged the Christians themselves to begin their long tradition of charities.

One thing about the Christians that annoyed many polytheists (and Jews) was their insistent preaching and proselytizing. There was resentment from the start between Christians and Jews. The Jews were trying to maintain their immunity from the required emperor worship, and the Christians seemed to them too unorthodox, too forward, too embarrassing and dangerous. The Christians reciprocated with resentment of their own, sometimes violently, for example in the mob's burning of the Serapeum around 485 A.D.

Jewish, polytheist, and Christian instigators typically roused mobs against one other. The polytheists were resentful at the loss of their preeminence, while the Jews no doubt were resentful at having lost the relative tolerance they had enjoyed under polytheist emperors.

We leave all those tormented souls, as we continue working backward—next, we'll peel away the layer of the imported Greek Olympian gods and goddesses.

Greek Olympian Gods

The Romans conquered Greece in the Second Century B.C. They had now become the owners of a culture so profoundly advanced that it conquered them in turn, much as they had conquered it. The Greeks were no strangers to the Romans. Rome sprang up with a network of magnificent Greek colonies to her south. The Romans had been trading with the Greeks for some time. The two cultures shared the lingering shadow of the Bronze Age in common. The Romans began by plundering Greece, and the plundering continued for centuries. The Romans also learned, admired, and imitated. Conservatives like Cato might be horrified at Greek customs (particularly, Athenian pederasty must have outraged the austere, conservative Romans), but the novelty and sophistication of the more advanced Greek civilization flooded Rome with new ideas.

Greek and Roman deities were not necessarily the same, but their worship in many cases fused over time, and moderns construct tables comparing the names various cultures gave to the same or similar gods. Roman and Greek (and Etruscan) deities often sprang from similar roots in the Bronze Age or even earlier. The collapse of Bronze Age civilization caused turmoil and migrations that spread some of the fundamental Mediterranean beliefs—notably the Oriental mystery cults involving themes of life, death, and rebirth. It has often happened in human history, and certainly in archaic Italy, that a new culture would move in on an older culture, and their religious beliefs would fuse together, leaving tangled threads of both the old and the new.

Mythologians like Sir James Frazer (*The Golden Bough*) and Robert Graves (*The White Goddess*) have pointed out that the Classical deities can also be grouped as sky deities vs. earth deities.

We find a good example in Egyptian religion. Originally, the various animal deities (the jackal, the falcon, the hippo, etc.) were all tribal totems, like those of the Native Americans. When the early pharaos united Egypt, they faced the delicate balance of making everyone happy and placing no god above any other. As a result, the pharaos fostered a complex and lavish network of cults embracing all the ancient deities. In practice, the cult of Amon acquired more power than some others over many centuries.

An alternative answer would have been to simply unite all the tribal fetishes into a single supreme deity, as the Hebrews may have done. In Egypt, one pharao tried this, with disastrous results. Amenhotep IV (pharao 1372–1354 B.C.) renamed himself Ikhnaton ('Aton is Satisfied') and insisted that everyone worship only one god, the sun, personified as Aton. He turned all Egypt on its ear, trying to make them monotheists, but in his fanatical zeal, his reign became one of terror. When he died, he had lost large segments of the empire, and he was widely hated. It's noteworthy that the hatred was not just for the physical, economic, and social harm he inflicted on his people, but because he was seen as harming Egypt at the core of her religious soul. That is a theme the Romans would well understand.

Among the earth goddesses we can put Kybele and Demeter, the *Magna Mater* (Great Mother) and Isis. Then, among the sky gods, we can put most of the Classic Greek pantheon (Zeus, Athena, Hera, et al). The earth deities seem more goddess-oriented, while the sky-gods seem more male-oriented.

Zeus (or *theos*, god) and Iuppiter, Jupiter (*dius* or *deus*, god + *pater*, father) seem similar. When the two enmesh, with Rome's conquest of Greece, Zeus is a more sophisticated Greek deity with a tangled web of mythology, wrapping himself around the simpler, starker father god of a more primitive agricultural people (the Roman *Iuppiter*). In this sense, Zeus seems more like a rich, spoiled playboy, while Jupiter seems more a stern, fearsome father god.

The Greek Ares and the Roman Mars are another case in point. Mars started his career as a Latin agriculture deity in charge of producing good harvests. Early on, he was known variously as Marmar, Marmur, Mamurrus, etc. Meanwhile, among the Greeks, there is an agricultural god named Ares with a similar job description.

The Greek Hera (wife of Zeus) sort of roughly matches up with Jupiter's wife Juno, and Athena finds that the girdle of Minerva fits. Interestingly, as it happens, Diana the man-hating huntress was originally a male deity—Janus, god of gateways and new years (after whom the first month of our year is named—January). The story of Janus/Diana in particular illustrates how these ancient deities morphed as they traveled through time and space.

Once we peel back the layer of Olympian sky gods, with all their interesting stories, we are very close to the source of our answers. We do have one more, thin layer to peel back—Etruscan religion.

Etruscan Deities

The Etruscans were Rome's neighbors north of the Tiber. The beauty and atmosphere of Tuscany are legendary, and one can easily imagine why for a time the marshy, gloomy Tiber delta stayed at the edge of the Etruscan mark. By 750 (the Romans said 753) B.C., the inhabitants of the Palatine Hill formed a community that was to grow into what we call Rome. By this time, the Etruscans had established a considerable confederation of city-states across northern Italy. Soon, they had small towns overlooking the Tiber Valley from the near north, as at Veii (just 26km or 16 miles away). The people living on the Palatine were not Etruscan, but affiliated with a very different group, the Latins, whose main centers were in the Alban Mountains just south of the Tiber. The Latins occupied a number of small towns closer to the southeastern region of what is now Rome, including the town of Tibur. North of there, the Sabine people from the Apennine foothills (and beyond them the Samnites) pressed in close enough to have small settlements on the northern hills (of the later Rome) including the Pincian and even possibly the Capitoline. For a time, the Palatine Latins had the breathing space to establish the core of a culture. Then the Etruscans moved in around 700 and established a monarchy that would last until 509 B.C. We learn more of how Lucumo and Tanaquil established the Tarquin dynasty when we visit the Temple of Semo Sancus, where Tanaquil's personal possessions are kept enshrined.

The Etruscans may have been descended from the Villanovans or come from Lydia in Asia Minor and set up camp all over northern Italy during the dark age following the collapse of Bronze Age civilization. Nobody knows for sure. They did pop up rather suddenly, with a full-blown, very impressive civilization. The Etruscans were unique. For one thing, their language was unlike any other. They had a simple alphabet modeled on the Phoenician, and moderns can read their words, but for the most part they are incomprehensible. Unlike virtually all their neighbors, the Etruscans treated their woman as beloved equals rather than property. Etruscan sexual acrobatics horrified the dour Romans and even shocked the romping Greeks. It was said Etruscan men and women would think nothing of copulating in the village square at high noon if the fancy happened to strike them. The high point of Etruscan civilization, 800–600 B.C., seems like a long, sunny day. From their tombs, moderns learn that the Etruscans enjoyed life to the fullest. Death was initially a continuation of life. They set up their tombs like imitation houses, with everything in them that a person would need— including coils of (stone relief work) rope on the walls, knives, wheels of cheese, goblets of wine, and tables heaped with food. Life was good, so hopefully one could continue living it in death. The standard Etruscan sarcophagus shows a happy man and his wife reclining together, wearing their long robes, he behind her and embracing her protectively and fondly as they smile at the viewer. Their wall art shows them hunting, fishing, almost dancing in the air for joy. Historically, during this period, they have taken over Rome, which is ruled by the Tarquins.

Around 390 B.C., disaster struck as about 300,000 displaced Gauls came pouring over the Alps and laid waste most of Italy. The Gaulish sacks wiped out Etruscan city-states, though some were rebuilt. The Gauls had broken the back of Etruscan power. The Romans came away in better shape than most of their neighbors. By now, the Romans had made themselves the senior member of a small alliance of local city-states called the Latin League. When the Gauls came knocking, the Romans made a deal. The Romans handed over the entire treasury of the Latin League, and in return the Gauls let the Romans step outside their city before sacking it. The other Latins, who had no money to offer, were killed and their cities were burned. Rome emerged from the Gaulish debacle stronger than any of her neighbors, and began her rise to power. The Etruscans, after the Gaulish disaster, began a dreadful decline, whose misery is reflected in their tomb art. One sees the arrival of frightening demons, where previously was happy laughter and flute music. A grim custom takes on momentum, which will have a grisly influence on all of Roman history, the funeral games.

Funeral games were nothing new. The Greeks practiced them, and the custom probably came over from Asia Minor in antiquity. The Greeks, though, forbade the use of weapons. Among the Etruscans, the funeral games began to involve combat. At first, the games had involved more or less friendly sparring. Then it became customary to have condemned criminals fight to the death. This happened in small numbers—nothing on the order of the wholesale butchery of the later Roman arenas. At a decent funeral, maybe four or six contestants would fight to the death, honoring the deceased and

The Etruscan pantheon came to closely resemble that of the Greeks, thus also later that of the Romans. Here are is a brief sampling of some congruent deities, listed in order by Greek, Etruscan, and Roman equivalents:

Zeus, Tinia, Jupiter (father god)

Hera, Uni, Juno (wife of father god)

Athena, Menrva, Minerva (Greek war goddess and protectrix of Athens matches up with Italian goddess of crafts and trade guilds).

Apollo, Aplu, Phoebus Apollo (Greek god of poetry and healing, worshipped by Sibyl at Cumae, took on many aspects across the Roman empire, especially including Phoebus as sun god; Romanized Celtic Apollo Cunomaglus, Hound Lord, for hunting, etc.).

Artemis, Aritimi, (Diana?) (daughter of Zeus and Leto; twin sister of Apollo; healing, but also brings disease; chaste; hunting but protective of animals; wrathful when provoked; the moon as Greek Selene, etc.)

Aphrodite, Turan, Venus (consort of Mars, goddess of fertility; Greek goddess of love, beauty, and sexual rapture; cognate of ancient Mesopotamian Ishtar and Syro-Palestinian Ashtart. Born when Uranus, father of the gods, castrated by his son Cronus or Chronos. Severed genitals thrown in to the ocean, which began to boil up and foam, and from the *aphros*, sea foam, rose Aphrodite. Married off by Zeus to Hephaestos, Vulcan, so that her beauty should not stir envy among the Olympians).

Dionysius, Fuflun, Bacchus (god of vegation, exuberance, gaity)

Other Etruscan deities were Artume (goddess of night and death, possible cognate with Artemis); Adunis (Adonis) . . . the list goes on, and the point is that the Olympian gods shared commonalities across the Italian and Balkan Peninsulas. However, the Romans were reluctant to fully adopt them, for reasons we shall see.

It remains to be said about the Etruscans that they were fatalistic. As long as things were going well, they were happy and dancing. As things began to go badly for them, particularly in the light of the Gaulish invasions, they began looking inward, as D.H. Lawrence said, or one might say, they were looking upward and outward. They were great diviners, and made a science of understanding portents in such things as the liver of a sacrificed animal, the flight of birds across the sky, or the path of a comet. They lived in a kind of mechanistic universe, a magical windup box, in which they were trapped and had no control, but with the proper magic they could 'see' the future; and they found it looking increasingly bleak.

entertaining the survivors. The Etruscans, despite their reputation for casual and high living, were among the most deeply religious people of their time. In time, the Romans simply swallowed the Etruscans up. We know that centuries later, the Emperor Claudius had an Etruscan wife. We know that the Romans clung to their Etruscan soothsayers and diviners. We know they honored the Etruscans by negation as much as affirmation. For example, after they expelled the Etruscan monarchs, the Romans kept the fasces (bundle of sticks symbolizing the unbreakable power of people when united) but tossed out the double-headed ax symbolizing the (Etruscan) king's absolute power over life and death.

Rome's Animist Roots

Now we come to the real thing, the Roman soul. This fundament, this rock-bottom layer, is totally different from all others. It is the animist layer, often difficult for modern monotheists (Christians, Jews, Moslems) to understand. Monotheists, who tend to live in a world of absolutes, have enough trouble understanding polytheism (more than one god, as in Hinduism). Significant modern cultures follow the third path, animism, in many parts of Africa, Asia, and South America. Particularly compelling is the example of Japanese Shinto, which can help us better understand the ancient Romans. We'll see that not only were the archaic Romans quite different from their polytheistic descendants, but, more importantly, the culture of animist Rome decisively defined the polytheism of the future, indeed the entire Roman culture, for many centuries to come. When the Romans persecuted the Christians, it was because they felt threatened at their animist roots (which included the key issue of emperor worship). They saw Christianity not so much as a philosophically abstract difference of opinion, but as a very real life and death threat to their way of life, to their very survival as a state and a people. From their perspective, Christians were a bunch of immoral atheists.

Japan's Animist Roots

As with Rome, we must peel back layers of history to get to the real thing. We must peel back the layers of state and Buddhism, which came across from China along with a smattering of Confucianism and Taoism.

One should not confuse Shinto and Buddhism. They exist side by side, but they remain distinct. Eighth Century Japanese rulers gave the name Shinto to the native religion (of the earlier Yayoi Japanese culture) in creating a state religion in which the emperor could be a living god. *Shin tao* (*shin*, gods + *tao*, way) is a Chinese term for 'The way of the gods.' Shinto is a more formal expression of a nameless, archaic Japanese native animism. What we need to peel back are the layers added on after the 8th Century. Successive governments of Japan, over many centuries, constructed a state religion out of Shinto. This state connection was severed in 1946, when Emperor Hirohito was forced to announce to his people that he was not a living god.

Buddhism, an offshoot of Vedic culture in India around 500 B.C., is in itself a very tolerant faith. Buddha, while seeking a path of enlightenment, neither discouraged nor encouraged the enormous pantheon of his Hindu ancestors. There is no creator god in Buddhism (as there is in Hinduism), but an endless cycle of birth and rebirth that can only be broken by achieving spiritual freedom through four great insights, leading to eight good ways to live, covering every aspect of life. One strives for transcendance through a combination of enlightened thinking and moral action. Buddhism is by far the dominant faith of Japan besides Shinto. The vast majority of Japanese practice both faiths.

Confucius (Latinized version of Kongfuzi or K'ung fu-tzu) was a contemporary of Buddha, but in China. Confucius taught a moral way of life based on benevolence, loyalty, respect, and reciprocity. Confucius created a religion that deeply affected Chinese culture. He defined five important senior-junior relationships (father-son, husband-wife, elder brother-younger brother, friend-friend). In either relationship, the senior partner must govern wisely and morally, while the junior partner must offer loyalty and respect. He taught that all people fall under the rule of Heaven, which is the principal source of order and laws under a Lord-on-High (Shangdi or Shang-ti) who gives to the human emperor a heavenly mandate to rule. Confucianism requires morality and proper relationships, plus proper sacrificing.

Having peeled back the layers of later religiosity, we come to a simple, rural animist faith based on *kami* (spirits). Freed of some eleven centuries of state and imperial burdens, modern 'Shrine' Shinto (as opposed to the defunct State Shinto) has begun to revert to its archaic roots, which in this book we'll call *kami-do*, way of the *kami* or spirits (very similar to Roman *numina*). Another term is *kannagara*, 'the way of the kami.' One refers to the archaic Roman animism as numenism (singular *numen*, plural *numina*, neuter gender; from *nuo, nutare*, to nod or assent—which implies that the gods communicate with humans, not in scriptures or words, but in gestures optimistically taken to be positive).

We don't expect an exact match between the two animisms (kami-do and numenism), but the similarities are both startling and useful in our effort to understand the archaic Romans; likewise, the ancient Roman numenism may help some to understand kami-do or Shinto a bit better.

However it was later made to serve the emperors and military rulers, kami-do is fundamentally a tolerant faith. Followers of kami-do easily accepted Buddha as another kami, or spirit. At the same time, kami-do is a very powerful force at the heart of Japanese culture.

Understanding Animism

Believers in kami (or *numina*, as the Romans called these spirits, from a word for 'nodding') are every bit as sincere, passionate, and devout as the most devout monotheist or polytheist. The two animisms were not necessarily all gloom and doom. Nature and the nameless deities were capricious, and a lot could go wrong— but precisely because of the emphasis on propitiation, if one did the right rituals in the right way at the right times, one was likely to avoid bad luck or evil fate.

The world of the Palatine Romans and of the Yayoi Japanese was a frightening and compelling one, and their response to it understandable. The archaic Romans, like the archaic Japanese, lived in a geothermally active and unpredictable world. What is the dominant symbol of Japan? Mount Fuji, a volcano sitting astride Tokyo, in a landscape riddled with earthquakes and vulcanism. One of the most enduring images of Rome is of nearby Pompeii being tragi-

Good story telling, whether by grandma or the court poet, plays a heavy role also. In Roman folkways the stories of state numenism tended to have a grim cast, emphasizing filial virtues, sobriety, patriotism, austerity, and the like. In Japanese kami-do, which stayed free of state definition until the 7th–9th Century A.D., tales like the following offer a delightful moment. The king was riding on his horse past a certain house, when a cat appeared on the porch and waved to him. The king, curious at this strange event, got off his horse and approached the cat to investigate. Just then, lightning struck the horse and killed it. Ever since, cats are honored in Japanese lore as protectors and bringers of good luck. That's why, when you go to your local Japanese restaurant, you are likely to see a happily grinning ceramic cat waving to you on the counter, usually with paper money or coins attached. With any luck, lightning won't strike your car while you wait for your sushi.

cally buried in ash from Mount Vesuvius. Right outside Rome, within view of the Vatican, are volcanic mountains. In fact, the Pope's summer retreat is at Lake Albano, whose water fills the cone of an inactive volcano. In their uncertain world, the earliest Latins huddled on their low hills under a dark and blustery sky. Though generally sunny and mild, the climate was colder and wetter than in later centuries, and Roman literature is replete with tales of lightning strikes and other supernatural portents. The corridors hewn into the rock under the Temple of Capitoline Jupiter were filled with bits of statuary and friezes that had been smashed by lightning and fell to the ground as terrible portents. Earthquakes shook the ground and steam rose from fissures. Birds dropped dead from the sky over gloomy Lake Avornus (Gr *aornis*, without birds) because (moderns understand, ancients didn't) of gas emitted from underground fissures; nearby lay the entrance to the underworld (*Avernus*), crossed in the epic poems of both Virgil (Chapter 6 of *The Aeneid*) and Dante (entering the *Inferno*). A bit further south at the Fields of Fire (Phlegraean Fields) near Naples, Pliny writes that one time 600 sheep keeled over dead in their meadows, overcome by poison gas. Nearby, at Cumae, the most famous Sibyl in Italy sat in her cave, swooning over dreadful revelations coming up in the hot breath of the underworld, and wrote down the future history of Rome (kept in the Temple of Capitoline Jupiter, and destroyed 83 B.C. by, you guessed it, lightning strikes that burned down the entire temple). The southern Italian landscape contains some of the world's biggest and most violent volcanoes, from Vesuvius to Stromboli and Aetna. These exploded capriciously and filled a sunny Mediterranean sky with violent black clouds laced with lightning and raining death for miles around. In fact, the earlier Bronze Age civilization in the eastern Mediterranean had been toppled by the explosion of Thera. The immediate area that would become Rome was a marshy swamp riddled with malaria and cholera. The Romans took their world on its terms, propitiating the forces that affected their lives, their families, and their state (e.g., Mars or Marmur, god of agriculture; Robigo, goddess who prevented blight; Febris, goddess who averts fever; Cholera, Fever). Moderns have, in fact, inherited a month named after Febris.

Animism permeates every minute the believer lives, everywhere he or she goes, everything he or she does. An important difference between gods and kami is that kami generally are local to some place, which they cannot leave, or they are specific to some thing. They aren't necessarily like guardian angels in monotheism, because kami can be either good or evil, or ambivalent. Kami are often capricious, like nature, hence they require constant propitiation and appeasement.

Few named deities exist with much of a theology or mythology surrounding them. Countless spirits exist, most nameless. Most of the spirits (kami, numina) are local deities associated with a stream, a boulder, a mountain, a grove of trees. By a twist, the central deity in kami-do is that of a sun goddess named Amaterasu, who created all. The archaic Romans had a sort of dark, foreboding fulminator (lightning-thrower) in Jupiter, but not yet the complicated Greek tales of skirt-chasing and marital infidelity—such things were inconceivable to the Puritanical Romans.

Animism has no founding figure (no Jesus, no Buddha), no written scriptures as such (no Bible, no Koran), no body of religious laws (no Canon Law, no Talmud), and no centralized authority (no Archbishop of Canterbury, no Pope).

Like the Yayoi Japanese, the Palatine Latins were animists. They had no scripture, no abstract moral code as we think of it. That's not the same as saying they didn't know right from wrong—quite the contrary.

Archaic Roman Animism

Numenism—buried in a stew of polytheism, yet dictating their flavorings by its robustness—offered the Romans great strength over time. Their numinism served them well because of its inextricable linkage with seasonal ritual and custom, involving core concerns like birth, death, child-bearing, honor, warfare, leadership, and more. It gave Rome a uniquely Roman religion that defined her culture apart from all others.

Lares (singular *lar*) were generally a pretty spooky bunch. They came in two varieties—public and household. Public lares were associated with cemeteries, and with the ghosts *(manes)* of the dead. Early Roman animists always revered their ancestors, often deifying them as *lares*. Luckily, only worthy ancestors could become lares and dwell in one's house. The public lares were of two sorts. The *lares praestites* (sort of meaning 'standing first among lares') who protected the entire city. Of lesser rank, but still very powerful, were the *lares compitales* (literally, 'crossroads lares' after *compita*, crossroads).

The domestic (*domus*, 'house') lares were ancestral ghosts, who lived in the home. Often it was only one such ghost, or it might be several. Domestic lares even had a leader, the *lars familiaris*, or

Remarkably, despite centuries of Christianity, some worship of the lares survives in modern Italian 'old religion' *(Vecchia)* or witchcraft *(stregheria)*, in the form of clan spirits called *lare*. These lare are associated with ancestor veneration, and are honored with shrines set up in the eastern side of the house. They receive offerings at the family shrine on important family milestones like births, weddings, and deaths. Interestingly, remembering the ancient *lares compitales*, streghe claim to be able to see spirits of the dead passing at night at crossroads.

founder of the family. In the Roman scale of things, 'worthy' might mean some dour old soul who had executed his own son for disobedience, or buried his daughter alive for infidelity, so 'worthy' is a relative term, not necessarily implying a sense of comfort to moderns. Every home worth its salt (to use the Roman expression) had a family altar called the *lararium*. Walking into a Roman home, one might expect to find a wooden closet resembling a coat vestibule. Chances were, it had two sets of doors. If the lower section contained dishes and other household items, opening the upper doors would reveal the lararium or household shrine. This shrine received regular offerings, including at all family meals. On festive occasions it might be open, and decorated with garlands of flowers, so that the ancestral ghosts could participate in the festivities.

The lares were a subset of a larger set of numina called the penates. As usual in animist societies, distinctions are often blurred. A family might have one or more lares, but the very word penates has no singular. However, it is derived from *penus*, 'kitchen cupboard.' Thus, in the simplest sense, the penates were kitchen gremlins. The hearth and the table were sacred to them. At every meal, the *paterfamilias* (head of the family) would first throw an offering (a crust of bread, a slip of wine) into the fire, before the family ate. A perpetual fire stayed burning in hearth to honor the penates, and on the table stood a salt cellar and fruits. As with the lares, the state itself had public penates. Aeneas was believed to have brought from Troy the eternal flame of Hestia, Greek for Vesta. Vesta was the Roman goddess of the household hearth, and intimately tied up with the penates of every home. The family meal was, in a real sense, a communal act of worship involving Vesta and the penates (including the lar or lares). Every home was, in effect, a temple of Vesta (all tied together supernaturally by the religious state). On the state level, there stood since earliest times in the Forum the all-important Temple of Vesta. No statue of Vesta was permitted in this temple, in an animistic refutation of the anthropomorphic deities imported from outside the nation. The Greeks might have their philandering Zeus, but the Romans would keep closest to their heart and hearth the chaste nuns of Vesta. Instead of a statue, an eternal flame symbolized Vesta's presence in the temple. Her priestesses were virgins selected in childhood, and dedicated through their fruitful years to remain in the temple and live chaste, pure lives. Anyone who offended a Vestal Virgin was severely punished, and the rare Vestal who strayed from her vows was buried alive or immured; in either case, lengthy purification rituals had to be performed on an emergency basis to prevent harm to the people, the city, and the state (which were all one). The Vestals observed many rituals and solemn days sacred to their goddess, including the Vestalia on June 9. On that day, only women were allowed to the temple, and they came barefoot from far and wide. Near the Temple of Vesta stands a Temple of the *penates publici*, the public or state penates.

Moderns have surviving statues of ancient Roman men, particularly from the Republic, wearing their finest togas, and holding images of their ancestors. Before photography in modern times, it

Like most peoples, the inhabitants of ancient Italy offered human sacrifice at some point. Dr. Amanda Claridge reports the find of a human sacrifice, not far from the center of the Roman Forum at the northwestern end. Modern archeologists doing depth soundings have discovered, buried deep within the soil that has accreted over thousands of years, the bodies of a man, woman, and child who were bound together and evidently purposely drowned during some dark time in distant antiquity. The Romans, who came later, are not generally known for human sacrifices (unless one considers the millions of victims of the arenas, circuses, and naumachia). However, the Romans were not above sacrificing humans when the state was in sufficient danger. Historians mention that, in 216 B.C. during the Punic Wars, the Romans buried two Greeks and two Gauls alive in the Forum; such vaults have been unearthed in modern times, unless these are chambers in which the occasional errant Vestal was entombed alive with her little lamp and a jug of water. Food for discussion: Was the burning alive of alleged witches and heretics by Christians a form of human sacrifice? Were the killings of women and children at the Salem, Massachusetts Colony human sacrifices to a grisly deity? Is the death penalty, surrounded as it is with state pieties, a form of human sacrifice?

was customary to pour a death mask—usually of wax or plaster—and this custom came from the Romans. It was the best way they had of preserving a snapshot of the person—perhaps in the sense that the recently deceased had one foot in the world of the living, and the other foot already in the spirit world (a very primitive afterlife). The resting expression of the peacefully departed suggests a sort of transfiguration. Speaking of same, another concept associated with deification is *apotheosis* (*apo*, 'from' + *theos*, 'god'). There is a splendid sculpture in the Forum, showing the apotheosis of Rome. What this means, in modern words, is that Rome (the city, the culture, the concept) at some point becomes deified, becomes a goddess (names of cities are feminine, whereas rivers, for example, are masculine). The sculpture, showing a beautiful woman in robes, rising up with outspread wings like those of an angel, captures the transcendant moment as the newly deified Roma, personification of the city, is accepted into a kind of Olympian 'up there,' perhaps on Olympus. Modern Christians, regarding such an apotheosis, whether it be of Roma, or the male Tiber, immediately think of angels or similar supernatural beings whose images have long been associated with wings. It is most likely that the picturing of angels (Gr *angelos*, messenger) as winged creatures comes from this prac-

A good illustration of this is in how the archaic Romans (Palatine-Capitoline Latins) handled the abode of their chief (polytheist) god, Jupiter, on the Capitoline without disturbing the preexisting spirits of the site. The Temple of *Iuppiter Capitolinus D.O.M.* (*Deus Optimus et Maximus*, Bestand Greatest God) was the most important and powerful center of their religion and state (which were one and the same, as in the later Shinto Japan). The Capitoline Temple was also called that of the so-called Capitoline Triad (Jupiter with his companion goddesses Juno and Minerva). These were housed in the largest and oldest Roman structure on the Capitoline Hill. As was common throughout Roman history, Etruscan diviners helped lay out the grounds and the structure. The Romans built the temple in the antique Etruscan style (a long, rectangular, open portico with columns overlooking steps on all accessible outside edges, and deep within, a recessed niche with side walls, or *cella*—a kind of apartment for each deity to dwell in. Archeologists have found evidence of worship on this site at least as far back as the Bronze Age. The Capitoline Hill was known to be inhabited by a considerable number of spirits or numina in bewildering profusion (genii, lares, penates, etc). When the Romans founded their temple, they could not simply pave over or displace these deities and so, as usual, they consulted the Etruscans. After much speculation (in other words, 'looking' or 'seeing') the Etruscans informed them which deities could be displaced and which couldn't. The archaic Romans were very scrupulous in their dealings with local deities. After all, most animist deities are local to a specific place. To displace a numen (or an unknown number of numina) from a hill, or a grove of trees, or cave, or a lake, could bring disaster on the state/people/nation (which were all one). A displaced numen, even a nice one, could become a fearsome, wandering, bloodthirsty demon—which was the growing theme of the declining Etruscans. When all the auguries were in, the Romans built this great Etruscan-style temple that would become a center point of their state—the largest building of its type ever built—so that it carefully incorporated the old deities into the temple complex. One was a tiny temple (maybe 5m or 15 feet square) for Feretrius or Iuppiter Feretrius, said to be the oldest in Rome. The origin of Feretrius is unclear, though he is associated with an oak tree, and he may have blessed weapons or contracts (the Romans brought spoils of victory to this temple in archaic times, as in 428 B.C. when A. Cornelius Cossus killed Lar Tolumnius, King of Veii, in battle. The name Iuppiter Feretrius is an attributive, meaning in this case that Jupiter has been aligned with an earlier local deity. Also nearby was a tiny but ancient temple of Ops (goddess of plenty). Ops probably was originally associated with harvests, but became identified with Saturn and Cronus, and thus with Cronus' consort Rhea. Festivals for Ops were held twice yearly—the Opsiconsivia on 25 August, and the Opalia on 19 December. Another tiny temple in the shadow of the Capitoline Triad was that of Fides (Faith, goddess of good faith, oaths, verbal contracts). Caesar kept the entire state treasury here, so dedicated was he to her reliability. The temple was actually in or very near the Temple of Iuppiter D.O.M., close to the cella of Jupiter.

tice. In a like manner, the picturing of saints (or Byzantine emperors) with halos (Gr *hal_s*, light) stems primarily from the cult of Sol Invictus (the Unconquered Sun), while a soft light background is more precisely known as a *nimbus* (cloud). Wings, halos, nimbi, all amount to ancient special effects to convey a message of sanctity.

Roman animism and polytheism remain distinct from one another, yet share generously overlapping borders. The Roman emperors, especially Hadrian, offered extreme religious toleration in exchange for fundamental respect of Rome (deified as Roma) and the Emperor (we'll discuss his deification in more detail shortly). The Greek polytheistic deities found a place within the sacred Pomerium, but the so-called Oriental and mystery religions generally did not. An exception might be the temples of Isis and Serapis, who gave their name to a district of Rome (Regio III), but their opulent temples sat at the edge of the Pomerium on the Esquiline slope beyond the *thermae* of Trajan and Titus. There were successive shrines on the Capitoline to Isis Capitolina (at several points, 28 B.C. under Augustus and 9 B.C. under Tiberius, destroyed by order of the Senate; and restored by the likes of Nero, Caligula, and Caracalla) but the key here is how well the associative (by location, Capitolina; or by association with some truly Roman deity) would pair a foreign deity with a Roman one. In time, the resistance to the powerful Isis lessened, and she was paired with various favored Roman goddesses. Isis was, among other things, a patroness of sailors. Deep in the Roman breast, in any case, the heartbeat was that of animism.

Comparing Numenism & Kami-do

One should in no way imply that there was ever any direct contact between archaic Palatine Latins and Yayoi Japanese. That makes it all the more interesting to compare the two, because the separate development of such startlingly similar impulses does imply their universality. We have already seen there is no scripture, no founder, no abstract moral code, and no centralized priesthood in the modern sense (like a Pope or an Archbishop of Canterbury).

The emphasis in animism is on ritual. The world can be a scary place, filled with capricious spirits, who must be kept appeased at

We can see hints of how religion defined every moment of private and public life, in the echoes that survive into our modern world. The days of the week are haphazardly named after ancient deities in both the Germanic and Romance languages: Sunday is the day of the Sun (Eng. *Sunday*, L. dies solis, 'day of the sun,' renamed *dies Dominica*, 'day of God' in Christian times; Monday is the day of the Moon (Fr. *Lundi*, It. *Lunedi*, from L. *Luna*); Tuesday is the day of Tiw, god of war (Fr. Mardi, Sp. *Martes*, from L. Mars); Wednesday is the day of wild-hunting Wotan (but in France and Spain, the day of messenger and healer Mercury, hence Fr. *Mercredi*, It. *mercoledi*); Thursday is the day of the thunder god Thor (Fr *jeudi*, It *giovedi*, Sp *jueves*, from L *Jovis* or *Jupiter*); Friday is the day of love goddess Freya (Fr *vendredi*, It *venerdi*, Sp *viernes*, from L Venus); Saturday is the day of Saturn (father of Jupiter, Gr *Chronos*).

In English, the months are January (from Janus, two-faced god of doorways and changing seasons, who had a young face in front and an old face in back, from which comes the modern custom of portraying the new year as a baby and the old year as an old man; he also did a strange switch by morphing in to the beautiful young huntress Diana); February is the month of Februaria, purgation; March is the month of the war god Mars; April is the month of *aperio*, 'opening' or 'appearance' or even 'coming,' as in *ad-per-ire*; May possibly comes from Maiesta, 'majesty,' Vulcan's wife and the loveliest of the seven sisters of the Pleiades; June may come from Juno, wife of Jupiter; July is named after Julius Caesar; August is named after Augustus (he's the one who made up this iteration of the calendar); while September, October, November, and December, are simply the ordinal numbers of the original Roman calendar (seventh month, eighth month, ninth month, and tenth month respectively).

all times. Proper performance with diligent attention to detail keeps the *numina* or *kami* happy. Rituals are performed at shrines, both in kami-do and in numenism. Spirits are local. The *numina* or *kami* are specific to streams, hills, groves, boulders, and similar natural phenomena; and to objects, particularly ancient ones that may be haunted by ancestral spirits. Specific types of numina are the lars or lares, like those of crossroads *(lares compitales)*. Even in modern Italian witchcraft, crossroads have special attributes; for example, at certain phases of the moon, initiates claim they can see the spirits of the dead at crossroads. Archaic Latin religion has special crossroads rituals.

Also of great importance are boundary markers. Boundaries are not just physical, but may represent spiritual borders. The city is enclosed not only within protective walls, but also within a spiritual boundary the Latins called the *Pomerium*. Romulus laid out the Pomerium of Rome by using a plow to lay down a furrow, in a precise manner according to auguries he received. When the Servian Wall went up, as a rule a certain amount of space behind the wall was left empty (the *agger*) for defensive purposes, but it also had spiritual implications.

Spiritual boundaries are critical in both numenism and kami-do. There is in fact a kind of ritual or spiritual geometry or geography involving boundaries and doorways. Consider the famous raked gravel-gardens of Japanese temples. These are spiritual surfaces on which the spirits inhabiting the temple walk. In kami-do and Shinto, the famed and elegant *torii* gates adorn every major shrine. These are spiritual doorways between our world and that of the kami. Also, one may see a boulder or other object with a heavy braided rope around it, with a knot tied like a belt. That is a spiritual boundary marker between the ordinary world and the spiritual world in which the object's kami lives. A locality or object may have an unknown number of kami or numina. For that reason, prayers Romans addressed to numina were often very carefully conditional, as in "Spirit, or spirits, known and unknown, who inhabit this place, we respectfully ask you . . ." The idea is to be respectful and not to insult the numina by our ignorance of their names and number. For example, the *Lacus Camenae* or Lake of the Camenae (a grassy or marshy area along the Via Nova, near the southeast end of the Circus Maximus, that had pure spring water) was said to be inhabited by an unnumbered and unnamed flock of water nymphs or fountain deities (later identified with the Muses of Poetry, or Camenae, from *carmen*, 'song,' from *cano*, 'sing'). They had a sacred grove, and a neighborhood, and a well-source named after them. There is a practical reason for this. The early Romans relied on the fresh, sweet spring water that is plentiful around Rome. Even after the arrival of great aqueducts, the Romans held in great esteem the healing qualities attributed to sacred springs like those of the Camenae[8].

Speaking of doorways: on the Palatine was a very ancient shrine called the *mundus*. Its key feature was a kind of manhole cover that the priests ceremonially removed three times a year on special feast days, so that the spirits of the underworld could come out and roam about. Why? It kept them happy. And some were probably the ancestors of living people. The reason why Augustus moved his home to the Palatine Hill was to associate himself with Roman antiquity. In establishing his dynasty and the empire, he did all he could to play upon Rome's past. He tried to portray himself as the Romulus or founder of a new Rome. He also commissioned the poet Virgil to write his epic *The Aeneid*, in which he connects Augustus' ancestors with the wise warrior Aeneas, who fled from burning Troy with his family and (allegedly) landed in the Alban Hills after an Odyssey-like odyssey around the Med.

Crossroads are very important. Boundary markers each have their specific local genii; at some early point, there evolves the named god Terminus as the official state personification of all boundary markers, with his own marker in the Temple of Capitoline Jupiter. The rural boundary stone genii (Termini) have their own annual rituals, the Terminalia, celebrated February 23. Roman society is property-oriented, with free enterprise playing a key role—so, despite the emphasis on serving the community and the state, the

As god of doorways and passages, Janus had a key shrine in the Roman Forum, which consisted of an arched, east-west passageway. The doors at either end were closed in times of peace, but open in times of war. Like the Japanese torii, this was a spiritual doorway. When Rome officially went to war, the gates were opened in solemn ceremonies; in times of peace, the gates were closed with thankful ceremonies. Janus was also honored during the *Portunalia* on 17 August, which honored the god of the river port (Portunus, whose name combines the concepts of 'door or gate' and 'Neptune.' He had a very ancient temple in the Forum Boarium).

delineation of property boundaries helps define the *pater familias* and the hierarchy of both house and state. The father of the family is the ruler and chief priest in the home, while the emperor is the father of the nation, ruler of the state, and chief priest to boot.

The animist year consists of a chain of feasts and rituals observed at the shrines and temples. Many are agricultural, like the worship of an earth goddess named Tellus, who is honored at both the *Paganalia* (*pagus*, countryside) in January and the *Fordicidia* (*fordi-*, referring to a pregnant cow + *cidia*, killing) in April. The latter promoted the fertility of cattle; the unborn calves were burned and the ashes sprinkled the following week during the *Parilia* or *Palilia*, a ritual for purifying sheep and shepherds, and reflecting the Palatine origins of Rome. The god Pales' name may be onomatopoeic, or derived from the sound sheep make: balare, to bleat. These are just a few examples; there are many more festivals with interesting origins in the archaic agricultural and herding culture and animism of the Palatine Latins.

The *lares compitales* (lares of the crossroads) receive honors during the Compitalia in January, right about the time of the new year (dedicated to Janus, god of doorways and gates, and also of beginnings).

These were more serious gods than the *penates*, or cupboard gods (from *penus*, cupboard), whose mischief was legendary around the kitchen. The world was filled with spirits or *numina*, and every place has its genius or *genius loci*. The term *genius* itself comes from the same root as *gens* ('tribe') and means 'begetter' (modern 'genetics').

Kami-do and numenism have other similarities. We noted the straw dolls used in modern Shinto rites, and these remind one of straw dolls woven from the wheat harvest, and thrown into the Tiber by Vestal Virgins. One can speculate about the meaning of these practices, lost in the mists of time, but it's probably safe to guess they have some connection with fertility prayers. In Japan, State Shinto absorbed the native animist (kami-do) religion along with Buddhist, Confucian, and other foreign influences. In archaic Rome, the official state polytheism absorbed the numenist roots of the Palatine Latins, yet that animism defined the polytheism as much as the other way around. One could argue that those very early deities, that are anthropomorphic in little more than name (perhaps 'personification' would be a better term than 'god of' or 'goddess of') and do not evolve complicated mythologies, are as much in the animist world as in the polytheist world.

Many of these are little more than named animist spirits, and most are quite charming. That includes, for example, such person-ifications as Anna Perenna (personification of the year; female); Cardea (of door hinges; f.); Forculus (doors; m.); Febris (fever; f.); Juturna (springs; f); Laverna (thieves and impostors; f); Picus (woodpecker owned by Mars; m); Tempestas (weather; f); Tellus (earth goddess); Tiberinus (Tiber; m); Vallonia (valleys; f).

It includes a large group of archaic agricultural and rural deities, covering every aspect of agriculture. These include Marmur (later the war god Mars); Collatina (personification of hills; f.); Consus (of the granary; m.); Convector (binding sheaves of wheat; m.); Fornax (prevents grain from burning in grain ovens; f.); Imporcitor (harrowing or breaking up hard earth in a field; m.); Insitor (sow-ing, m.); Messor (reaping; m); Nodutus (knots and joints of the stems of grain plants; m); Obarator (manure spreading atop fields; m); Sterculinus (general manure spreading; m); Occator or Sarritor (hoeing; m); Pales (shepherds and sheep; m or f); Patelana (husks of corn as they are open to let the ears emerge; f); Volutina (husks of corn when they are folded over the ears); Pomona (fruit; f; wife of Vertumnus, god of orchards and fruit and of the changing sea-sons); Promitor (distribution of the harvest; m); Reparator or Re-darator (second plowing; m); Robigo (f) or Robigus (m) (prevents crop mold, mildew, and grain rust; m); Rusina (fields and farm-land; f); Segetia (grain crops ripening above ground; f); Seia (sown seed; f); Silvanus (woods and farmland; m); Spiniensis (digging out thorn bushes, *spina* being a thorn; f); Subruncinator (weeding; m); Tutilina (harvested and stored grain; f); Vervactor (first plowing of fallow land; m); and so on.

Personifications also included abstract ideas: Concordia (peace, f.); Bellona (war, f.); Carna (health, f.); Fides (faith and contracts); Honos (Honor, f.); Juventas (Youth, f.); Mens (mind or good think-ing; f); Virtus (moral excellence; m).

One of the gods of special interest is Terminus, official state god of boundary markers with his own boundary stone in the Temple of Jupiter D.O.M. on the Capitoline. There were as many Termini as there were boundary markers in the Latin region. Like many of the deities mentioned here, Terminus had his own festival of special rituals and celebrations (the Terminalia, 23 February) and his own temple.

Another god of special interest is Portunus, who started out as a god of gates and doors and also came to be the god of the river port. His special symbol is the key. He has an ancient and famous temple in the city harbor markets.

Yet another such deity is Venus, originally an Italian goddess of fertility in fruits and flowers, who acquired many attributes (for example, *Venus Cloacina*, or Venus of the City Sewer, and *Venus Veticordia*, Changer of Hearts).

Personifications could include simple local or Italian variants of the mother or earth goddesses (Dea Nutrix or Nourishing Goddess; Bona Dea or Good Goddess; Rumina, goddess protecting mothers suckling their babies; et al), which would later be enmeshed in complex deific mythologies brought in with the Oriental cults of late Republican times, and more so in Imperial times. Many personifications and deities are difficult to peg into a single category, because the lines evolved over time in an often blurry fashion.

A good example of personification leading to deification in our scheme is that of Lara. Her name is also Mania (not necessarily from the Greek 'madness,' but from *manes*, Latin for departed soul. Manes collectively represent (there is no singular) the numen (soul or spirit) of the deceased, while a *lar* is more of a tutelary (guardian) spirit. Lara is the mother of the lares. She also talked too much, and Jupiter cut her tongue out, after which she is known also as Muta and has a shrine near the Lake of Camenae near the Porta Capena. With this nomenclature and mythological baggage, we may see her as one of innumerable animist water spirits (nymphs) who gets a name (is personified as Lara or Mania, mother of lares or manes) and then achieves a place in the polytheistic pantheon in which Jupiter lives (not so much the stern, distant sky god of the Palatine Latins, but more the capricious Zeus).

Kami-do likewise has myriad nameless spirits or kami, but also personified kami, and some deities enshrined in ancient folk-tales of religious import—most notably, Amaterasu, sun goddess and creator.

In the end, the numenism of the Palatine Latins would constitute the real core of the later state polytheism of both the Republic and the Empire. Puzzled moderns ask "How could they actually believe in deities like Zeus or Hera, which may seem rather shallow and silly from a modern viewpoint?" The answer is complex (because the ancient religions were complex) but fundamentally, personifications and deities were merely surface manifestations of much deeper ideas. It was the animist underpinnings that held the state together, assured victory in war, assured health and good harvests in peace, and brought ships safely across dangerous seas. To a modern person, atheism means nonbelief in supernatural beings. When the Romans went through periodic pogroms driven by fear and opportunism, they persecuted Christians whom they called them atheist. This term also meant something a bit different than in the modern sense. It meant someone who disregards the complex traditional rituals and propitiations that guarantee the survival of the state. It is someone who refuses to participate in emperor worship which is an essential part of the state religion—and is therefore an enemy of the state, of the people, of the emperor, and so forth.

Why deify emperors?

Moderns will need to absorb this explanation in steps. In the Jewish, Christian, and Muslim traditions, the commandment "Thou shalt not place strange gods beside me" is a chilling admonition against deifying cows, spear-throwing giants, or for that matter emperors.

Even the worst of emperors was a prisoner of procedure, and knew it. He owed his office to a complex of traditions, and those like Nero and Caligula who played havoc with procedure tended to have very short reigns. Even so, for example, Nero and Caligula built some of the finest buildings in Rome; well, there was a very fine civil service and engineering department doing the heavy lifting, but the emperor got to add his two sesterces.

When the emperors built great structures, it wasn't just with the sense of helping people or for that matter showing off. Those, and the idea of leaving a legacy, were all motivators, but there was something more fundamental. Whether it was a temple, or a bread kitchen for the poor, or a month of circuses in the spirit of *munificentia*, the emperors were not just showing off or being egotistical—they were performing an ancient religious or priestly role in providing for the city's survival and growth. Dedicatory events were accompanied by exacting religious rituals that went on for days, as well as auguries and public festivals. Religion and the state were one and the same.

The universe of the archaic Roman was filled with spirits or numina (as in kami-do). Every field, every rock, every grove, every stream, possessed its specific local spirit. In general, the spirits were called numina, and these came in a variety of flavors. *Lemures*, or *Larvae*, were the spirits of dead household members who haunted the halls all year, but especially during their festival days in May. By contrast, *Manes* were the divine dead more generally (including one's ancestors) who were solemnly worshiped during the Parentalia. The *Lares* were the household gods, whose images were kept in the *lararium* or household shrine, along with ancestral death masks. It's easy to see, then, how ancestor reverence and ancestor worship become blurred. Since the world is filled with mostly nameless spirits, and since the dead join those spirits, then honoring the dead with religious rituals becomes *de facto* a religious act. Sometimes, a Roman family deified a particularly revered ancestor—that is, one prayed to him by name, remembered his deeds, asked for his help. Like his uncle, Julius, Augustus himself was deified after his death, but not in life. Most emperors were in fact not deified in life, and many weren't accorded this great honor in death either. It has been suggested, also, that statues of Augustus' genius proliferated as objects of worship during his lifetime, no doubt urged on by his energetic propaganda and self-promotion. If the genius of the *paterfamilias* (father of our family) could be worshiped in the household lararium since archaic times, then why not the genius of the *pater patriae* (father of our country)? Call it getting a jump on things. That neatly parallels the fact that the eternal flame in the Temple of Vesta was the state representation of the hearth flame in every household, and reinforces our understanding that the state was at a significant level an extension of the family.

The deification of Augustus (reigned 27 B.C. to 14 A.D.) had an interesting and important twist. When he died, the long list of titles bestowed on him by the Senate included *Caesar Divi Filius*, or 'Caesar, son of the Deified One.' The implication is that, in life, something of the deity of the dead ancestor Julius Caesar rubbed off on him. So, while the Senate wasn't ready (or abject enough) yet to deify the still-breathing Augustus as their successors would in another half-century fearfully do for the mad Caligula, the Senate did take a sort of intermediate step of preparing him to become a divine ancestor while still alive, by wrapping him in the spiritual mantle of Caesar.

The original monarchs (the Etruscan overlords) had done all the priestly rituals. After they were expelled, the Romans of the Republic set up a system to ensure no tyrant could ever take charge again. The Republic set up a system called the *Rex Sacrorum*, or King of Sacred Things, and made sure there was a separation of temple and state in that the two consuls who ruled were not also state priests (even though the state itself and the religion were one and the same). So when Augustus created the empire, he knew exactly what he was doing, and started pulling that priestly mantle back over himself. Very cleverly, he capitalized on the ancient ancestor worship tradition to have Julius Caesar deified, thus guaranteeing his own *post mortem* deification, and hoped to set in motion a chain of deifications for the rest of his dynasty. His successor Tiberius (reigned 14–37 A.D.), held titles including *Divi Augusti Filius*, or Son of Divine Augustus, which sets up the chain of ownership on the launch toward *post mortem* deification; but Tiberius died disliked and undeified. His successor, Gaius, had a good start and was initially well-liked; then some sort of illness fell over him, and history recalls him for his short (37–41) reign as the terrifying Caligula,[9] who forced his living deification upon a trembling Senate.

The animosity between many emperors and the Senate was an ironic fact. The Senate, which ran the government, represented those 300 wealthy families who had consolidated virtually all the wealth of Rome to themselves by the late Republic.

The senate, like the dictators and then Augustus to whom they sold their souls, had finished off the Republic. As dishonest as

Augustus while clinging to their money and power, they kept alive the fictions of the Republic, which included their own existence as a governing body, while the emperors gradually usurped more and more Senatorial power. As early as Tiberius' reign, it was not unusual for a senator to be dragged from his home on some pretext and killed. Under Caligula, it became the norm—they were hauled out of the Curia while in session, and murdered wholesale along with their families and slaves. Caligula declared himself a god, erected a temple to himself, and extracted huge amounts of money from wealthy patricians to serve in his priesthood. Caligula had long, intimate conversations with the full moon and with Capitoline Jupiter. His list of titles at the time of his assassination does not include references to divine origin or deification. Neither did those of Claudius or Nero (last of the Julio-Claudians). Some emperors, like Antoninus Pius, might deify a beloved wife or other relative, but have the decency to wait until death for their own honor. One of the finer monuments of the Roman Forum is the Temple of Deified Antoninus and Deified Faustina. Earlier, Hadrian deified his deceased male lover, Antinous.

When Constantine emancipated the Christians by the Edict of Milan (313), he set in motion a process that followed its own irresistible path, like a rushing river finding its channel. As the state weakened, the church stepped in to take its place. As the legions departed forever from the far-flung provinces of the vanishing Western empire, Christian missionaries went forth to those same former provinces which were now ruled by 'barbarians.' That is an often deceptive term, a Roman pejorative, that does not take into account the fact that in many cases, in Britain for example, some invading Germanic tribes blended with some remnants of Romanized British civilization and spawned a new hybrid civilization whose rulers pragmatically saw the benefits conferred by clerics educated at Rome, Alexandria, Hippo, and the like. It was a Christian, Merovingian king, Charles Martel, who was able to stop the sophisticated and militarily successful Moors at Poitiers in 732. It was a Frankish king, Charles the Great, whom Pope Leo III crowned Holy Roman Emperor in the

Lateran at Rome on Christmas Eve 800. The fragmented kingdoms of Britain lay half under Anglo-Saxon and half under Danish rule—it would be interesting to know when the last ecdysiast climbed into the warm, steamy waters at Bath for some civilized relaxation. From Ireland came a steady stream of Christian missionaries to Britain, to Germany, to as far away as modern Russia. The Byzantine state would continue to style itself 'Roman' until its fall to the Ottoman Muslims in 1453. Except for the Byzantines, the last actual embers of Ancient Rome had long since gone out. The diocesan structure of the late empire lived on in the ecclesiastical organization of Christendom, which dominated the West. The ancient plantation system (*latifundia*) survived in the feudal system, using both serf and slave labor.

The list of things Roman is endless and pervasive—but Rome herself was no more. Rather, she was now a Medieval Rome that would in time morph into Renaissance and Counter-Reformation and ultimately modern Rome. What disappeared, when Rome went from a world metropolis to a small village for many centuries, were not the Romans so much—they dwindled in number but did not disappear— but what disappeared was the ancient, animistic religion and its later polytheistic overlays. The mystery cults hardly matter, nor do the gods informed by Greek mythology. What matters is the things the ancient Romans did in archaic times to make them the Romans of ancient times. These things stopped being believed and ritually acted upon when Christianity won the day and became the official state religion, intolerant of any other religions or even its own heretical sects. They had been dying out anyway, with many Romans drifting off to increasingly alien religions from afar. The extended family of the Pontiffs and the Vestals disappeared, and with it Roman state and culture. Ironically, the old ways persist into modern times in many rural settings of greater Italy, and even more ironically, one sees echoes of ancient practices in every nook and cranny of Christianity.

Constantine understood that the ancient religion had become moribund, and he needed a new religious glue to hold the empire together. The chaos of the 3rd Century had shattered the faith of all but a few like the 'apostate' Julian—and the machinery set in motion by Constantine was able to handily stamp out all opposition, even from an emperor (Julian) trying to revive the corpse of Romanitas. The point ultimately is that, in answer to the question 'when did ancient (Western) Rome stop existing?', there is a lengthy road map of points stretching over several centuries, and definitely ending by, say, the breaking of the aqueducts in the 6th Century, but a good answer to the question is: when the eternal flame went out in the Vestal Temple. And even that in itself isn't the point. Ancient Rome, as such, stopped being Ancient Rome when her people gradually turned away from the animist rituals of their national childhood. The Vestal cult was banned just before 400, merely a final flicker of a long-dying flame, and the Goths and their allies sacked Rome ten years later in 410. The many things we moderns do, from building banks like ancient temples to worshiping on altars and using holy water, seem very Roman, and on the surface they are, but intrinsically that which was ancient Roman, or in a broader sense the creation of Classical Mediterranean civilization, has gone. The things we have inherited are like the lingering vapor of breath on a window, long after the person who looked in for a moment has passed on and will never return.

APPENDIX C

OUR ITINERARY

The Republican city was divided into four roughly equal sections, numbered I, II, III, and IV in a counter-clockwise manner. The common center point probably lay between the Velia and the Oppian Hill. Augustus Caesar, in the 19th year of his emperorship, or about 7 B.C., replaced the traditional four divisions of the City of Rome with a more manageable fourteen new districts *(regiones)*.

Eight of these circumscribed the area within the ancient city walls of Servius (4th Century B.C.). The other six new districts were created beyond the ancient walls to reflect the city's expansion. The imperial capital was by then probably the largest city in the world, with an estimated 1.2 million souls; with countless more living in the region around Rome. This included the Tiber outflow area toward Ostia on the Tyrrhenian Sea coast, in the Tiber delta. It also incorporated the hilly, mountainous areas surrounding Rome on three sides (the Alban Hills to the south, the Bracciano region to the north, and the Campanian region to the east). From two documents (the *Notitiae* and the *Curiosum*, collectively known as the Regionary Catalogs) compiled by city engineers in the 4th Century A.D., we get the strong idea that Augustus divided the city as evenly as possible into districts to equally apportion population segments. Initially, he then created one major fire and police barracks for every two districts. Engineers could get a handle on such issues as getting in enough water on the aqueducts, and planning for new road projects. In the following table are the districts in numerical order, running roughly counter-clockwise.

Districts in Numerical Order

Regio I.	Porta Capena (Capena Gate)
Regio II.	Caelimontium (Caelian Hill)
Regio III.	Isis et Serapis (temple area; Isis & Serapis)
Regio IV.	Templum Pacis (Temple of Peace)
Regio V.	Esquiliae (Esquiline Hill)
Regio VI.	Alta Semita (High Lane)
Regio VII.	Via Lata (Broad Street)
Regio VIII.	Forum Romanum (Roman Plaza)
Regio IX.	Circus Flaminius (Flaminian Raceway)
Regio X.	Palatium (Palatine Hill)
Regio XI.	Circus Maximus (Great Raceway)
Regio XII.	Piscina Publica (Public Pool)
Regio XIII.	Aventinus (Aventine Hill)
Regio XIV.	Trans Tiberim (Across the Tiber)

Augustus' redistricting plan remained in place through the rest of the western imperial age (which most historians say ended 476 A.D. when the Goths deposed the last Roman emperor, Romulus Augustulus, and installed Odoacer as King of the Romans, ruling from Ravenna). Some of the city districts are still discernible in the 21st Century; for example, ancient *Transtiberim* is the modern Trastevere.

Here is the sequence of our itinerary, whereby we'll better understand the city in light of her developing history.

Our Itinerary

Regio XIII. Aventinus (13. Aventine Hill)

Regio XI.   Circus Maximus (11. Great Raceway)

Regio VIII. Forum Romanum (7. Roman Plaza)

Regio X.   Palatium (10. Palatine Hill)

Regio XII. Piscina Publica (12. Public Pool)

Regio I.   Porta Capena (1. Capena Gate)

Regio II.   Caelimontium (2. Caelian Hill)

Regio III. Isis et Serapis (3. Isis & Serapis)

Regio IV. Templum Pacis (4. Temple of Peace)

Regio V.   Esquiliae (5. Esquiline Hill)

Regio VI. Alta Semita (6. High Lane)

Regio VII. Via Lata (7. Broad Street)

Regio IX. Circus Flaminius (9. Flaminian Raceway)

Regio XIV. Trans Tiberim (14. Across the Tiber)

The Regionary Catalogs are a fascinating study in themselves. They contain the information below (with some slight discrepancies, particularly in *Regio XI*). Not shown here is the fact that each district had exactly two *vicomagistri* (sort of local mayors or magistrates, where *vicus* means neighborhood or street and *magister* means master or magistrate). The Regionaries also give a rough cross-dimension of each district, not shown here. What is worth pointing out is that the number of *vici* (neighborhoods) and *aedicula* (neighborhood shrines) is always the same, reflecting the inherent civic religiosity of the Romans. Each neighborhood would have had some sort of central plaza, maybe with a fountain and a shrine in its center. I took the term lacus (lake, trough, what have you) generally to refer to a main water outlet, possibly a *castellum* or storage unit associated with an aqueduct.

Regio	vici	Neighb. shrines	insulae	Great houses	Grain stores	baths	Water mains	Mills & bakeries
I	10	10	250	120	16	86	87	20
II	7	7	600	127	27	85	65	15
III	12	12	757	160	18	80	65	16
IV	8	8	757	88	18	75	78	15
V	15	15	850	180	22	75	74	15
VI	17	17	403	146	18	75	73	16
VII	15	15	805	120	25	75	76	15
VIII	34	34	480	80	18	85	70	20
IX	35	35	777	111	25	63	120	20
X	20	20	642	89	44	44	84	20
XI	21?	21?	600?	88?	16	15	20	16
XII	17	17	487	123	27	63	81	20
XIII	18	18	487	130	35	60	88	24
XIV	17	17	487	80	35	60	87	24
Totals	246	246	8382	1642	344	941	1068	256

The statistics given here would reflect conditions in the 4th Century, that is, over 300 years following the reapportioning by Augustus into 14 districts. We assume the original redistricting was to divide the population into even slices, and dynamic urban changes over three or four centuries shifted things about.

The discrepancies in the Palatine District (XI) may be understandable in light of the fact that the Regionary catalogs date from a time when the emperors had moved their capital(s) elsewhere, and the Palatine began to revert from a single huge palace to a growing multitude of lesser palaces. That's long after our walk in Rome, at a time when successive emperors starting with the Flavians were both undoing the damage of Nero's vast palace that sprawled over half the city center, and building up a great palatial complex atop the Palatine. It's questionable that there would be room for any *vici*, or common neighborhoods, around 150.

TOPOLOGICAL NOTES

Districts

Augustus partitioned the city into 14 districts *(regiones)*, which remained standard (with some shifting of borders to keep the population census even among districts) until medieval times. These maps show the central districts (1, 2, 3, 4, 8, 9, and 10) arguably intersecting at a point west of the Colosseum, possibly at the site of Nero's giant statue. It appears to be one Roman mile west to the Milliarum Aureus (Golden Milestone)—all of this is simply conjecture. Somewhere in or near the Roman Forum, the major roads of Rome in and out between city and empire were supposed to make a ghostly intersection. The milestones, however, began counting from the city gates rather than the city center. It seems reasonable to speculate that this apparent disjunction between reality and symbolism echoes that remarkable dicotomy in the Roman mind between the material world and the spirit world, within the dual realities of numenism. At the same time, one advises caution before taking conjecture past hypothesis.

Hills

Rome is famed as Urbs Septicollis (City of Seven Hills) but one can quibble about that number. 'Seven' refers to the hills within the Servian Wall city of the early to mid Republic (Capitoline, Palatine, Aventine, Caelian, Esquiline, Quirinal, and Viminal). However, Platner is reluctant to admit the Esquiline, because its plateau really lies outside the Servian Wall. Instead, he notes that its two westerly spurs, the Oppian and Cespian, arguably form two hills inside the Pomerium. Platner also notes that 'Esquiline' probably comes from *ex colo* (outside the settled region) and didn't originally denote a hill so much as a *pagus* (countryside, land outside the city walls).

Aqueducts

The city had at least ten major aqueducts, and numerous added spurs leading to specific sites.[10] The Romans built their first (Aqua Appia) in 312 B.C. and their last (Aqua Alexandrina) in 226 A.D. Several aqueducts brought in water from the Anio Valley east of Rome (Aqua Anio Novus, Aqua Anio Vetus, Aqua Marcia, Aqua Tepula, Aqua Julia, Aqua Claudia). Agrippa built the Aqua Virgo to bring water from the north, down through the Campus Martius, to supply his large public baths. Augustus built the Aqua Alsietina to bring water from the west to his naumachia, an artificial lake for sea battles outside Transtiberim. The Alsietina had the reputation of least tasty water, while the Marcia probably had the best. Trajan built the last major aqueduct—from the west, the Aqua Traiana—in concert with his improvements on Claudius' harbor.

APPENDIX E

OUR ITINERARY AND REGIONARY CATALOGS

On the map showing main itinerary highlights, not shown are the opening chapters on the Ostian Way and the final chapter on the road leading to the new Port of Claudius and Trajan. These are the references on the map (numbered in black) to selected sights:

1. Hill of Shards, Chapter 6
2. Porticus Aemilia, Ch. 8
3. Sublician Bridge, Ch. 10
4. City river port, Ch. 11
5. Circus Maximus, Ch. 12
6. Capitoline Hill, Ch. 14
7. Forum Romanum, Ch. 17
8. Palatine Hill, Ch. 18
9. Public Pool, Ch. 20
10. Appian Way Terminus, Ch. 24
11. Carriage trade area, Ch. 26
12. Temple of Mars, Ch. 25
13. Lateran estate, Ch. 30

A Walk in Rome: Itinerary

Note. As a hypothetical recreation, idly searching for possible lines of connection that may or may not exist, I have elaborated on a suggestion by Platner ("Regiones Quattuordecim," p. 446) that "Regiones I, II, III, IV, and X all met at some point near the Meta Sudans," and in the above picture extended the border of Regio VIII to that point also. The more accepted view is given in my sketch (at right from Platner, *Topographical Dictionary,* figure p. 394), discussing the Pomerium. It is possible the original four Republican regions did intersect on the Velia, which would make this area a significant place—one that Augustus might have wanted to keep as a center of his redistricted city, even if not all 14 districts physically intersected there. The view that Augustus' original redistricting was just a practical way of dividing the city into equal and manageable portions according to the census of the time can still accommodate this hypothesis, if imperfectly. One factor that teased me into this speculation was that anomalous, elongated, narrow extension of Regio I to the Colosseum Valley. That the Capena Gate opens upon the venerable Appian Way suggests added weight. It's as if, for some reason, they absolutely had to make the pieces fit the puzzle.

The Milliarum Aureum (Golden Milestone) is an imperial construct of Augustus and Agrippa, as Lanciani informs us (*Ruins and Excavations*, P. 280), and it is not unreasonable to think that later emperors would want to elaborate on this locus of their ownership of the world.

From the Milliarum Aureum to the Porta Caelimontana in the Servian Wall is one Roman Mile (1000 passus). Why the Porta Caelimontana? Probably because it was the best straight shot to retrofit by line of sight from that gate into the Forum without intervening hills. The halfway-point is right about in the archaic stagnum of the Colosseum valley where Vespasian laid out the Colosseum. Is it possible, then, that the delusional Nero wanted to figuratively stand astride this golden mile, and so he picked the halfway point of the line between the gate and the milestone marker in the Forum? The Flavian Amphitheater of Vespasian was already in place, and in any case the Velia would have provided more solid ground for his colossal statue. This statue stood in the vestibule of his Golden House, and therefore had to play a focal role in his entire scheme (including realigning part of the Via Sacra along which the golden mile in part runs).

As an interesting side note, both Lanciani and Claridge mention that Hadrian's architect De(me)trianus or Decrianus used 24 elephants, pulling a great wooden scaffold containing the 100 foot statue upright, to move it closer to the Flavian Amphitheater, thus making room for Hadrian's Temple of Venus and Roma.

AUTHOR'S NOTES

In weaving together historical journalism, story telling, and tour guiding, I confess that I have taken liberties to bridge some of the many gaps in our knowledge of ancient Rome. This is a work of nonfiction, yet it has been necessary to fill in gaps with reasoned fictions. I have created some of it, like the Balneum in the Vicus Horse Head, from pure speculation. I have taken a few liberties, speculating about the Milliarum Aureum and several other items. For example, I wanted to put in the Mundus, but nobody knows where that lay, so I placed it on the Palatine. I would urge the reader to verify every fact, every claim offered here, from at least one other source before committing it to a reference work or school paper. I think you'll find that most of what I have written comes from reliable primary or secondary sources, and I offer a selective bibliography. I hope this book will offer a pleasurable tour, without cost of shoe leather.

Non-English words. To keep down the number of italicized words, I have tried to follow the convention of italicizing a word in its first appearance, and thereafter treating it without emphasis, like any English term.

Eras, Years, Dates. For our convention, we use B.C. and A.D. In the modern multicultural age, one often sees C.E. (Common Era) instead of the older A.D. (*Anno Domini*, Year of Our Lord). Likewise, one may see B.C.E. (Before Common Era) instead of B.C. (Before Christ). To save eye strain, we may leave off A.D. with references to some common-era years, while explicitly calling out B.C. dates.

Languages. As a general convention, a Latin word is given emphasized (underlined or italic) and its translation follows parenthetically in single quotes. Comments, if any, also appear in parentheses. E.g., *Rumo* ('river,' archaic pre-Latin name of the Tiber, which may have given Rome her name, as opposed to the more fanciful story about wolf-nurtured Romulus).

Double quotes are reserved for dialog.

'Modern' (with a capital M) always refers to the era of automobiles and space ships (20th Century and after). 'Current' (initial cap or lower case) always refers to the 2nd Century when our Walk in Ancient Rome takes place. 'Ancient' generally refers to the older period of the Republic. 'Archaic' may refer to the Monarchy and earlier periods including the Bronze Age.

Banks of the Tiber may be referred to as cityside or citerior (hither) vs. cross-Tiber (transtiberim). References to 'left bank' and 'right bank' can confuse the reader and I avoid them here. Almost the entire ancient city lay on the east side of the Tiber, except for Regio XIV (Transtiberim, today Trastevere) with its Jewish quarter; plus the Janiculum Hill; and the Vatican Hill, location of some public gardens, and buildings including the Circus of Nero and Gaius. This is where St. Peter is said to have been crucified upside down about 61 A.D. (89 years ago).

Time of Day not always sequential. I have taken the liberty of placing our vignettes (Policeman, Priest, etc.) at various times of day. Assume that you, the traveler, spend several days and nights in the city, but not all stops are mentioned. For millennia, it has been the tendency of Romans to stay indoors during the heat of day, especially in summer. At about 9 or 10 p.m. a pleasant breeze blows through the streets, and people throng outdoors for an hour or two; though shops are closed, restaurants serve dinner to families and groups. Modern Rome at night is considerably safer than Antonine Rome.

Time of Year Ambivalent. We may imagine some scenes at different times of year—whatever is best suited to put the reader into a vivid, lifelike presence in ancient Rome, which is the primary mission of this book. I have purposely allowed for seasonal and descriptive latitude to achieve advantages of mood and setting for best artistic effect. A quick rundown of the climate follows. During archaic times, the weather tended to be colder, wetter, and more overcast as in modern times in the U.K. or northwest maritime continental Europe. By current (Antonine) times it is more like the modern: in summer, hot and stifling July/August; in autumn (fall), overcast, rainy in November; winter, from December through February, chilly with occasional overcast; spring, starts overcast, becomes balmy and sunny, clear and pleasant.

SELECTED REFERENCES

Special thanks to Mr. Bill Thayer, for his generosity and kindness in making available the resources on his extensive website, *Lacus Curtius: Into The Roman World* (hosted by the University of Chicago).

Adkins, Lesley and Roy A.: *Handbook to Life in Ancient Rome* (Oxford University Press, London, 1994).

Balsdon, J. P. V. D.: *Life and Leisure in Ancient Rome* (The Bodley Head, London, 1969). Also by Balsdon: *Roman Women* (McGraw-Hill, New York, 1969).

Baring, Anne and Jules Cashford: *The Myth of The Goddess, Evolution of An Image* (Viking, New York, 1991).

Boyle, A. J. and Roger D. Woodard: *Ovid Fasti* (Penguin Classics, London, 2000).

Braudel, Fernand: *Memory and the Mediterranean* (Editions de Fallois, Paris, 1993; translated from the French in 2001 by Siân Reynolds for the Vintage/Random House edition, New York).

Canfora, Luciano: *The Vanished Library: A Wonder of the Ancient World* (1987 Sellerio editore, Palermo; translated into English by Martin Ryle; reissued 1990 by the University of California Press, Berkeley).

Carcopino, Jérôme: *Daily Life in Ancient Rome* (Yale University Press, New Haven, 1940).

Chevalier, Raymond: *Roman Roads* (University of California Press, Berkeley and Los Angeles, 1976).

Claridge, Amanda: *Rome: An Oxford Archaeological Guide* (Oxford University Press, London, 1998).

Connolly, Peter and Hazel Dodge: *The Ancient City, Life in Classical Athens & Rome* (Oxford University Press, Oxford, 1998).

Frazer, James: *The Golden Bough* (Penguin, London, 1996).

Hamilton, Edith: *The Roman Way* (W. W. Norton & Co., New York, 1932).

Heurgon, Jacques: *Daily Life of the Etruscans* (Librairie Hachette, Paris, 1961; translated by James Kirkup for the 1964 MacMillan edition, New York).

Lanciani, Rodolfo: *Ancient Rome in the Light of Recent Discoveries*, 1888 (reissued 1967 by Benjamin Bloom, New York); *The Ruins and Excavations of Ancient Rome*, 1897 (reissued 1979 by Bell Publishing Co., a division of Crown Publishing Co., in conjunction with Arno Press, Inc.); and other works by Lanciani including the *Forma Urbis Romae*.

LeGlay, Marcel, Jean-Louis Voisin, & Yann Le Bohec: *A History of Rome, Second Edition* (Presses Universitaires de France, Paris, 1991; translated 1994 by Antonia Nevill for the 1996 edition published by Blackwell, Oxford, U.K.).

Johnson, Paul: *A History of Christianity* (MacMillan Atheneum, New York, 1976).

Mattingly, H. (1948; revised: S. A. Handford, 1970): *Tacitus, The Agricola and The Germania* (Penguin, London, 1970).

Matyszak, Philip: *Chronicle of the Roman Republic, The Rulers of Ancient Rome from Romulus to Augustus* (Thames & Hudson, London, 2003).

Payne, Robert: *Ancient Rome* (Horizon, New York, 1966; reissued by iBooks, New York, 2001).

Platner, Samuel B. and Thomas Ashby: *A Topographical Dictionary of Ancient Rome* (Oxford University Press, London, 1929; available on the University of Chicago Library website).

Scarre, Chris: *Chronicle of the Roman Emperors* (Thames & Hudson, London, 1995).

Smith, William: *A Dictionary of Greek and Roman Antiquities* (John Murray, London, 1875; available on Mr. Thayer's website).

Smith, William: *Smaller Classical Dictionary* (Dutton, New York, 1958).

Stambaugh, John E.: *The Ancient Roman City* (Johns Hopkins University Press, Baltimore, 1988).

Stockton, David: *The Gracchi* (Oxford University Press, Oxford, 1979).

Talbart, Richard J. A.: *Atlas of Classical History* (Croom Helm Ltd., London, 1985; reissued 2002 by Routledge, London).

Toussaint-Samat, Maguelonne: *A History of Food* (Bordas, Paris, 1987; translated from the French 1992 by Anthea Bell for the edition of Blackwell Publishing, London).

Though it would be impracticable to list all the resource books I consulted more casually, the following were also useful and enjoyable to varying degrees (in some cases nearly landing in the above category):

Ambrosini, Maria with Mary Willis: *The Secret Archives of the Vatican* (Little, Brown, New York, 1969).

Ballard, Robert with Toni Eugene: *Mystery of the Ancient Seafarers; Early Maritime Civilizations* (National Geographic Books, Washington, D.C., 2004).

Boardman, John et. al.: *The Oxford Illustrated History of the Roman World* (Oxford University Press, Oxford, 2003).

Churton, Tobias: *The Gnostics* (Barnes & Noble, New York, 1987).

Constable, Nick: *Historical Atlas of Ancient Rome* (Checkmark Books/ Facts on File, New York, 2003).

Coogan, Michael D.: *The Oxford History of the Biblical World* (Oxford University Press, Oxford, 1998).

Cowell, F. R.: *Life in Ancient Rome* (Perigee/Putnam, New York 1961).

Davies, J. G.: *The Early Christian Church* (Henry Holt & Co., New York, 1965).

Grant, Michael: *The Art and Life of Pompeii and Herculaneum* (Newsweek, New York, 1979); *The Twelve Caesars* (Scribner's, New York, 1975).

Hamblin, Dora Jane & Mary Jane Grunsfeld: *The Appian Way, A Journey* (Random House, New York, 1974).

Jones, Prudence and Nigel Pennick: *A History of Pagan Europe* (Routledge, London, 1995).

King, Ross: *Michelangelo and the Pope's Ceiling* (Penguin, New York, 2003).

Knopf Guides (numerous authors and authorities listed): *Rome* (Nouveaux Loisiers/Gallimard, Paris, 1994; translated by Louis Marcelin-Rice and Kate Newton for the 1994 Knopf edition, New York).

Lewis, Jon E.: *The Mammoth Book of Eyewitness Ancient Rome* (Robinson, London, 2003; Carroll & Graf, New York, 2003).

Lombardo, Stanley (Transl.): *Homer, The Iliad* (Hackett/Cambridge, Indianapolis, 1997).

Mannix, Daniel P.: *The Way of the Gladiator* (iBooks, New York, 1958 and 2001).

McGregor, Horace C. P. (Translator) *Cicero: The Nature of the Gods* (Penguin Classics, London, 1972).

Messadié, Gerald: *A History of the Devil* (Editions Robert Laffont, Paris, 1993; translated from the French by Marc Romano for the 1996 Kodansha America edition, New York).

Nappo, Salvatore: *Pompeii, A Guide to The Ancient City* (White Star S.r.l., Vercelli, Italy; translators A.B.A. Milan for the 1998 Barnes & Noble edition).

O'Grady, Joan: *Early Christian Heresies* (Element Books/Barnes & Noble, New York, 1985).

Pescarin, Sofia: *Rome, A Guide to The Eternal City* (White Star S.r.l., Vercelli, Italy; translators A.B.A. Milan for the 1999 Barnes & Noble edition).

Portella, Ivana (Della): *Subterranean Rome* (Arsenale Editrice, Venice, 1999; translated from the Italian by Caroline Higgitt with Goodfellow & Egan Publishing Management, Cambridge, U.K., for the 2000 English Language edition published by K_nemann, Cologne

Potter, T.W. and Catherine Johns: *Roman Britain* (The British Museum Press, London, 1992).

Rodgers, Nigel with Hazel Dodge: *The History and Conquests of Ancient Rome* (Anness, London, 1994).

Scarre, Chris: *The Penguin Historical Atlas of Ancient Rome* (Penguin, London, 1995).

Starr, Chester A.: *A History of the Ancient World* (Oxford University Press, Oxford and New York, 1965).

Rolfe, J.C.: Suetonius, The Twelve Caesars (Loeb Classical Library, Harvard University Press, 1997–98).

Veyne, Paul: *Did the Greeks Believe in Their Myths?* (Editions du Se-euil, Paris, 1983; translated into English by Paula Wissing for the 1988 University of Chicago Press edition).
Veyne, Paul (Editor): *A History of Private Life, I, From Pagan Rome to Byzantium* (Editions du Seuil, Paris, 1985; translated into English by Arthur Goldhammer for the 1987 Belknap Harvard University edition, Cambridge, Mass., U.S.A.).
Williamson, G. A. (Transl.) *Eusebius, The History of the Church from Christ to Constantine* (Penguin, London, 1965).
Wurman, Richard Saul: *Rome Access* (Access Press, New York, 1990). Note especially the wonderful sections "On A Typical Roman Day in Ancient Times" and "Via Sacra."
Zoll, Amy: *Gladiatrix, The True Story of History's Unknown Woman Warrior* (Berkley Boulevard, New York, 2002).

Throughout the process, I had the advantage of living in San Diego with its many excellent book stores and a solid Public Library, all staffed by helpful professionals. I referred often to Cassell's Latin Dictionary (MacMillan, New York, 1968, 5th Edition), as well as to Webster's New World Dictionary and the American Heritage Dictionary, both of which have good etymological citations. Finally, also, I have the good fortune to live in the age of the Internet, to which I constantly turned for quick bits of this or that information. One strong source is my on-line subscription to the Encyclopedia Britannica, which offers authoritative articles by academically credentialed men and women at the top of their fields. Again, I must thank Mr. Bill Thayer for his excellent website, Lacus Curtius, from which I learned a great deal that was helpful in writing this book. There are numerous other websites dedicated to the study and enjoyment of Ancient Rome lore. Among them are:

David Camden's Forum Romanum (http://www.forumromanum .org/);
Jona Lendering's Livius: (http://www.livius.org/);
Domenico Carro's Roma Aeterna: (http://www.romaeterna.org/);
Rome art links by Dr. Whitcomb: (http://witcombe.sbc.edu/ ARTHrome.html#Roman)

Laurence Wright offers a copy of Smith's Smaller Classical Dictionary
    on line: (http://www.classicaldictionary.bravepages.com/
    1.htm#START)
Bullfinch's Mythology: (http://www.bulfinch.org/fables/welcome
    .html)
Maps of Rome: (http://garyb.0catch.com/rome-map/index.html)
More maps:
    (http://intranet.dalton.org/groups/rome/RMaps.html)

There are many more such helpful and enjoyable websites, and
searches on terms like "Ancient Rome" (or more specific terms; e.g.,
"Ancient Rome mosaics Ostia") may bring some pleasant surprises.

ENDNOTES

CHAPTER 1

1. During nearly 2,000 years leading to modern times, it's estimated the shoreline moves westward two to three kilometers, leaving the old port of Ostia stranded inland.

CHAPTER 2

2. For a broad historical perspective on Rumo and his world, see Appendix A.

3. As late as 846 A.D., during the initial vast sweep of Arab Islamic conquest, Saracen pirates enter the Tiber, sail past Ostia to Rome, and attack the Vatican during the papacy of Sergius II. Using the fortifications of Hadrian's Tomb, the pope fends off the pirates and begins a new era of fortifications.

CHAPTER 13

4. Rodolfo Lanciani (*The Ruins and Excavations of Ancient Rome,* 1897) offers these representative altitudes above sea level (which I have rounded to the nearest meter, and in parentheses rounded to the nearest foot): Quirinal 63m (207ft), Small Gardens 56 (183) to 63 (207), Viminal 57 (187), Oppian 55 (180), Esquiline 54 (177), Cespian 51 (167), Palatine 50 (164), Caelian 48 (158), Capitoline 46 (151), Aventine 46 (151), the lesser Aventine 43 (141), Mons Aureus near the Porta Metronia of the Aurelian Wall 46 (151), Mons Citorius 24 (79).

5. Actual elevations at any given point may vary noticeably, as in the heights of the Capitoline areas given by Samuel Ball Plattner in his *A Topographical Dictionary of Ancient Rome* (Oxford University Press, 1929).

CHAPTER 17

6. See Appendix B for more information

APPENDIX B

7. The word 'cult' or 'cultus' here is interchangeable with the terms 'religion' or 'belief system.' The word cult actually comes from the Latin 'colui,' which means to grow or—more closely—to cultivate, as in tilling the earth (*agricola*, farmer=*ager* or *agri*, earth + *colui*). As a counterpoint, the word *religio*, 'religion' in ancient Rome had positive connotations, but could also negatively imply ignorance and superstition. As to the etymology of 'superstition,' it is generally taken to be *super*, above + *stare*, stand, but an alternative might be: *su*, self + *perstire* (from *stare*, stand) like 'persist,' suggesting someone who stubbornly clings to or wraps himself in a belief that the speaker views negatively. Cicero (*De Natura Divorum*, The Nature of the Gods, Penguin, HCP McGregor, transl.) suggests 'superstition' comes from *superstes*, survivor, which he relates to people desperately praying for their children to live beyond them. Regarding 'religion,' Cicero says it comes from *relegere*, to read again and again in the proper performance of exact rituals. Some will find Cicero's assumptions tenuous. McGregor suggests *religare*, to bind or bind again, which seems reasonable, given that some religions practice real or symbolic binding. The prefix *re-* is given by Cassell as back, or against, or again. Possible *leg-* etymologies might include *legare*, to appoint, to send a message or messenger, to bequeath or ordain: *legare, religare*.

8. Lanciani, RAEOAR, p. 47

9. Ironic, because it means 'little boots.' His father, Germanicus, adoptive heir of Tiberius, was a popular general, whom the paranoid Tiberius ordered murdered. Germanicus used to take his family along on campaigns, and his little son was the darling of the legionaries. He would accompany his father, dressed in a tiny uniform including the red sandals of royalty, so the soldiers gave him the nickname by which he is unofficially remembered (more properly, he is Gaius). His cruel reign is one of history's most notorious. As violent and capricious as he was, he was surpassed in loathing by his successor-Nero.

APPENDIX D

10. Connolly & Dodge, p. 130